MW00477093

Routes of Remembrance

BAYO HOLSEY

Routes of Remembrance

REFASHIONING THE SLAVE TRADE IN GHANA

The University of Chicago Press » CHICAGO & LONDON

BAYO HOLSEY is assistant professor of cultural
anthropology and African and African American studies
at Duke University.

The University of Chicago Press, Chicago 60637
The University of Chicago Press, Ltd., London
© 2008 by The University of Chicago
All rights reserved. Published 2008
Printed in the United States of America

17 16 15 14 13 12 11 10 09 08   1 2 3 4 5

ISBN-13: 978-0-226-34975-6 (cloth)
ISBN-13: 978-0-226-34976-3 (paper)
ISBN-10: 0-226-34975-6 (cloth)
ISBN-10: 0-226-34976-4 (paper)

Library of Congress Cataloging-in-Publication Data

Holsey, Bayo.
  Routes of remembrance : refashioning the slave trade in
Ghana / Bayo Holsey.
    p. cm.
  Includes bibliographical references and index.
  ISBN-13: 978-0-226-34975-6 (cloth : alk. paper)
  ISBN-10: 0-226-34975-6 (cloth : alk. paper)
  ISBN-13: 978-0-226-34976-3 (pbk. : alk. paper)
  ISBN-10: 0-226-34976-4 (pbk. : alk. paper)
  1. Slave trade—Ghana—History. I. Title.
  HT1394 .G48H64 2008
  306.3'6209667—dc22
                                        2007038227

♾ The paper used in this publication meets the
minimum requirements of the American National
Standard for Information Sciences—Permanence of
Paper for Printed Library Materials, ANSI Z39.48-1992.

History, despite its wrenching pain,
Cannot be unlived, and if faced
With courage, need not be lived again.

» MAYA ANGELOU

In memory of all of the victims of the slave trade,
on both sides of the Atlantic.

CONTENTS

ACKNOWLEDGMENTS

I have incurred a number of intellectual and emotional debts along the road to finishing this book. It has at times been a difficult journey, but it has also been filled with moments of great joy and laughter. Above all, it has given me the opportunity to meet people and build friendships that I hope to carry with me throughout my life.

I want to thank first the people of Cape Coast and Elmina who welcomed me into their lives and generously shared with me their thoughts and experiences. I especially must thank Alexandra Mensah and the entire Mensah family for opening up their home to me. I am forever grateful to the staff of Cape Coast and Elmina castles for their assistance and hospitality in allowing me access to the castles. Special thanks to Naana Ocraan, Leo Yankson, Kingsley Kofi Yeboah, Kwesi Essel Blankson, Charles Adu-Arhin, Stephen Korsah, J. Wallace Kwaw, Felix Nguah, and all of the tour guides who allowed me to observe their tours and were an immense help to me. I also benefited from the expertise of Nkunu Akyea, James Anquandah, Kwadwo Opoku-Agyemang, Akosua Perbi, Akosua Darkwah, Edward Apenteng-Sackey, and Robert E. Lee. Jamil Idun-Ogde and Richard and Joyce Mensah proved to be great friends, as did Vanessa and Kafui Tetteh, who always opened their home to me during my forays into Accra. Their generosity has been truly remarkable. Finally, I sincerely thank Ato Ashun, who introduced me to many of the people interviewed in this book and often served as an interpreter. This project would have been impossible without him. Both as a research assistant and a cherished friend, I am forever deeply indebted to him. The kindness of all of these individuals makes every trip to Ghana a homecoming.

Several people have had the patience to read entire versions of this project. For reading this book in its earliest incarnation, I thank my dissertation committee, including my advisor, Sherry Ortner, whose critical perspectives were invaluable. I am grateful also to Lesley Sharp for her careful reading of drafts and her insightful comments and to Lee Baker for his long-term support and friendship. Lee is a model of mentorship to whom I owe so much. In addition, Jacqueline Nassy Brown and Brian Larkin provided many important comments and suggestions.

I thank David Brent at the University of Chicago Press for his belief in the project and tireless effort to make this book come to fruition. An extremely careful and diligent anonymous reader provided excellent feedback. Ralph Austen, who revealed himself as my other reader, kindly shared his great knowledge and insight to help me to improve this project. Any shortcomings are, of course, my own.

I also thank those who have read various portions of the text for their time and help. Charlie Piot, Harvey Neptune, Orin Starn, and Randal Jelks have provided constructive criticism. I thank also Karla Slocum and Kia Cauldwell, who became invaluable interlocutors during the final stages of this project. I am grateful to Jemima Pierre, who has graciously offered me her insights and friendship. Many thanks also to Keith Piper for his encouragement, affection, and inspiration. I can never thank these individuals enough for engaging with my work and providing emotional support.

I extend my gratitude also to friends and mentors at Columbia University, including Jafari Allen, Paulette Young, John Jackson, George Bond, Robin Kelley, David Scott, Mahmood Mamdani, Elaine Combs-Schilling, Farah Griffin, Steven Gregory, Sandhya Shukla, and Maxine Weisgrau, who saw me through the earliest stages of my anthropological career. The fieldwork and writing stages of this project were generously supported by the National Science Foundation Pre-dissertation Fellowship and the Ford Foundation Disseration Fellowship. It was also made possible by the Ann Plato Dissertation Fellowship at Trinity College. I am grateful to Margo Perkins, Johanna Fernandez, and the entire Anthropology Department at Trinity for their support and encouragement. I was also aided by a postdoctoral fellowship at Northwestern University. I thank the department of African American Studies at Northwestern, especially Martha Biondi, Celeste Watkins-Hayes, Mary Patillo, Richard Iton, Sandra Lee Richards, and Dwight McBride.

My colleagues at Duke University have been a constant source of inspiration to me. Special thanks to Thavolia Glymph, Wahneema Lubiano, Mark Anthony Neal, Michaeline Crichlow, Anne-Maria Makhulu, Charles Payne, Maurice Wallace, Richard Powell, Sandy Darity, Sherman James, and Karla Holloway. I also appreciate the support of Anne Allison and the faculty of the Cultural Anthropology Department. Members of the Franklin Humanities Institute 2005–2006 Seminar, Indigeneity and Diaspora, including Orin Starn, Tina Campt, Christoff Galli, Micaela Janan, Ranjana Khanna, Leela Prasad, Linda Rupert, Karin Shapiro, and Yektan Turkyilmaz, provided greatly enriching conversations.

Many friends not yet mentioned have provided invaluable support to me over the years. I thank William Michael Smith for his unwavering friendship. I also thank Ann Payne, Stephanie Blackman, and Lara Holliday. I am so grateful that our childhood friendship continues today. Thanks also to my Durham posse, Rhonda Jones, Karen Jean Hunt, and Erica Edwards for keeping me sane, or at least trying to. I extend my deep thanks and love to Zaje Harrell, my dearest friend and confidante. I could never have made it to this point without her, and I am continually honored to be her friend.

Finally, I thank my family, to whom I owe everything. I thank all of my aunts, uncles, and cousins, my dearly missed grandmother, Jane Seaman Smith, my grandparents, George and Cecil Taylor, my wonderful father, Khalim Piankhi Holsey and his wife Farhaana Holsey, my brilliant and beautiful sisters, Yasmin and Sheba Holsey, and Nile and Imani Holsey Wortham whose boundless energy and glee always make me laugh out loud. More than anyone, my amazing mother, Lois Taylor Holsey, has been deeply committed to this project, reading drafts, traveling to Ghana to visit me, and constantly reminding me to believe in myself. I can never thank my mother enough for being a model of both the highest intelligence and the deepest generosity. To all of those who have provided such great love and encouragement, I say thank you, and I love you.

A NOTE ON AKAN ORTHOGRAPHY

Many historical and contemporary texts transcribe Akan words using an English orthography. When referring specifically to words in these texts, I use their same orthographies. Akan orthography, however, has been used to transcribe Akan words spoken by the individuals interviewed in this text. This orthography includes the vowel sounds ɛ, pronounced like the "e" in "let," and ɔ, pronounced like the "o" in "not." It also includes the consonants "ky," pronounced like the "ch" in "chair," and "hy," pronounced like the "sh" in "shirt."

INTRODUCTION

As soon as one enters the town of Elmina, on the coast of Ghana, one notices the castle. On a clear day, its majestic size and stark whiteness stand against the bright blue of both sky and ocean with arresting beauty. The same holds true for Cape Coast, its neighboring town, with its own massive and awesome castle. These castles have stood on the shore since the era of the Atlantic slave trade, during which the Dutch and the British used them as their headquarters. Today they seem out of scale with the rest of the towns' modest buildings, and so too is the attention they have received. The castles have been conserved and have become major tourist destinations, particularly for African Americans and others of African descent. Their conservation has been part of a larger trend over the past two decades of diaspora tourism, which is centered around these two towns and commemorates the Atlantic slave trade. The towns host a biannual festival called PANAFEST, a celebration that aims to reconnect Africans in the diaspora to their African "roots," as well as an annual Emancipation Day celebration. As a result, scores of diaspora tourists arrive most every day on tour buses and in private cars to see the castles and, in particular, to see the dungeons in which enslaved Africans were kept centuries ago, awaiting their forced migration to the Americas. The castles have become sites in which these tourists can imagine the suffering of their enslaved ancestors and ultimately celebrate their survival. Cape Coast and Elmina have indeed become places of pilgrimage for many black subjects throughout the world.

These castles have also become key sites for historical inquiry about the slave trade and the making of the black diaspora. But for me as an anthropologist, gazing at the castles and thinking about the painful history that they evoke made me want to make sense of this history within the larger story of the lives of the men and women whom I came to know in Cape Coast and Elmina. I wanted to explore what it means to live, quite literally, in the shadows cast by these castles. This book undertakes a journey into the politics of memory in Cape Coast and Elmina in order to examine the emergent identities fashioned in the wake of the slave trade. It does so not only to explore the effects of the slave trade on the lives of the men and women who live on this small stretch of the West African coastline but also as a contribution to a much larger discussion of the effects of the slave trade on the construction of black subjectivities throughout the world.

MY EXAMINATION OF THE POLITICS of memory in Cape Coast and Elmina proved to be a formidable task. As soon as I began to search for collective memories of the slave trade, I found that the high visibility of the slave trade within the tourism industry stands in sharp relief to its practical invisibility in other arenas of Ghanaian society, where it is rarely mentioned. When I asked local residents whether or not they had ever learned about the slave trade from any sources outside of the tourism industry, from members of their families or other people in their communities, they told me that they had not. They most often replied by stating, "Nobody remembers anything about that," or, even more intriguing, "Nobody talks about that," expressing great reluctance to discuss it. They did not offer stories about what once transpired in the castles' dungeons but rather suggested that this history has been forgotten. Many told me that the castles are just for tourists and expressed little interest in them.

What is the reason for their disinclination to discuss the slave trade? The more time that I spent in Cape Coast and Elmina, the more I began to see that local residents are regularly assailed with European popular and academic historical narratives about the slave trade. Within these narratives, Africans on the continent are denounced for being outside of the march of progress that is seen to define human history as both victims and perpetrators of the trade. In this context, local residents seek to distance themselves from the slave trade in order to avoid its stigmatizing effects and ultimately to attempt to improve their position in the "global ecumene" (Hannerz 1992).

At the same time, however, as a result of the tremendous growth of diaspora tourism, some local residents, particularly adolescents, have become interested in going to the castles and learning about the slave trade.

Many of them have as a result begun to discuss the slave trade as part of a critique of racial oppression in ways that draw upon diasporic examples. In contrast to the majority of local residents who sequester the slave trade, they center it within constructions of their history. Their approach to history appears at first glance to be diametrically opposed to the stance of other members of their communities. I came to believe, however, that they share similar motivations. Faced with the flawed logics behind European fabrications of the inferiority of Africans and people of African descent that are the legacy of the slave trade, I argue throughout these pages that both groups attempt to mend this image, in one case, by stitching over this history, and in the other, by refashioning it. They are both, in this way, engaged in agentive and empowering acts.[1]

To set the stage for the chapters that follow, I first discuss the ways in which the residents of Cape Coast and Elmina navigate around European histories about the slave trade in order to construct different narratives of the past. I then elaborate on this process by demonstrating the significance of viewing these towns as part of the Atlantic world. Next I turn specifically to the role of the African diaspora and the tourism industry and its attempts to publicize the history of the slave trade in productive ways. Finally, I discuss the larger implications of this example for the study of collective memory.

Navigating History

For centuries, European ships docked at West Africa ports, including, for much of this time, at Cape Coast and Elmina. Their hulls were loaded with captives who were transported to the Americas in horrific conditions to labor against their will and without remuneration. And yet, most popular constructions of European and American histories are told as narratives of progress, stressing development, modernization, and capitalism (see Chakrabarty 1992). Within such narratives, the slave trade is presented as an aberration. It appears, in other words, as "a premodern residue that disappears once it is revealed to be fundamentally incompatible with enlightened rationality and capitalist industrial production" (Gilroy 1993, 49).

While these narratives stress the West's triumph over slavery, and thereby diminish it within a larger story of an emerging "modernity," they often paint the slave trade as crucial to an understanding of Africa's past and present. In contrast to the grand histories of Europe, Africa is characterized solely by this "primitive" past from which, they suggest, it has yet to escape.

This characterization is accomplished through several techniques. For one, indigenous forms of slavery on the African continent are often raised in order to make the case that this institution was the foundation upon which the Atlantic slave trade was built, that slavery is in fact an institution that belonged first to the African continent. Popular presentations today continue to describe the perversion of African families who owned slaves. But the history of the Atlantic trade also brings its own damning narratives. Many descriptions of this trade have focused on the terror and insecurity of West African regions where slave raiding was once rampant, depicting them as the savage bush. In addition, there are narratives that take their aim at the entire continent of Africa, describing it as a cursed land because of its participation in the slave trade. These accounts do not examine Africa's entrapment within global processes; rather, they describe the slave trade as an early moment in its internal combustion.

In Cape Coast and Elmina, the displacement of the slave trade from public history arenas results in part from these constructions of history and their attendant dangers. As a result of their "long conversation" (Comaroff and Comaroff 1991) with Europe, I argue, residents of Cape Coast and Elmina sequester discourses that map the slave trade onto their families, region, and nation from the public domain in an attempt to reform the image of themselves that is projected to a global audience.

Indeed, when I asked questions about the slave trade, men and women in Cape Coast and Elmina often insisted that it was not their history, for their ancestors had never owned slaves, had loved ones captured, or participated in captures. These responses require some complex navigations of historical evidence. Histories of slave owning have become part of private family discourses not often shared with outsiders in part in order to avoid providing any more fodder for European images of the perversion of African families. Additionally, histories of slave raiding are displaced onto the northern savannahs. Cape Coast and Elmina, their residents' argue, were places where slaves captured in the North were brought to be sold to Europeans and generally not sites of the actual procurement of slaves. By constructing this history and thereby distancing themselves from slave raiding, they avoid the special stigmatization that this aspect of the slave trade seems to attract.

By sequestering the slave trade, residents of Cape Coast and Elmina attempt to create respectable histories and thereby make an argument for their inclusion in the global order on better terms. In addition to hiding and displacing negative histories then, they embrace narratives that tie them to global processes. For instance, regional histories in Cape Coast and Elmina highlight the past cosmopolitanism of the coast that the presence of European traders produced. Like many European histories, in the process, they diminish the slave dealing between coastal merchants and Europeans within a larger picture of an emerging transnational economic order. Doing so also allows them to critique their contemporary decline that has resulted from the dissolution of their ties to Europe. Similarly, national histories stress colonialism and the independence struggle, thereby demonstrating the country's political maturity. The symbolic and real capital granted to nation-states contrasts sharply to the censure faced by an undifferentiated Africa, which is seen only as the land of the slave trade. To keep the latter image at bay, national histories must make the slave trade a minor addendum to the larger story of the emergence of the modern nation-state.

While these acts have an empowering effect, they have not tended to be viewed in this light. When confronted with sequestered histories, there is a tendency in the West to stress the importance of "breaking the silence." This desire has many roots, including Western psychotherapy, which suggests that trauma can only be cured through the discursive repetition of a narrative of the traumatic event (Leys 1996). But as many scholars have pointed out (see especially Battaglia 1992; Carsten 1995), silence is not always a symptom of a damaged psyche or of censorship from an outside power. Silence can also be a strategy that groups employ in order to negotiate oppressive conditions. In this way it can be productive of particular kinds of identities and positive possibilities.

Understanding precisely how sequestering the slave trade is an empowering act requires attention to the rules and agendas that guide historical discourse in southern Ghana. "In every society," Foucault argues,

> The production of discourse is at once controlled, selected, organised and redistributed according to a certain number of procedures, whose role is to avert its powers and its dangers, to cope with chance events, to evade its ponderous, awesome materiality. In a society such as our own we all know the rules of *exclusion*. The most obvious and familiar of these concerns what is *prohibited*. We know perfectly well that we are not free to say just anything, that we cannot simply speak of anything, when we like or where we like; not just anyone, finally, may speak just anything. (1972, 216)

The rules of exclusion at play in the assertions of men and women in Cape Coast and Elmina that "no one remembers anything about the slave trade" include prohibitions against public discussion of slave ownership or slave status within coastal families. They also involve the public disavowal of slave raiding and dealing as elements of the histories of Cape Coast and Elmina. In addition, they require downplaying the slave trade within national histories. As a result of these processes, discussions of the slave trade are sequestered into specific domains including private family discussions, references to northerners, veiled allusions, and minor sections of school textbooks. This sequestering, although always incomplete, is an attempt to protect notions of family, region, and nation and to imagine their improved status. These rules for the production of discourse demonstrate concerns for the portrayal of Cape Coast and Elmina not only within the boundaries of these towns but also within a global context.

As a result of their perceptions of the power that Europe has had (through its control of the Atlantic trade and its colonial power) and continues to yield (through, among other things, foreign aid), many Ghanaians have felt compelled to respond to European discourses. They may contest these discourses or appropriate them toward new ends, but nonetheless they must acknowledge and grapple with them. Their "conscription" (see Scott 2004) to these discourses is indeed what is implied by the invocation of a metropole-(post)colony imagined geography. Not only did these discourses emerge out of a past conversation with European traders and colonialists, but southern Ghanaians are still involved in a conversation with Europeans through international law, development discourses, and popular and academic histories, leading them to persist in their practices of sequestering the history of the slave trade. Indeed, in many ways, their identities are forged not through the discursive construction of the slave trade as their historical experience, but rather through the silence that surrounds it.

Atlantic Pasts

Many theorists have similarly noted a reluctance within various West African communities to discuss the slave trade.[2] Rosalind Shaw notes a fundamental problem in studying memories of the slave trade, namely, the unwillingness of most people to talk about it. She quotes Edward Ball, who describes an interview with a Sierra Leonean, stating, "Speaking through an interpreter, in Temne, he began by saying that the slave business was finished and that therefore it should not be spoken about" (Shaw 2002, 1). Robert Baum (1999) notes that in his initial interviews in Esulala, a Senegalese community, he was first told that slavery had never existed. These scholars have addressed the question raised by this silence by demonstrating that the slave trade is indeed invoked in ways other than explicit references to it within public speech. In this way, they contest the popular notion that silence regarding the slave trade is evidence of the absence of moral indignation concerning it within African societies and the judgment of these societies that it does not warrant commemoration. Certainly, as Shaw reminds us, "there are other ways of remembering the past than by speaking of it" (2002, 2). This insight leads her to distinguish between two types of memories, discursive and practical, which refer, respectively, to "explicit, intentional narrative accounts of the past" and those memories that are "embedded in habits, social practices, ritual processes, and embodied experiences" (2002, 7), with her focus being on the latter. Similarly, Baum examines shrines in Senegal devoted to slaves (1999). Other examples include Suzanne Blier's examination of the use of carved figures to depict slaves as ritual objects in southern Benin and Togo (1995), and Judy Rosenthal's exploration of the honoring of former slaves in Ewe Vodu rituals in southern Togo (1998). Indeed, with a few notable exceptions,[3] most scholars of collective memories of the slave trade in Africa use ritual as their primary site of analysis.

The focus on ritual and discourses about the spiritual realm underscores the idea that there are multiple ways to remember the past outside of the conventionalized arena of explicit verbal accounts. These scholars furthermore suggest that such silence in this arena derives from local logics. Shaw, for instance, draws on Jennifer Cole's examination of the lack of discussion of colonialism among the Betsimisaraka in Madagascar in which she argues that their process of remembering is "not the heroic history of events reflected in Merina and French archives" (1998, 614); rather, for them, "to remember is to draw a connection or link between themselves and the particular person or practice they remember. It is to recognize and thereby create the power of the persons who are remembered. Considered as a whole, Betsimisaraka theory holds that to remember is more than simply to recall a specific event or fact. It means defining their place in the world, asserting links with particular people and places while rejecting others" (1998, 616; quoted in Shaw 2002, 8). In this context, Cole plays on the double meaning of remembering: to recall the past as well as to re-member or to re-constitute it in order to discuss the ways in which memories may serve to reconstruct societies whose coherence has been threatened by tragic events. She notes that re-membering often involves "deliberate forgetting" (1998, 621), a process by which groups remember one set of relationships by forgetting another. Drawing on this work, Shaw observes that among the Temne of Sierra Leone, discursive memory similarly serves to evoke a connection to the past and empower the individuals being remembered. She argues, therefore, "In most cases, the violence of the slave trade and the moral difficulties it entailed would preclude its being an attractive choice for the drawing of such connections" (2002, 8). Similarly, Ralph Austen accounts for the absence of stories about the enslavement of innocent women and men among the Duala of Cameroon by explaining that "[t]his extremely antisocial, indeed inhumane, characteristic of the slave trade cannot, apparently, be discussed openly by the Duala and their neighbors, just as it is absent from the more plausibly historical oral tradition of many African societies that we know to have been engaged in such traffic on a larger scale than the Duala" (2001, 234). He suggests that judgments of the immorality of the slave trade are inherent to West African societies and independent of European discourses.

These scholars have demonstrated that the slave trade is indeed recalled in unconventional ways such as ritual or practical memory. They also note that it is referenced incidentally within narratives that purport to address other histories. In this way they have succeeded in broadening our understanding of how the past is *remembered*. There is room, however, to deepen our understanding of how and why particular histories are *sequestered* from the public domain. We might certainly probe further the question of why the slave trade is an unattractive history within conventional arenas of public history. Only through a close examination of those arenas and the histories that groups *do* explicitly produce and liberally share (those histories that have in this way become conventionalized) can we begin to answer this question. For this reason, instead of searching for hidden, implicit memories of the slave trade, this book focuses primarily on public, explicit constructions of the past. In part 1, in particular, I examine the ways in which the slave trade often serves as their foil and try to explain how and why the slave trade troubles them in this fashion.

Such an analysis reveals that while there are certainly local logics behind many African constructions of the past, these constructions are also shaped by global logics and, in particular, by the negative effects of many European narratives. They are products of a long conversation with Europe and the world at large, a conversation that has been shaped by forms of surveillance under colonialism as well as present-day development discourse with its Africa-as-failure mantra and the endless instantiations of Western ideologies of antiblack racism. Residents of Cape Coast and Elmina, in other words, seek to re-member themselves not only to themselves but also to a global audience. I suggest then that not only do they imagine the past in a strategic manner but that the context that their strategies attempt to negotiate includes the numerous ways in which they have been stigmatized through Europe's construction of the Atlantic slave trade. Their constructions of history are not simply rooted in local logics, they are also routed through the Atlantic.

Many of the conventionalized histories in Cape Coast and Elmina belong to genres that are widely recognized throughout many parts of the world and will certainly be familiar to Western readers such as family histories, church discourses, and histories taught in schools. Their familiarity is no coincidence. For these histories to make sense of coastal Ghanaians' place in the world, they must use terms that can be understood within a global context. I do not want to suggest here that all historical discourses have these concerns, only that constructions of history that do should be no less studied than witchcraft beliefs, mythic histories, and divination practices. After all, not all African productions of the past represent radical departures from the dominant terms of European historical consciousness. Many, including those listed above, are sites for the production and representation of the past that respond to Western categories on their own discursive terms.

These processes include, as I have noted, the sequestering of the slave trade, but they also entail the embrace of a separate set of European narratives about the Atlantic era. In particular, many local residents embrace narratives that describe their towns as enclaves of European modernity and, along with them, images of their towns' cosmopolitan pasts. Even some of the smallest gestures take up this agenda. During the time I lived in Ghana, for example, almost every day I walked over the bridge that spans Benya lagoon in Elmina and would see a colorful spectacle of brightly painted canoes waiting for the tide to allow them to go out to sea. Many of the boats display flags of various nations—Canada, England, France—a strange sight on boats that are clearly of local origin. I finally asked a friend why the fishermen displayed those flags on their boats, to which he replied that they simply copy the flags that they see on ships out at sea. But their mimicking seems also to recall a past in which Elmina was a famous port city, where ships from many nations regularly docked. Indeed, the Atlantic era forms a central part of local constructions of history here, despite the fact that today the only boats that dock in Elmina are small canoes, and one of their few ties to international commerce is through a fisherman's gaze at distant ships at sea. The invocation of global sites as seen through the use of national flags as decorations on fishing boats is repeated throughout Elmina. The maintenance of colonial place names such as Trafalgar Square and Buitenrust Lane are other examples of this practice. Similarly, local residents have applauded

1 Canoes with flags, Elmina

efforts to conserve the many old Dutch merchant homes, particularly on Liverpool Street, which runs from the lagoon bridge through the center of town. The name invokes another famous port city with which many Elminans seek to compare their town. In addition, the Dutch cemetery near the center of town is well kept and often pointed out to visitors.

Likewise, Cape Coast is home to Victoria Park, where a bust of Queen Victoria is still displayed. A small, brightly painted bridge in town bears the name London Bridge. There are also several European-style homes in Cape Coast, particularly along Commercial Street, Jackson Street, Garden Street, Coronation Street, and Beulah Lane. These reminders of the Atlantic era are but small examples of local attempts to construct an image of globality within their productions of regional histories, an image that matches some European discourses about these towns.

Such characterizations are perhaps troubling to some because they uphold connections to Europe and even the employment of European narratives as the source of symbolic capital. But the fact that attempts to gain symbolic capital entail the adoption of European criteria should not be surprising. In their discussion of the Tswana's opposition to missionaries, Comaroff and Comaroff note that they couched their critiques within

2 Fort St. Jago, Elmina

Eurocentric logics. For example, they describe a conversation between the Tswana and missionaries about what makes rain as follows: "In being drawn into that conversation, the Southern Tswana had no alternative but to be inducted, unwittingly and often unwillingly, into the *forms* of European discourse. To argue over who was the legitimate rainmaker or where the water came from, for instance, was to be seduced into the modes of rational debate, positivist knowledge, and empirical reason at the core of bourgeois culture" (1991, 213). Similarly, Ashis Nandy argues that the means of acculturation "produce not merely models of conformity but also models of 'official dissent' . . . Let us not forget that the most violent denunciation of the West produced by Frantz Fanon is written in the elegant style of a Jean-Paul Sartre" (1983, xii; see also Tsing 2005).

To be sure, a desire to represent those discourses that do not conform to Eurocentric narratives is what has led many anthropologists to formulate theories of alternative modernities. While scholars may celebrate these alternatives, the price of being labeled parochial is high. As James Ferguson notes, "[W]hat is lost in the overly easy extension of an ideal equality to 'modernities' in the plural are the all too real inequalities that leave most Africans today excluded and abjected from the economic and institutional

3 Historic home in Cape Coast

conditions that they themselves regard as modern" (2002, 559; see also Ferguson 2005; Hountondji 1983; Mudimbe 1988). With this recognition, we can no longer simply celebrate the continuation of practices of localization that reject Western norms; we must also pay attention to attempts to challenge global exclusion through the production of images that portray Africans as well positioned within an imagined European order. These attempts form an integral part of the life-worlds of many African people. Such an analysis does not deny the ways in which such assertions are always ambivalent and often openly overturned by competing discourses.

To this end, *Routes of Remembrance* examines the imbrication of coastal Ghanaian subjects within these discourses, not as their helpless victims, but rather as agentive and *well-versed* subjects. In stressing their deep literacy in the terms of Western narratives, I am suggesting not simply that these men and women are made by the forces of Western hegemony but that their practices of self-making consciously and strategically utilize its categories and terms. They utilize them even, and perhaps especially, when refuting the characterizations of their societies that these categories and terms entail.

In the context of these various complexities, local residents' embrace of those European discourses that cast them in a favorable light does not mean that they do not also hold the possibility of arriving at novel places. Such transformations occur not only through refutation but also in moments of

4 Historic home in Elmina

seeming conformity. Richard Werbner suggests that postcolonial relations are characterized by toying with power, a connivance with a wink (1996). Drawing on Achille Mbembe (1992), he argues that this interpretation "moves our understanding of playfulness in the face of tyranny—be it bureaucratic, charismatic, domestic, nationalist or otherwise close to home— from an overemphasis, in socio-political theory, on resistance to a perception of connivance" (1996, 2). Unfortunately, connivance is rarely studied by scholars out of a fear, Sherry Ortner (1995) notes, that to do so would compromise their representations of resistance (see also Abu-Lughod 1990).

While resistance suggests a rejection of normative terms, a conceptualization of connivance leads us to understand a negotiation of these terms that occurs only through a complete competency in them. The wink is an apt metaphor to describe a common response to the harsh realities of postcolonialism. It points to the strategic presentation of a particular image of self and leaves open the possibility of other beliefs or indeed alternative modernities at the same time that individuals may seek to position themselves within Western discourses. In *Routes of Remembrance,* various strategies that aim to exclude the slave trade from discourse and thereby define a belonging to "modernity" constitute this wink.

Scholars have long noted that in the African diaspora, a similar winking gesture, a split vision or double consciousness (Du Bois 1989; see also Gilroy 1993), derives from the experience of the slave trade. Most of these studies have, however, failed to view African societies as also inheriting this Atlantic past. At the same time, Africanists have tended not to discuss this gesture as an effect of the Atlantic economy. In West Africa, perhaps particularly in the parts that are situated on the Atlantic shore, African subjects not only shoulder the legacies of colonialism, they also bear the burden of responding to representations born out of the slave trade. This is, indeed, the burden of blackness that, while strangely ignored in much of Africanist literature, manifests itself in a variety ways in Ghana. I propose then, a view of contemporary African societies within the geographies provided by theories of postcolonialism as well as those provided by theories of the black Atlantic in order to attend to the ways in which both colonialism and the slave trade shape contemporary African subjectivities (see also Pierre 2002; Piot 2001).

Diasporic Engagements

If we take seriously the ways in which African subjects are entrapped in conversations with Europe, we should likewise take seriously the ways in which they may find resources to negotiate their entrapment within discourses produced by groups that are similarly ensnared. This focus forces us to pay attention to conversations that connect specifically black groups in the circum-Atlantic world. Indeed, as I stated above, the rules of exclusion regarding the slave trade are currently being challenged as the result of another transatlantic conversation in which residents of Cape Coast and Elmina are increasingly involved, a conversation with the African diaspora. While there is a long tradition of the interchange of ideas across the Atlantic that has involved Ghana, today diaspora tourism is one of the main catalysts for these conversations. The greater affordability of jet travel has enabled the growth of this industry over the past two decades. Whereas the ship was once the key symbol of black Atlantic travel (Gilroy 1993), today planes are the more relevant image.

For the most part, diaspora tourism discusses the slave trade in order to detail the origin story of the African diaspora. It takes diaspora tourists to the very spaces where slaves were forced into the hulls of slave ships to embark on the Middle Passage after inhabiting a similar hell in the bowels of the slave dungeons. Revisiting this history, however, does not necessarily challenge dominant Western discourses. By stressing that this horror has ended, diaspora tourism often in fact reifies popular narratives that paint the slave trade as the prelude to "modern" freedom in the West. In doing so, it also provides the necessary conditions for contrasting constructions of the slave trade as an indelible stain on the African continent. For this reason in particular, many Ghanaians who encounter diaspora tourism simply disregard its narratives and continue their practices of sequestering the slave trade.

Others, however, have begun to refashion these representations of the slave trade. In contrast to critiques of African actors within the web of power created by the Atlantic trade, they focus on this web of power itself, one that represented a new global terrain characterized by racial terror, sexual violence, and economic exploitation.[4] These strategies recall diasporic counternarratives. While, as I mention above, blacks on both sides of the Atlantic critique the ways in which they are viewed by the white/Western world, a crucial difference is that throughout their history, diaspora blacks have openly referenced the slave trade in some of these critiques. They have sought to disrupt the West's claims to progress and rationality by representing rather the presence of this past in the present. In contrast to celebratory discourses about slavery's end, individuals like Toni Morrison (1987), Derek Walcott (1990), and Keith Piper (1996), for instance, demonstrate that "history is not 'history,' not a property of the past but the property the present inherits as its structuring material *and* the property (both affective and instrumental) the past holds in the present" (Baucom 2005, 330). Their counternarratives of slavery point to the permanence of an always-gendered racial terror (Gilroy 1993) and force us to recognize, as Bauman argues with regard to the Holocaust "the double-sidedness of modern social arrangement" (1989, 28).

The African diaspora, as part of the West but made distinct by the implications of its blackness, is of course uniquely positioned to critique Western assumptions. Thus, Michel-Rolph Trouillot refers to the Caribbean as an example of the "other from within" (2002, 228; see also Campt 2004, 102). He argues that this narrative of Caribbean history "suggests much less the need to rewrite Caribbean history than the necessity to question the story that the North Atlantic tells about itself" (2002, 222). In other words, this positionality points not simply to the African diaspora having a different history, but also to its ability to throw into question the assumptions of European histories.

Today, some Ghanaians are finding ways to make similar critiques by pointing to the slave trade as a key moment of their own engagement with the West. Contrary to popular paradigms, they argue that the slave trade represents not only the history *of* Africa but also the history of the West's impact *on* Africa. These discourses appeal to youth in particular, who are most exposed to diaspora tourism. They provide them with a language with which to contest their contemporary oppression and through which they can embrace a transnational black identity. This adoption represents the latest instantiation within a long history of black Atlantic identifications in Ghana. Recent neoliberal policies have driven their current popularity. Indeed, Ghana's dismal outlook with regard to the global economy has led to a slow shift in perceptions of history in Ghana that reveal skepticism toward the promises of nationalism. The current moment then brings a negotiation in which the distinct positionalities of West Africa and the African diaspora are being questioned and rethought. In this sense, Ghanaian remembrances are increasingly routed not only through dominant Western narratives but also through those of the African diaspora.

Place, Memory, and Identity

The emphasis on the transnational nature of collective memory has implications beyond the history of the slave trade. With a few notable exceptions (see, especially, Schwenkel 2006; White 1995; Yoneyama 1999), collective memory is viewed to delimit the membership in a given society. In other words, even as groups reflect upon global forces such as colonialism and capitalism, they do so, most argue, according to local logics (see especially Comaroff and Comaroff 1993). As a result, these processes seem to only shore up the local. Of course, local beliefs and practices are transformed in the process, but the idea of "the local" is maintained and perhaps strengthened as a result. For members of these communities, the story they tell to themselves about themselves, to use Geertz's (1973) phrase, is undecipherable to anyone outside, save a dedicated anthropologist.

Given the focus on syncretism within most other arenas of social life on both sides of the Atlantic, it is curious that scholars have not by and large placed constructions of history within this context. To be sure, the representation of the local specificity of collective memory embodies an important theoretical shift by de-universalizing European theories of historical consciousness. It points to the fact that these theories are inherently cultural and therefore not applicable in every society. The appeal of the notion of local productions of the past, like the appeal of the notion of alternative modernities, is, of course, its ability to oppose an image of a complete Western hegemony that sweeps the globe, erasing all cultural diversity. Few any longer believe that such is the fate of the world. But as this project demonstrates, not only discourses that arise from the specificities of local contexts but also those that emerge through transnational dialogues may provide alternatives to dominant Western narratives.

Through an examination of the latter, we can examine how individuals aim not only to tell a story to themselves about themselves but also to speak to the larger world. While the chapters of this book address historical discourses specific to different groups, namely, families, regional communities, and the nation, as well as a shifting and unstable black Atlantic, their analyses seek to challenge the notion that collective memory is an internal product of any one group. I explicitly posit, therefore, that while individuals situate themselves within particular social groups and use their constructions of the past to attempt to define them, these groups and the discourses that they produce are always in conversation with larger social contexts.

As should be clear, I am interested here in the perceived consequences of various historical narratives. In his seminal work on nationalism, Benedict Anderson (1991, 6) argues that "communities are to be distinguished, not by their falsity/genuineness, but by the style in which they are imagined." Similarly, in his discussion of the status of both slavery and Africa in the historical consciousness of Africans in the diaspora, David Scott suggests that anthropologists move away from concerns regarding authenticity and instead attempt to "describe the tradition of discourse in which they participate, the local network of power and knowledge in which they are employed, and the kinds of identity they serve to fashion" (1991, 280). As I demonstrate below, there are many styles by which groups imagine the past, and it is an interest in the style of this imaginative feat, and not an interest in judging their histories against the fantasy of a complete history, that propels this study. The important question here is not the historical accuracy of these histories but rather the process and effects of their construction.

Many scholars have argued that collective memory should not be viewed to be simply strategic, as simply concerned with "the politics of the present," some in response to Halbwachs's (1980) argument that collective memory serves to cement the bonds of group affiliation. They have addressed constructions of the past both in their institutional forms (Connerton 1989; Handler and Gable 1997; Gillis 1994) and in their ritual and everyday manifestations (Cole 2001; Shaw 2002; Stoller 1995) in order to explore the complex set of forces that constructs them. Because they are constructed intentionally for the public arena, however, within the histories that I discuss, what they represent as well as what they leave out must be viewed with an eye toward their strategic aims.

In addition, scholars have noted that there are always multiple versions of history. To be sure, the dominant constructions of history that I describe in the pages that follow are not mobilized by every resident of Cape Coast and Elmina. Some of the family, regional, and national histories in part 1 are specific to a particular class. Nearly all are most familiar to individuals who have had some schooling and speak some English, who read newspapers or at least watch television or listen to the radio, and who attend church. This description, however, fits a large percentage of the residents of these towns. What I seek to draw attention to then is the formation of conventionalized representations of the past as those narratives that a large number of people in Cape Coast and Elmina can recognize and articulate *even if they choose to contradict them.* Indeed, as I discuss in part 2, the youth who, through their encounters with diaspora tourism, produce alternative narratives, do so with a full awareness of these conventionalized narratives.

In addition, the question of audience is crucial. The telling of family histories in the presence of nonkin, the recounting of community histories to strangers, and the writing of academic histories in the context of the dominance of European historiography are frameworks that are central to an understanding of the content of historical narratives in Cape Coast and Elmina. Even when residents tell stories to each other, the West is present as a ghostly audience, as these conversations are ways of embracing an "imagined cosmopolitanism" (Schein 1999). It is imagined because "participants in this cosmopolitanism do not meet face to face"; nevertheless, what prompts it is "a longing for horizontality, for eradicating the differentials of power and wealth that otherwise amount to exclusions" (Schein 1999, 360). Recognition of the importance of these frameworks led me to examine the implications of my subject position, as I was at times the intended audience for these narratives. When I was the interlocutor, my status as nonkin and stranger certainly mattered. In many ways, I represented "the West" to my informants, but at the same time, the length of my stay and the close relationships that I formed with many of them served to cast me as a trusted friend. My blackness also allowed many to engage in racial discourses that they might not have otherwise. My complex status as both stranger and temporary community member, both Westerner and black person, both American graduate student and later professor, and as a young woman prone to ask challenging questions provided a rich context for discovering the complexities of coastal identities.

The Atlantic Littoral

As I hope to show, Cape Coast and Elmina are located both literally and figuratively on the edge of the Atlantic world. While there are many differences between the two towns that I discuss in the following chapter, they share a past status as ports of Atlantic trade. The significance of their position on the coast to their constructions of identities and histories cannot be overstated. For people in these towns, the sea is central to their lives. I, in fact, refer to them throughout the book as "coastal residents" (although it should be noted that this designation refers here specifically to residents of these two towns and not to all of the inhabitants of the entire stretch of coast in Ghana). Many of the men are fishermen, and in Elmina, an estimated one-quarter of women are involved in the smoking, processing, and marketing of fish (Arhin 1995). In addition to fishing, salt mining is another major industry in this region. But these two towns are also and importantly located a two to three hours' drive from Accra, the capital of Ghana, and Cape Coast, which was the former capital of the British colony and home to many of the early nationalists leaders, is now the capital of the Central Region, an area that includes the center of the coastal area, west of Accra and east of Sekondi. It has approximately 100,000 residents. Elmina has a population of only 20,000. Outside of fishing and salt mining, many residents are petty traders who trade their wares at small roadside kiosks or at one of the central market places. The recent elaboration of the tourist market here has led to the development of two luxury hotels and several three-star hotels, which provide jobs for a fortunate few. Outside of these jobs, however, the tourism industry has in fact brought little development to these towns.

Because of Cape Coast's position as the capital of the Central Region, although it is a small town, it has many amenities. There is a Barclay's Bank, the Center for National Culture, a sports stadium, and many regional government offices. It also has a bus station with daily service to Accra, Kumasi, and other cities and towns. Between two of my visits in 1999 and 2001, two department stores sprang up on the main road in town as well as a large Internet cafe. Cape Coast was the site of the earliest missionary activity in Ghana, and the Anglican, Methodist, and Catholic churches are evidence of this past. More recently, the Presbyterian and African Methodist Episcopal Zion churches and countless charismatic churches have been built in Cape

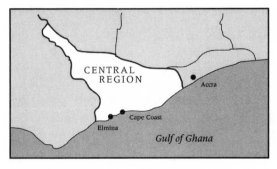

5 Map of Ghana

Coast. In addition, Cape Coast's missionary history made it the site of the first European schools in Ghana, and it remains its most important center for secondary education. There are several secondary schools in Cape Coast, including some of the most prestigious schools in the country. Perhaps most significantly, Cape Coast is also home to one of the five major universities in Ghana, the University of Cape Coast. As a result of the numerous schools here, a large percentage of the region's professional class is made up of teachers.

In contrast, Elmina has seen little development since the departure of the Dutch in 1872. It has no schools of national repute and one rural bank. There are no major office buildings in Elmina and in fact, until recently, not a single pay phone in the entire town. Residents have had to rely on a handful of communications centers or travel to Cape Coast to make calls. The major religion in Elmina is Catholicism, but other churches include the Methodist, Anglican, and charismatic churches. The state bus system does not operate a station in Elmina, and the main Accra-Takoradi road bypasses the town, attesting to its marginal status.

Cape Coast and Elmina are located eight miles from one another, and residents of each town regularly travel to the other by way of shared taxis or by "tro-tros," which are small buses or vans. There is regular commerce between the two towns, and many people commute daily between them. Also, many of the region's hotels are situated on the road between Cape Coast and Elmina because of their treatment by the tourism industry as twin cities. These towns have seen little economic development. They in fact lack any major industries, leading many residents to dream of better lives elsewhere. Indeed, while the landscape of Accra has become dotted with skyscrapers and is crisscrossed by motorways conjuring tales of modernization, Cape Coast and Elmina were left with crumbling buildings that seem to tell a story of defeat. Coastal identities are fractured by past wealth and present poverty, early political activity and present political marginalization, and the status of these towns as the destination of tourists from throughout the world and sites that few residents find the means to leave. These contradictions as well as the towns' economically marginalized status within a marginalized nation are crucial to an understanding of local constructions of history and, in particular, the status of the slave trade within coastal historical narratives.

The Project

Routes of Remembrance is based on an eight-year engagement with Ghana. Since my initial visit there in 1999, I have traveled to Ghana many times, attempting to find answers to the questions with which I was first confronted. I spent twelve months in Cape Coast and Elmina in 2001 and have made four additional research trips of one to two months in length. During this time, I attended community events, sat in on history classes at local schools, observed numerous tours at the castles, and observed PANAFEST and Emancipation Day celebrations in 1999, 2001, and 2005. In addition, I interviewed local residents, students, tour guides, tourism officials, teachers, education officials, and both Ghanaian and international tourists.

The chapters that follow are divided into two parts. Part 1 discusses arenas in which local residents seek to sequester the history of the slave trade. Part 2 explores the current renegotiation of the history of the slave trade as a result of the diaspora tourism industry. Chapter 1 situates the study historically by examining the development of discourses about families, the coastal region, and the nation during the Atlantic and colonial eras. I discuss the ways in which notions of families were altered to account for the growing population of enslaved individuals that existed within them. I then examine the formation of regional identity beginning in the last two decades of the nineteenth century. I argue that in their construction of an urban coastal identity, early coastal elites eschewed discussion of the Atlantic slave trade. These residents stressed instead their incorporation within the European order to argue that coastal elites should be incorporated into the British colonial apparatus. I also discuss the beginnings of a larger national identity that responded in part to European histories that defined all of the inhabitants of the Gold Coast collectively as a degenerate population as a result of the slave trade.

In chapters 2–5, I examine how contemporary subjectivities are shaped by notions of identity that were forged during earlier periods. Chapter 2 discusses the place of domestic slavery within constructions of family histories. I focus on this topic not only because domestic slavery increased as a result of the Atlantic slave trade but also because I learned that when I brought up the topic of slavery, domestic slavery is what first leapt to mind, which is in large part a result of the use of the same term for both. I argue that with regard to family histories, in public, individuals often flatly deny that members of their families were enslaved, while in private settings, stories of past enslavement are common. The sequestering of family histories of slavery from public discourse, which occurs through claims that no one remembers anything about domestic slavery, serves to guard against the stigmatization of family members and thereby to define families in accordance with the terms of modern legal apparatuses.

Chapter 3 addresses regional histories by examining the ways in which coastal residents, who seek to distance themselves from the stigma of past vulnerability to enslavement, place this stigma instead onto northerners. The result has been the development of a stark division between the North and the South that arose from the geography of the slave trade and continues today based in part on the oft-cited notion that the North represented a past pool of potential slaves. In chapter 4, I argue that coastal residents replace narratives of enslavement with stories of their past integration into the Atlantic economy on favorable terms. These narratives allow for the construction of critiques of the present based on a conceptualization of past glory and recent decline or, in other words, following Ferguson (1999), a notion of abjection. Such constructions require downplaying the slave dealing that occurred on the coast in order to focus specifically on the effects of the postcolonial moment.

Chapter 5 explores national histories by examining history textbooks and classrooms. It argues that these arenas have been heavily influenced by European colonial historians whose histories of colonial Ghana, then the Gold Coast, used the slave trade in order to brand Ghanaians with a racial stigma. School textbooks in particular have been sites in which European historians have highlighted the slave trade in order to create an image of African savagery. In attempting to write against this legacy, postcolonial Ghanaian textbook writers have marginalized the history of the slave trade, making it subsidiary to the story of colonialism and independence. Through schooling then, the slave trade became a present if embattled part of national history. These various strategies of sequestering the slave trade operate by alternately repositioning it within private discourses, discourses about northerners, and subsidiary histories of the nation, all of which function to minimize the effects of the history of the slave trade on coastal residents' constructions of their contemporary identities.

In part 2, I turn to the tourism industry's centering of the slave trade. Chapter 6 addresses this development as an outcome of an Afro-Atlantic dialogue (Matory 2005) involving African-American expatriates and tourists, local authorities, and international organizations like the Smithsonian. This dialogue has led to the conservation of the castles, the development of three museums within them, and the celebration of PANAFEST and Emancipation Day. The development of the castles as tourist sites has been hotly contested, both by African Americans residing in Ghana who insisted that the castles be treated as the sacred abodes of the spirits of those enslaved and by many Ghanaians who insisted that the interpretation of the castles' histories not be limited to this sorrowful past. These sites have nonetheless produced very particular narratives about the slave trade that remain in many ways problematic to their local audiences.

Chapter 7 explores these problems and the ways in which local residents negotiate new discourses that have entered into the discursive field through the route of diaspora tourism. While diaspora tourism has faced opposition from Ghanaians who question the emphasis placed on a marginalized history, the tourism industry, which responds to an emerging global dialogue regarding the slave trade that is equally contested, has nonetheless introduced new possibilities for the discursive mobilization of history within emancipatory projects.

In essence, this project examines the slave trade within many arenas, including the incomplete silences surrounding it in family and community histories, to its troubled presentation in classrooms and nationalist narratives, and finally, to its great elaboration by the tourism industry. This is a story of a series of global conversations and their production of varied and circuitous routes of remembrance.

PART I »

Sequestering the Slave Trade

1 » *Of Origins*

MAKING FAMILY, REGION, NATION

C ape Coast and Elmina, although minor towns in a small West African country, were once essential sites in the Atlantic trade and, as such, had famed reputations in Europe. Elmina, as the site of the first European-style building in West Africa, earned the appellation *Aborekyir kaakra* or "little Europe" (Wartemberg 1950, 25). In the early part of the nineteenth century, Cape Coast was known as the "Athens of the Gold Coast" (Arhin 1995, 3). These appellations demonstrate the construction of both towns as central nodes in the Atlantic world. They also point to the processes through which Cape Coast and Elmina were remade through reference to Europe. Indeed, contemporary subjectivities in Cape Coast and Elmina must be understood within the context of the transformations wrought by the Atlantic trade and the encounter between coastal residents and European peoples, power, and practices.

In contrast to most historical studies of this region, which attempt to de-fine continuities within the large swath of geography that would become the Gold Coast, I focus on the continuities between two of its specific nodes.[1] As the headquarters of the British and Dutch, respectively, on the coast, Cape Coast and Elmina were the two most important port cities for Atlantic trade on the Gold Coast. They shared a status as cosmopolitan trading centers. For this reason, while they were separated in the past by their membership within different political alliances, the processes through which they came to understand their place in the Atlantic world were quite similar. Moreover, the focus on these urban spaces as opposed to the rural areas surrounding them is important because as Margaret Priestley notes, "Maritime towns rose to prominence around the forts and became the focal points of a wide, commercial network extending along the seaboard and into the hinterland" (1969, 12–13).

The inhabitants of these towns were truly "Atlantic creoles" (Berlin 1998). Their societies were formed through a complex interplay of race and gender that necessarily characterizes creole societies. These towns not only hosted European traders, they also became filled with traders and laborers of various kinds from other African regions, creating ethnically diverse populations. Many men understood the intricacies of doing business with both African traders from the hinterland and Europeans. Many women negotiated various types of romantic relationships with European men and were often involved in their own business dealings as well. Some of the residents of these towns attended European-style schools starting in the eighteenth century and converted to Christianity. In these ways, their encounter with Europeans defined their romantic, economic, and social relationships. It therefore played a key role in the formation of families, the emergence of an urban coastal identity, and the development of a larger national identity.

These past relationships with Europeans, furthermore, continue to define coastal residents' understandings of these identities today. In particular, as I argue in this chapter, their intimacy with Europeans forced them to navigate European discourses about the slave trade, and ultimately led them to sequester it from constructions of their histories. For this reason, I will explore the history of this sequestering before turning to discussion of contemporary identity constructions. What follows makes no attempt to represent a complete history; rather it examines some key elements of the Atlantic and colonial eras that are central to the story that follows.

I begin here with a general discussion of the design of the Atlantic world from the point of view of coastal residents, followed by sections devoted to the making of notions of family, coastal identity, and national identity. These sections are meant to provide an historical background for the complimentary chapters in part 1.

A Brief History of Two Slave Ports

Cape Coast and Elmina began as two small fishing villages named Oguaa and Edina, respectively. Oguaa was founded by the Guan people in the thirteenth or fourteenth century as part of the Fetu kingdom. Edina belonged to both the Fetu and Komenda kingdoms. During the fifteenth century, an

Akan-speaking[2] group migrated to the coast from Techiman, a northern town, and soon became the dominant group throughout the coast, including in Cape Coast and Elmina. Today known as the Fante, this group shares a language (also called Fante) as well as certain social institutions including the *abusua*, or matrilineal family, and the *asafo*, a set of military companies to which every member of a given society belonged and in which membership was passed down patrilineally. They also shared similar religious beliefs (Priestley 1969, 17–19).

It was also during the fifteenth century that the Portuguese began trading expeditions to what would later be known as the Gold Coast. They sought to seize control of trade in this region from Muslim traders in North Africa and to establish a new route to the Asante goldfields. Their first contact with the Gold Coast was at Edina, and there they discovered a vast supply of gold. They began trading guns, brass and copper objects, and cloth in exchange for gold and soon decided to establish trade in Edina, which they named *A Mina*, or "the mine," which would later be transformed into "Elmina" (Lawrence 1964, 103). They chose a site between the Benya lagoon and the sea in Edina as the most strategic site on which to establish the base of their trading activities, and, in 1482, the Portuguese captain Don Diego d'Azambuja gained permission from a local king, Kwamena Ansa, to build a fort, which he named São Jorge da Mina, or Saint George of the Mine (Sarbah 1968b), on this piece of land that he rented annually.

The Portuguese soon discovered the existence of a burgeoning market for slaves in the Asante kingdom. They thus began importing slaves from the kingdom of Benin in present-day Nigeria as well as from the Congo to sell to Asante traders. These slaves were transported through São Tomé, which became a slave depot, to Elmina to exchange for gold. The Portuguese trade itself increased the demand for slaves because slaves were needed to serve as porters to transport trade goods between the coast and the Asante kingdom and to work in its gold mines (Vogt 1973). In the fifteenth and early sixteenth centuries, slaves accounted for 10 percent of the Portuguese trade, involving the importation of 10,000–12,000 slaves between 1500 and 1535 alone (Wilks 1993, 24). The Asante also received slaves from the North from Hausa and Mossi traders. They had established a trade with northern territories prior to the arrival of the Portuguese. Before the increase in the demand for slaves, the majority of this trade involved salt, cloth, and brass and copper items. During the sixteenth century, northern groups like the Wangara traders began providing slaves to the Asante in greater numbers (Wilks 1993).

The Portuguese traders themselves also kept slaves to serve them at the castle and sent several of them to Lisbon in the early part of the sixteenth century. Some of these slaves were later shipped to the Spanish holdings in the Americas. In 1532, a Portuguese ship named Santo Antonio transported 201 Africans directly from São Tomé to the West Indies, marking one of the earliest Middle Passage voyages (Vogt 1973). Most of the slaves were bought in the kingdom of Benin and not in the Gold Coast because the Portuguese feared that their capturing of slaves would upset the gold trade there. To prevent this outcome, slave capture was forbidden within ten leagues of Elmina Castle (Rodney 1969, 14).

Other European nations soon followed the Portuguese in their desire to enter the trade on the Gold Coast. Dutch, Swedish, Bradenburgers, French, British, and Danish companies were all among the parties that eventually established forty-three principal forts and castles along the west coast of Africa, thirty-two of these on the Gold Coast (Lawrence 1964, 14–15).[3] The Dutch established a fort at Mouri, ten miles east of Elmina, and sought to monopolize trade on the coast. After several attempts, they captured Elmina Castle from the Portuguese in 1637 and expanded the trade from Elmina (DeCorse 2001, 23). The rise of sugar plantations in the Dutch colonies in Brazil soon prompted the Dutch to enter the transatlantic slave trade, but they, like the Portuguese before them, took few slaves from the Gold Coast, preferring to secure slaves from the kingdom of Benin. They continued to emphasize the gold trade as their primary trade on the Gold Coast until competition with the British encouraged them to increase their participation in the slave trade.

Meanwhile, a little further down the coast, various European powers fought to establish a presence in Oguaa because of its strategic position on a cape jutting out into the sea. The Portuguese called this town Cabo Corso, meaning "short cape." In the 1650s, the Swedes were granted land from the Fetu king to build a fort, which they named Fort Carolusburg after King Charles X of Sweden. After several exchanges, the fort ended up in the hands of the Dutch. The worldwide competition between the British and Dutch during this period included conflicts over their West African trading posts. A group of British merchants known as the Company of Royal Adventurers was the major competitor of the Dutch West India Company for control of trade on the coast, and in 1664, the British captured the fort and renamed it Cape Coast Castle, a corruption of the Portuguese Cabo Corso. In 1672, the Royal Africa Company took over the assets of the Royal Adventurers, who had been ruined financially by the war, and made the fort the headquarters of their West African operations and expanded it into a true castle (Lawrence 1964, 183). Between 1700 and 1807, the British exported 408,460 slaves from the Gold Coast, accounting for approximately 13 percent of their total slave exports from West Africa (Richardson 1989, 13).

By the early eighteenth century, the two major slave-trading powers on the Gold Coast were the Dutch, who occupied fifteen forts with their headquarters at Elmina, and the British, who occupied nine forts with their headquarters at Cape Coast (Feinberg 1989, 41).[4] These groups were aligned with the people in the towns who monopolized the African side of the trade. Both towns operated as independent city-states, although Cape Coast was closely allied with the Fante Coalition, an alliance of states that came to dominate the coastal region in the eighteenth century from the area just east of Elmina to just west of Accra. Elmina, on the other hand, remained wholly outside of the Fante Coalition and was allied instead with the Asante, an expansionist kingdom situated in the hinterland (McCarthy 1983).

Despite occasional cases, elites in Cape Coast and Elmina had little fear of enslavement. Not only were they granted protection from enslavement, but also some became prominent traders, serving as intermediaries between traders from the hinterland and the European companies. One example is Edward Barter, a native of Cape Coast and one of the most influential African traders. He was sent to England to be educated, sponsored by the Royal African Company. When he returned to Cape Coast in 1693, he was employed by the British. He soon gained in importance until all trade that was conducted in Cape Coast passed through him (Daaku 1970).

Birempon Kwadwo was another prominent member of the coastal African trading community. He was born in the 1700s and became one of the chief traders in Cape Coast. Known by the British as Cudjo Caboceer,[5] he was often entrusted by them with large sums of money with which to buy slaves. One recorded story claims that Kwadwo would often retain some of the slaves he bought with this money as his domestic servants (Graham 1994). When the British asked for the slaves, he told them that some of the slaves had died and showed them recently filled graves where he claimed they were buried. In this way, Kwadwo peopled four villages that became part of Cape Coast. The British continued to hold Kwadwo in the highest regard, which attests to their ignorance with regard to his ruse, and in 1774, presented him with two silver goblets with an inscription that read, "A present from the committee of the company of Merchants Trading to Africa to Cudjoe, [*sic*] Caboceer for his faithful service and adherence to the subjects of his most sacred Majesty King George III, Anno Domini 1774" (quoted in Graham 1994, 8).

In Elmina, the position of *makelaar,* or broker, was the official designation of the West India Company's African commercial agent. Abocan became *makelaar* around 1712. He became quite wealthy and owned a fleet of small boats, a salt village, and a body of retainers. Feinberg (1989) notes that he also paid the Dutch to free a number of slaves owned by the company. Jan Nieser of Elmina was a local merchant who established connections to Louyssen and Son, one of the largest commercial houses for slaves in the Netherlands, through which he was able to establish himself as a private trader. In 1794, he reported that he could obtain five hundred slaves per year (Lever 1970, 255). During this period, with the development of a small class of extremely wealthy African traders, the basis for social status shifted to being determined almost wholly by wealth. In addition to wealth generation, involvement in the slave trade clearly allowed local traders to control who was and was not enslaved.

Throughout the eighteenth century, the Asante sought to wrest control of the trading route to the coast from the Fante Coalition, which led to a succession of wars between the Coalition, which fought on the side of Cape Coast with the support of the British on one side, and Elmina and the Asante, who were supported by the Dutch on the other.[6]

The British abolished the capture and transport of slaves in 1807, and the Dutch in 1814, but the slave trade continued long after this time. The year 1807 also marked the Asante invasion of the coast, which led to the destruction of many Fante villages, although Cape Coast was not directly attacked (McCarthy 1983). George Maclean was appointed governor by the British Committee of Merchants in 1830 and attempted to restore peace between the Fante and the Asante by treaty in 1831. He extended British judicial jurisdiction over parts the coast. During this same period, the Dutch began recruiting for soldiers from the Gold Coast to fight for them in Indonesia. Many of these recruits were slaves brought down from the hinterland. After they served their tour of duty, they were brought back to Elmina where many settled down in an area that became known as Java Hill, thereby adding to the coast's unique cultural mix.

In 1834, the British government abolished slavery in its colonies. During this time, an illegal slave trade continued that supplied slaves to Brazil and Cuba (Getz 2004, 32). In part to curb this trade, in 1844, the British Crown took control of the parts of the coast that had traditionally had a British presence, shifting what had been mostly a merchant presence to a limited colonial rule.

With the resultant slowdown of the slave trade, the Dutch were no longer able to remain profitable in their operations on the coast, so in 1872, they ceded Elmina Castle to the British and left the Gold Coast. The loss of these important allies would have dire consequences for the residents of Elmina. Throughout the Atlantic era, Elmina had been aligned with the Asante, who sought to wrest control of the trading route to the coast from the Fante Coalition, which had the support of the British. In 1873, the Asante defeated the Fante alliance, but soon afterward, the British in turn defeated the Asante kingdom during the Anglo-Asante war of 1873–74, after which the Gold Coast became a full-fledged colony. During a later expedition, the British imprisoned the *asantehene* (Asante king), Prempeh I, at the castle and later exiled him. In addition, because of Elmina's alliance with the Asante, they exiled the *ɔmanhene* (Fante king) of Elmina, Nana Kobena Igyan, and burned the part of the Elmina township where the lower classes lived to the ground.

The displaced residents rebuilt their homes in another part of the town; however, they could not reconstruct their former status in the Atlantic order within the emerging British colonial order. Because of the opposition that its residents had staked against the British, the British had poor relations with Elmina after its defeat and the town slumped into decline. When the British declared all of southern Ghana their colony in 1874, they made Cape Coast its capital. The second half of the nineteenth century marked the era of legitimate trade based primarily on palm oil and gold. Cape Coast, which was the greatest benefactor of this trade, developed a class of merchant-princes during this era. It also established a professional class of doctors, lawyers, teachers, catechists, and civil servants who would form the basis of the Gold Coast intelligentsia of the various nationalist campaigns.

Making Families

MARRYING EUROPEANS

Over the course of the roughly four hundred years during which Cape Coast and Elmina were the center of various European projects on the Gold Coast, Europeans formed a distinct community with which local residents had numerous kinds of interactions. Most of this community consisted of employees of the major European trading companies. Between 1673 and 1713, the number of employees of the British Royal Africa Company stationed at Cape Coast fluctuated between thirty-nine and 115 (Davies 1957, 247–48). At Elmina, the Dutch West India Company had between seventy and one hundred men stationed at the Castle during the eighteenth century (Feinberg 1989, 35), dropping to between five and twenty in the early nineteenth century (Yarak 1986, 34).[7]

A significant feature of the European community on the coast was that it was composed almost entirely of men. Few European women traveled with men to Cape Coast and Elmina. One Dutch official sent his wife back to the Netherlands because he feared the sexual advances of other European men with her being the only white woman there (Feinberg 1989, 86–87), and in fact, European companies discouraged their male employees from bringing their wives with them. A climate to which Europeans were unaccustomed as well as their susceptibility to tropical diseases were additional factors that dissuaded women from traveling to the coast.

Given the lack of European women, the fact that European men formed relationships with local women is not surprising. For many of these women, such relationships were quite attractive because they represented a major avenue to elite status. In addition to relationships of trade then, the creole nature of the coast is also exemplified by the sexual and romantic relationships between European men and African women. For the very reason that they demonstrate the marriage of African and European life-worlds, which is a key fact for thinking through coastal residents' contemporary ensnarement by European discourses, not only with respect to local families, but also with respect to their regional and national identities, I discuss these relationships at some length. Men formed these relationships either by purchasing women as slaves or by taking free women as mistresses or wives. Relationships between enslaved women and European men were founded on the condition of female powerlessness. Any man who had the means could buy a female slave and take up residence with her. Even if the European man gave her her freedom, that freedom was undoubtedly contingent on her continued relationship with him. As she was a slave, she likely would have been brought from a distant region and therefore have no family or means of protection. While these relationships can only be understood as being based on female subjugation, relationships between free women and European men, as demonstrated below, were much more complex.

These relationships were usually unofficial liaisons resembling common law marriages. This practice was encouraged by the Dutch West India Company. Ann Stoler describes a similar sanctioning by the Dutch East Indies Company in Indonesia, which viewed these relationships as "a prerequisite for quick acclimatization, as insulation from the ill-health that sexual abstention, isolation and boredom were thought to bring" (1989, 637).[8]

The British likewise encouraged relationships with local women, referring to this practice as "country marriage" (Priestley 1969). A nineteenth-century account of country marriage describes it as follows:

> [W]ith some it appears to be a practice when they become settled in Business for any length of time to form a connection with some native Molatto Girls for the time they remain in the country. When they amass Wealth enough to retire to Europe they leave to the Girl a certain proportion to subsist upon thereafter, But as there are no laws, nor stated customs, to regulate this proportions, the matter entirely depends upon the liberality of the individual . . . Such Compacts are considered as long as the parties reside on the coast as sacred and valid as marriages with us, and I know of many instances after the parties living together for years and having children to have the compact sanctioned by marriage itself. (quoted in Brooks 1962, 76)

The nature of these "marriages" is difficult to ascertain. While one might assume that it was a form of sexual slavery, not only does it appear that women had some measure of control over whether or not to enter into these relationships, they also were about much more than sex. They entailed living together, raising children, and in all ways sharing their lives. Natalie Everts notes that for European men, "their African family was the only way to experience some family bliss" (1996, 50).

From the perspective of African women and their families, these marriages certainly did not conform to the most common form of Akan marriage in which arrangements are made by the families of the bride and groom and which requires the presentation of gifts or *consawment* to the bride's family (Sarbah 1968a, 45). With regard to the Ewe of southeastern Ghana, Sandra Greene (1997) argues that because of the perceived risks involved, marriage to stranger men was considered most appropriate for slave women within local families who would be unwilling to allow their proper daughters to enter into such unions. In Cape Coast and Elmina, the daughters given by local families to European men may have been slaves. However, family histories suggest that at least some were free women (see chapter 2).

These relationships may have been understood as a version of *newewe awar*, or "lover marriage," an indigenous Akan form of relationship similar to the Western notion of common law marriage, in which the husband does not present *consawment* to the family and therefore has no guarantee of his wife's fidelity; however, he gains paternity rights to their children and the obligation to support them (Christensen 1954).[9] In the case of such marriages to European men, African families were unlikely to protest the circumvention of their authority because of the benefits that such marriages bestowed on them.

Christensen (1954) argues that women (of free descent) benefited most from these lover marriages because they retained greater freedom within the relationship, as well as the power to end the relationship. Women may not have had full liberty to leave their European husbands, but given the support that her *abusua,* or matrilineal descent group, would provide, one can imagine that extrication from the relationship could be accomplished. At the same time, women were not guaranteed to inherit from their European husbands. Indeed, some European men made stipulations in their wills that their children inherit from them but that barred their wives and their wives' families from obtaining any of their estates (Everts 1996).

On the other hand, many European men provided financially for their country wives. Richard Brew, a European trader in Cape Coast, was married to a local woman, Effua Ansah, and had two children by her. On the death of Effua's mother, he made a contribution for the funeral expenses as demanded of family and friends, thus conducting himself as true husband in the local framework. In addition, Brew named Effua and their two children beneficiaries of his will. At his death, the executors of his will not only handed over his estate to his African family but also gave them a gift of four gallons of rum, in accordance with local practice for his funeral (Priestley 1969, 108). This example illustrates that despite the lack of compulsion, many men treated their marriages as serious and somewhat official relationships. Given this tendency, women who entered into relationships with European men most likely expected that they and their families would benefit financially from them. Indeed, Everts (1996) suggests that many mothers wanted their daughters to find European common law husbands because of the economic benefits that such marriages had for African families.

With regard to the emotional component of these relationships, at least some men appear to have felt true affection for their country wives. A letter written by Richard Miles suggests that his relationship with a local woman was one of more than mere convenience. A British trader who had returned to England, Miles expressed his desire to continue a relationship, not only with his children, but also with their mother. He returned with his son whom he sent to a boarding school that other members of his family had attended and told his coastal correspondent, "You may tell the mother but as I am not yet settled I let her remain. Should I go to the Coast next year I can bring her of [*sic*] with me" (quoted in Priestley 1969, 107). Assuming that his desire to bring Sal, his country wife, to England is sincere, this letter suggests that at least some of these relationships were based on love and were not simply a means of sexual fulfillment for European men in the absence of European women.

Likewise, at least some women felt true affection for their country husbands. A nineteenth-century merchant observed one woman's reaction to the departure of her husband from the coast. He recounts her tearful good-byes on the beach before he boarded the ship, "'William you must go quik [*sic*] God bring you back to your Mary William no stop long time in England if you no come back quick your poor Mary must go die' . . . I left the poor girl on the beach all suffused in tears and crying as if her heart would break" (quoted in Brooks 1962, 77).

On the other hand, there is evidence that at least some country wives had extramarital affairs with local men. The scope of this problem led the West India Company to take measures to protect Europeans against adultery by establishing penalties for such action (Feinberg 1989, 89). Their capacity to engage in outside relationships, even if this behavior was contested, suggests that country wives gained a measure of sexual freedom in contrast to wives of proper Akan marriage. While they gained legitimate paternity for their children, a life of relative wealth, and the potential to inherit that wealth from their husbands, they retained the ability to seek sexual and emotional intimacy elsewhere. In this way, they subverted both European and African men's attempts to control them and their bodies.

Certainly, as objects of simultaneous desire and disdain by European men, African women were often despised for the contradiction that they revealed in European racist logic. Thus, relationships between European men and African women made manifest what Stoler refers to as "the simultaneous confirmation and compromise of racial hierarchy" (Stoler 1989, 688). In other words, European men's sexual access to local women cemented notions of white male privilege, but their affection and desire for these women challenged notions of African inferiority.

Some African women became proper wives of European men, their marriages having been negotiated through their families and their husbands paying *consawment* to them. Feinberg (1989) identifies at least seven of these marriages in Elmina during the eighteenth century. These marriages sometimes involved women from important local families; thus, these unions served to create alliances between Europeans and the local elites (McCarthy

1983, 44). These women and their families gained wealth and entrance into the European trade, some wives even becoming partners in their husbands' business ventures. Many African wives, regardless of the legal status of their marriages, played an important role in their husbands' business affairs. One nineteenth-century observer remarked, "The Girls are very useful to the men in Business. Their knowledge of the native tongue renders them almost indispensable with every trading establishment" (Brooks 1962, 76). There is also evidence that these women were able to influence their husbands' views, sometimes swaying them to support local causes in opposition to European policies (McCarthy 1983, 47).

Undoubtedly, one of the greatest motivating factors for women to become country wives was the benefits that these marriages would have for their children. The matrilineal family structure of the Fante accounts for the ease with which these relationships were integrated into coastal society. The children of African women and European men (known as "Euro-Africans")[10] were incorporated into the mother's *abusua* in exactly the same way as any other children would be and were not favored over non-European children (Everts 1996, 48). Mothers and their families were in charge of the upbringing of children. Fathers who sought to take control of their children's upbringing often found that they could not wrest control from the *abusua*. Because only the very wealthy could afford to send their children to school in Europe, the majority of fathers surrendered responsibility for their children's education to the mother's family. Nonetheless, mothers of Euro-African children had high hopes for their children's careers. Euro-African men often entered into service for the West India Company and some became successful traders. They had special status under Dutch law and formed the *Akrampa asafo* Company (Yarak 1989).

Perhaps because they were accustomed to being intimately involved in all aspects of their children's lives, some mothers felt emboldened to confront the West Indian Company concerning their sons' careers. One such woman approached the commander at the fort in Butri concerning her son's reassignment to a post at Shama, some distance away. She complained to the commander that she did not want her son sent away, and he agreed to send someone else in his place (Everts 1996). The boldness that mothers of Euro-African children exhibited as well as the apparent standing that they had with European companies suggests that bearing these children conferred upon them a special status with attendant privileges within the European order. These women had great influence over the lives of their children, who were often incorporated at least partially into the European society, and such control over these liminal Europeans presented a threat to the European order. In successive generations of the trade, many of the children of European men and African women came to form an elite class on the coast. Indeed, many of the most prominent local traders on the coast were Euro-Africans.

Many Euro-African women became wives of European men as well. Having been raised within the cultural milieu of European society on the coast, marriage to European men provided a means to remain within that elite universe of wealth and influence. Elizabeth and Catherine Dawson were the daughters of a European trader and a local woman from Cape Coast. Elizabeth married James Jackson, an English merchant who was part of the Royal African Corps. They built a four-story house on a street that came to be named after them as one of the most prominent families in the town. Her sister, Catherine, married Frank Swanzy, who was the founder of the famous trading company, F&A Swanzy Brothers. After both her sister Elizabeth and her husband died, Catherine married her sister's widower, James Jackson. She continued to run Swanzy Brothers herself and became the wealthiest and most powerful woman in Cape Coast (Graham 1994). The power of Euro-African women to influence the European trading community derived from their own liminal positions, with their marriages providing entrance into European coastal society while they remained firmly entrenched in the local African community through their strong ties to their *abusua*. This dual position is illustrated by their dress; they dressed in a flamboyant style from the waist up and like other local African women from the waist down (Bosman 1967, 142).

OWNING SLAVES

With the growing development of elite families, both those of European traders and those of African merchants, more and more individuals were retained on the coast as slaves to serve them. The estate of Carel Ruhle, an Elminan Euro-African trader, included 205 slaves, and his brother's estate included 112 slaves (Yarak 1989). Many slave owners were women and either wives of European men or Euro-Africans. Yarak (1989) notes that Carolina Huydecoper, a wealthy Euro-African woman, inherited six slaves from her father-in-law in 1818 after the death of her husband. Likewise, Jones (1995) notes that in 1873, Mrs. Swanzy owned up to eighty slave women.

Slavery existed among Fantes, and indeed throughout West Africa before the arrival of Europeans; however, it was a very different institution from slavery in the Americas (see Perbi 2004 for an extended discussion). Many historians have argued that in West Africa, although they occupied positions at the lowest level of the status system, the basic humanity and membership of slaves in their masters' societies was rarely questioned before the advent of the Atlantic trade. R. S. Rattray argues that the rights of slaves in Asante "seem in many instances practically the ordinary privileges of any Ashanti free man, with whom, in these respects, his position did not seem to compare unfavourably" (1969, 42). In contrast to Asante, Fantes had a much less stratified society. Not only were there fewer persons of unfree status before the height of the Atlantic trade, but indigenous status had little significance. Thus, slaves had many rights, including the right to bear arms, the right to legal redress, and, most importantly, the right of incorporation into the families of their masters (Yarak 1989). A common understanding about slavery was that domestic slaves could be incorporated into the families that owned them, and their children were considered to be full-fledged members of those families. Female slaves usually married free men within the lineage, and their children had only to reckon their descent through their father's matrilineage to become incorporated into the family (Sarbah 1968a). Incorporation was more difficult for the descendants of male slaves, who in all likelihood would marry a slave woman and therefore have no claim on their owner's matrilineage. But male slaves had the right to inherit from their masters if there were no other appropriate heirs. Many male slaves became heads of the lineages that had owned them in this way (Klein 1981). Individuals often recount stories of slaves who became wealthier than their masters. Rattray notes that the Asante had a term for slaves who became wealthy: ɔdɔnkɔ sene Kanis, which means, "a slave who is more powerful than an Akan" (1969, 41). Regardless of the actual frequency of this occurrence, the continued mention of its existence by individuals today suggests a strong continuing belief in the notion of incorporation.

Before the height of the Atlantic trade, different terms had described people who sold themselves, people taken in lieu of debt, and bought people. As a result of the destabilization of northern regions, this last category, nnɔnkɔfo (singular ɔdɔnkɔ), became the dominant type of slave during the nineteenth century (McSheffrey 1983) as victims of wars and raids in areas deep in the hinterland were brought to the coast and sold as slaves. The North became such an important source of slaves that the term "ɔdɔnkɔ" (plural nnɔnkɔfo),[11] which originally referred to a bought person came to mean a person from the North (Rattray 1969, 35). The incidence of domestic slavery on the coast increased during this time because many of these same captives were purchased by local elite families who, as a result of their trading activities, had the means to buy slaves. *Nnɔnkɔfo* served in many occupations: as agriculturalists, miners, skilled artisans, porters of trade goods along trade routes, soldiers, and household servants (Christensen 1954, 39). Some slaves, known as "garden slaves," worked on plantations in outlying areas (Yarak 1989). Despite the increasing slave population on the coast, a plantation economy never developed on the coast, in part because of the resistance of slaves to the harsher discipline and treatment that plantation economies such as those found in the New World seemed to require (Yarak 1989).

Many slave women were bought for the express purpose of marriage, which gave the advantage for men in these unions in that their children would belong to their lineages and not to that of their wives, as is the normal practice in a matrilineal society (Rattray 1969). Claire Robertson and Martin Klein (1983) argue that the majority of domestic slaves in West Africa were women, desired for their domestic labor as well as their reproductive capabilities. In his study of the Euro-African population of Elmina, however, Yarak (1989) finds that the majority of the slaves in Elmina were men and concludes that instead of marrying slaves, a larger proportion of elite men in Elmina compared with other places may have sought to marry elite women.

The number of domestic slaves on the coast increased again with the abolition of the transatlantic slave trade and the beginnings of legitimate trade. With the termination of this trade, the price of slaves dropped dramatically, allowing African elites the opportunity to acquire slaves in large numbers (Klein and Lovejoy 1979; Lovejoy 1983). The increase in the slave population meant the need to formalize the procedure for dealing with them.

While the process of incorporation had long been necessary in order to absorb subsequent generations of slaves, as a result of increasing British judicial control over the course of the nineteenth century, assimilation was codified as a legal right. During this time, the British instituted customary law, which involved the codification of what they understood to be local customs. The right of slaves to incorporation was codified in the form of two key laws. The first stated that slaves who had been freed had the right to be incorporated into the families of their former owners. In 1871, the judicial assessor of Cape Coast consulted two local chiefs regarding the rights of slaves. In response to the query by the court, "Do persons who have been made free retain any relationship to the family of which they were members?" the chiefs responded,

> though the master had made them free, they retain relationship to their master, because they did not belong to the place where they were freed . . . If a slave was a Fanti, when he was freed by his master he goes to his relations; but if not a Fanti, but Donkor,[12] he retains his relationship to the master because he knew no one else and would not be able to find his way to his country, and if his master had any relations he sticks to them. Persons freed have the right to go where they like, but their master looks after them that they may not be molested. (Sarbah 1968a, 9)

This law recognizes the problem that arises from an individual's inability to identify his or her lineage. Slaves are considered to be kinless; their enslavement removes them permanently from their old lineages such that they lose the ability to identify themselves through any of the normal modes.

Among the Fante, individuals identify themselves as belonging to the Fante ethnic group, then by hometown, which is the place where the head of their lineage is situated, and then by clan, which refers to their matrilineage, including all those who trace their descent to a common female ancestor. If someone cannot identify these aspects of their identity, he or she cannot be incorporated into normal modes of relating (see Perbi 2004). Descendants of slaves fall into this category because knowledge of origins is quickly lost and therefore must be replaced with the origin stories of their families of incorporation. The chiefs' interpretation of customary law was accepted by the court, and subsequent decisions have upheld this interpretation. First-generation slaves were most vulnerable to discrimination because they bore what were known as tribal marks as a result of scarification practices that served to announce their foreign status. Because all northerners were associated with slavery, the marks of northern groups were considered to be marks of enslavement.

When the British declared the Gold Coast their colony in 1874, they outlawed domestic slavery. The notion of incorporation then became crucial in order to avoid a large population without familial support of any kind. Incorporating freed slaves into one's family, furthermore, was the only way to legally keep them in one's household after this time. Emancipation, therefore, further codified notions of the kinship of slaves by declaring all former slaves family members.

The second law that defined the right of slaves to incorporation within the families of their owners is the law that forbids the disclosure of an individual's slave ancestry. Kwame Arhin (1983) traces this law back to the reign of Osei Tutu (1680–1717), the Asante ruler who, after conquering many lands and incorporating them into his kingdom, declared that the origins of people from those conquered lands were to be forgotten. Carl Reindorf describes this law: "Whoever dares tell his son: these people were from such and such a place, conquered and translocated to this or that town, was sure to pay for it with his life. Neither were such people themselves allowed to say where they had been transported from. Considering these captives as real citizens, any rank or honor was conferred freely on them according to merit, but not otherwise" (1950, 54). Bowdich (1873), Reindorf (1966), and Rattray (1929) note the popular expression of the prohibition against disclosing another person's origins, *obi nkyerɛ obi ase* ('no one must disclose the origins of another'). Evidence from later lawsuits demonstrates that this principle remains part of contemporary law (see chapter 2). Thus, not only were freed slaves incorporated into families, but by this law, mention of their past slave status was forbidden. Freed slaves and their descendants, however, could not become chiefs and often were barred from inheriting land, suggesting that their slave ancestry was raised at key moments. Outside of these moments, however, the history of slavery within families became sequestered from public discourse.

Making Regional Identity

THE HINTERLAND

While domestic slavery shaped new definitions of family, the processes by which those slaves as well as slaves destined for export were acquired shaped new definitions of regional identities. In the early part of the Atlantic trade, as a result of the rise of the Denkyira and Akwamu kingdoms, their conquering of their neighbors, and the resultant production of war captives that could be sold to Europeans, members of coastal and near-coastal communities made up the bulk of those enslaved. During the eighteenth and nineteenth centuries, residents of Cape Coast and Elmina as well as other Akan-speaking peoples remained involved in wars that produced slaves (Perbi 2004, 34).

After 1700, however, in addition to these individuals, many slaves originated from the northern savannahs. Asante traders traveled north to major slave markets where they could buy slaves from Mossi and Hausa traders in exchange for kola nuts and salt. In 1701, the Dutch presented the Asante leader Osei Tutu with gifts as part of their request that he direct his traders to their forts. In 1703, the English also approached various inland traders in order to express the interest of the Royal African Company in trading with them (Daaku 1970, 33–34).

The expansionist policies of the Asante also led to their ability to provide large numbers of slaves for the transatlantic slave trade beginning in the eighteenth century. In 1732, the Asante invaded Gonja, a northern territory, and the Gonja were forced to pay tribute to the Asante in slaves. In 1751, the Kpembe became a vassal state of the Asante kingdom and were similarly forced to pay an annual tribute to the Asante of one thousand slaves, and the Dagomba became indebted to the Asante for two thousand slaves to secure the release of their chief (Der 1998, 10).

In order to fulfill the Asante demand for slaves, these groups in turn began raiding decentralized northern communities, including the Grunshi, Konkomba, LoDagaa, and Talensi. In his analysis of the northern savannahs, which became known under colonialism as the Northern Territories, Jack Goody notes that decentralized communities such as these became the source of slaves for raiders from centralized states like the Gonja and Kpembe who had the "means of destruction," namely, guns and horses (1971).

The slave trade began a process by which many northern communities, which were already distant from the centers of the Atlantic order and therefore vulnerable to slave raiding, sought further distance from agents of the Atlantic trade in an attempt to reduce their vulnerability. As these communities sought to escape slave raiders, they retreated into remote areas, altering their relationship to the landscape. By moving to hiding places such as area caves, building walls surrounding their villages in order to protect themselves, like the wall around the village of Gwollu (Der 1998), and relocating to the hills that were less accessible by horseback (Goody 1971), they "produced" their remoteness (Ferme 2001).

In addition to physical remoteness, communities also sought distance from objects associated with the slave raiders as local shrines began to develop prohibitions designed to protect their communities. In the Tong Hills, horses and cloth were associated with Mossi raiders and were therefore considered to be ritually impure and were not allowed near ritual shrines (Allman and Parker 2005, 61–62). The shrine at Senyon also prohibited horses from entering the town because of their association with slave raiders (Goody 1971, 60). Goody (1971) notes that the village of Senyon was never raided by Samory, an infamous slave raider, purportedly because of the presence of the Senyon Kupo shrine, whose power Samory feared. He argues that many centralized communities that engaged in slave raiding had been influenced by Islam, while the decentralized communities that were commonly raided worshiped earth shrines. Despite their profession of Muslim faith, many slave raiders continued to respect these shrines and attested to the spiritual superiority of the communities in which they were located. Thus, the technological inferiority of acephalous communities was balanced by their spiritual superiority (Goody 1971, 64–65). Indeed, spirituality formed perhaps the most important form of resistance to enslavement.

While the retreat of acephalous communities was certainly an important strategy for protection, at the same time it cut them off from the flow of goods and wealth emerging from this slave-trading economy, thereby further diminishing their chances to be incorporated into the Atlantic order as anything other than slaves.[13] At the height of the slave trade, European companies stationed on the coast of Ghana came to view the hinterland as a vast pool of potential slaves. At the same time, European companies had codified coastal residents' immunity from enslavement in order to ensure their cooperation. In this context, Europeans and southern Ghanaians alike began to argue that these northern groups were not fit for anything but slavery. The remoteness of northerners from the point of view of Europeans, who rarely ventured from the coast, led the Europeans to view their enslavement as not just the result of geography or lack of weaponry but as the result of their status outside of the Christian, "civilized" Atlantic order that linked the West African coastal communities, Europe, and the New World. This Atlantic order was of course rooted in the savagery of the slave trade. Europeans, however, ignored the significance of their own "necropolitics" (Mbembe 2003) and concentrated all of the savagery of the slave trade onto a point outside of their direct influence, that of the acquisition of slaves in the North.

During the slave trade, Europeans on the coast described northerners as cannibals in the interior "whom one could hardly call human. They have a particularly wild nature, a physiognomy like that of a tiger" (Rømer 2000, 28). Such descriptions were used to explain the prevalence of slave raiding: after all, it was due to the "wild nature" of the North's inhabitants. Notions of their savagery also provided a convenient rationale for the enslavement of people from the North: as they were less than human, they were natural slaves. In this way, victims and perpetrators of slave raids were grouped together under the same stigmatized identity. They were all, it was argued, outside of the civilized world that Europeans were attempting to extend into West Africa.

Coastal elites, on the contrary, who were immediately incorporated into the Atlantic order, succeeded to a large extent in maintaining protection from enslavement through their further incorporation, a feat at which, from the point of view of Europeans, a point of view that would heavily influence coastal residents, northerners failed. While Europeans constructed narratives about northern inferiority, thereby further encouraging their retreat from the Atlantic order, they simultaneously constructed narratives about coastal superiority. Austen and Woodruff Smith identify a statement from the *Gentleman's Magazine* of London in 1792 that "Africans were stupid in proportion to their distance from the converse of coastal Negroes" (quoted in Austen and Smith 1969, 77). Brodie Cruickshank, a European official, writes of northerners, "They are naturally a very obstinate, perverse, and self-willed race, upon whom it is difficult to make any impression by kindness ... It is only by comparing the native Fantee with these, that we are sensible of the great advancement of the former, who appears a very civilized being in comparison with this foreign race" (1966, 2:244–45). As these remarks reveal, enslavement served to mark for Europeans a radical distinction between northerners and coastal residents. Many coastal elites accepted European stereotypes of *nnɔnkɔfo*, a term that began to imply inferiority.

By supporting the logic that defined northerners as appropriate subjects to enslave, they further guaranteed their own immunity from enslavement. In 1823, a European observer remarked that the term *ɔdɔnkɔ* "in the Fantee language, signifies stupid fellow, or ignorant man from the back country" (Adams 1966, 44). Those who were enslaved came to be viewed as deserving of their enslavement because of their backcountry status and unruly nature, while coastal elites' supposed higher level of civilization accounted for their immunity from enslavement. The 1841 remarks of the *asantehene* sum up well this unruliness. He is reported to have said, "The small tribes in the interior fight with each other, take prisoners and sell them for slaves; and as I know nothing about them, I allow my people to buy them as they please: they are of no use for any thing but slaves; they are stupid, and little better than beasts" (quoted in Allman and Parker 2005, 31). He paints a picture of northern savagery, but more specifically, he suggests that their *alien* nature, as people of which he knows nothing, justifies their enslavement. Discussions of northerners then became one arena in which southerners elaborated on the slave trade because it allowed them to define themselves in opposition to those enslaved.

After the Asante invasion of the coast in 1807, not just the North but also the South faced especial danger and violence, producing slaves for the illegal trade. Although the British abolished the slave trade in the same year, ports east of Cape Coast and outside of the sphere of British influence remained active (Getz 2004, 31–32). Thousands of individuals fled to Cape Coast for protection. This town thus gained even greater importance as a haven within an environment of pervasive danger. By the time southern Ghana became a British colony in 1874, such dangers were largely quelled. The North, in contrast, remained a dangerous landscape. The last decades of the nineteenth century were in fact a time of great instability in the North. It was during these years that Babatu and Samory, two infamous figures in the history of the slave trade, undertook regular slave raids in the North to capture slaves both for domestic use in the Asante kingdom, until their defeat by European forces at the end of the nineteenth century (Der 1998, 25). Views of the North that developed during the Atlantic era set the stage for its exploitation during the colonial era as a labor reserve. This pattern, as I discuss in chapter 3, continues to have consequences today.

THE COAST

Throughout these different phases of the slave trade, despite the fact that the Europeans had granted coastal residents legal protection from enslavement, not only did rival Africans pay no heed to these laws, but Europeans themselves at times overlooked them as well. Feinberg's example of an incident of illegal enslavement on the coast illustrates this point. He recounts that on May 23, 1746, seven residents of Elmina who had been hired to paddle a canoe of slaves to a ship docked offshore were seized once on board and placed in chains along with the other slaves. An uproar arose in Elmina over the unlawful seizure of these men. Director General de Petersen assured their families that the men would be found and returned. In 1749, five of the men were finally found in Surinam. They were taken to the Netherlands at the expense of the West India Company and were returned to Elmina in 1750. The other two men had died in the interim, and their families were compensated in an official settlement (1989, 142).

Because of the dangers of their misrecognition as enslavable subjects, coastal residents stressed their identity as urban, cosmopolitan individuals. The adoption of outward signs of their special status vis-à-vis Europeans provided a measure of protection by distinguishing coastal residents from the *nnɔnkɔfo*.[14] Cruickshank writes, "There are few houses now, however, in the neighborhood of Cape Coast, and other principal towns, in which many of the comforts and luxuries of civilized life are not to be found," and he goes on to note that the tendency "at present is strong towards a higher standard of excellence in the objects of their pursuit, which are chiefly based upon an anxious desire to imitate European habits of life" (1966, 2:294).

Education was one key means of assimilation. The first European schools were founded by European companies inside the castles. Philip Quaque is credited with establishing the castle school at Cape Coast in 1766, and Jacobus Capitein expanded the castle school at Elmina in 1742. Both of these men were Africans who received religious training in Europe. Capitein became the first African chaplain of the Dutch Reform Church, and Quaque the first African chaplain of the Church of England. These early schools served Euro-African students as well as the children of African traders. Besides reading, writing, and arithmetic, they focused heavily on religious instruction. In this way, they resembled English charity schools for the poor of the same period (Foster 1965, 45). The rationale for both types of schools was the belief that education, particularly religious instruction, could serve to combat the supposed natural tendencies among both Africans and the European poor toward "unsocial" behavior (Graham 1971, 12).

The Cape Coast School, which grew out of the castle school, continued to enroll male students into the nineteenth century. In addition to the Cape Coast School, in 1836, the Wesleyan Mission established the Wesley Girls School as a separate school for girls. In 1876, the Wesleyan Mission established the first secondary school in Ghana, which would later become known as Mfantsipim School.

By the nineteenth century, elite status was defined not simply by economic class, but also by the level of assimilation into European cultural practices. The significance of African assimilation led Europeans on the coast to distinguish between what they deemed the "better" and "poorer" classes (Gocking 1999, 53). The better class distinguished itself by its dress, which for men included woolen jackets and trousers and for women frocks and blouses; through residential segregation, with the better classes occupying large homes in well-planned neighborhoods; and through membership in religious and secular organizations (Gocking 1999, 53–54). The better class also made use of European imported goods, including ceramics, glass, and metal objects. One European observer described approvingly the homes of elite Africans stating, "But the houses inhabited by natives in the service of Europeans begin to show another appearance; one finds there are more paintings, the mirror tends to be bigger and often has a gilt frame. Here one finds a moderator-lamp, there is a tea-service, and in another house a curious collection of champagne, wine and beer glasses, or even a pile of old books" (quoted in DeCorse 2001, 175). The overall qualification for membership in the better class was the adoption of signs of European culture. Thus, cosmopolitan tastes served to cement one's identity as a coastal elite.

One such elite, James Hutton Brew, was a member of a prominent African merchant family that descended from an Irish trader and the editor of the *Western Echo*, a Cape Coast newspaper. Through his editorials, he promoted social occasions such as concerts, teas, and dinner parties as well as improvement societies, including the Freemasons, the Good Templars, and the Gold Coast Temperance Society. Many improvement societies were aimed at women, whose behavior was seen as the marker of the level of civilization of the entire society. Brew complained, for instance, of "heathen" women who did not cover their breasts (Gocking 1999, 54). He implored Gold Coasters to follow the example of the Creoles in Sierra Leone, who, he wrote, represented a "loftier order of Christian civilization" (Gocking 1999, 55). Thus, through newspapers and other media, discourses about the proper appropriation of European cultural norms circulated throughout literate coastal society.

Certainly, embracing the idea of assimilation to European cultural norms had advantages for Europeans and coastal residents alike. For Europeans, it was a means of social control. Timothy Mitchell argues that colonization "refers not simply to the establishing of a European presence but also to the spread of a political order that inscribes in the social world a new conception of space, new forms of personhood, and a new means of manufacturing the experience of the real" (1988, ix; see also Comaroff and Comaroff 1997). But mimicry can also be a powerful political tool among the colonized to gain freedom by throwing into question the assumed difference between colonizer and colonized. This leads Homi Bhabha to refer to mimicry as menace (1994). Many scholars have theorized formalized and often ritualized forms of mimicry, but few have addressed mimicry as everyday practice. As an exception, Evelyn Higginbotham (1993) examines the cultural practices of African American Baptist women in the early 1900s and what she terms "the politics of respectability," or their adherence to European American norms of behavior including dress, temperance, and the adoption of "polite manners" as a strategy to gain respect and power in a white-dominated society. She describes the subversive force of their appeal to respectable behavior: "[S]uch appeals were also explicit rejections of Social Darwinist explanations of blacks' biological inferiority to whites. Respectability was perceived as a weapon against such assumptions, since it was used to expose race relations as socially constructed rather than derived by evolutionary law or divine judgment" (1993, 192). In Ghana, not only did the adoption of European cultural traits challenge racist constructions of African inferiority, it also protected coastal residents from enslavement and later cemented their class privilege. Thus, the notion of the mimic as a cultural traitor must be reexamined in light of this analysis (see chapter 4). Indeed, coastal elites' treatment by Europeans as equals in a context in which other peoples had been routinely reduced to chattel demonstrates the expediency of their self-fashioning.

After the turn of the century, such a notion was so well ingrained in the minds of local residents that a play parodying Fante assimilation was a huge hit. The 1915 play, *The Blinkards,* was written by Kobina Sekyi, a writer and important Fante political figure. In it he describes a garden party at which the guests play tennis and croquet, wear European clothes, including gloves and parasols for the women, and are admonished to speak English. Those who have been to England are touted as the models for others to emulate and even serve as mentors for young people whose parents wish to have their children trained to "act British." Sekyi also describes an improvement society, the Cosmopolitan Club, at which men read "How to Be a Gentleman" and discuss the importance of wearing European clothes and eating European food. In one scene from *The Blinkards,* Mr. Okadu, in many ways the hero of the story because he has been to England but still appreciates his native culture, imitates some of his contemporaries who he surmises are overly impressed by anything British and who reject those who do not ascribe to their belief in assimilation. He takes out a looking glass and handkerchief, chalks his face white, and delivers his monologue:

> I'm learning to be British and treat with due contempt
> The worship of the fetish, from which I am exempt . . .
>
> I'm clad in coat and trousers, with boots upon my feet;
> And *tamfurafu*[15] and Hausas I seldom deign to greet:
>
> For I despise the native that wears the native dress—
> The badge that marks the bushman, who never will progress.
>
> All native ways are silly, repulsive, unrefined.
> All customs superstitious, that rule the native mind. (1974, 47)

The reference to Hausas could refer to Muslims or northerners more generally, many of whom lived on the coast at this time and would have been identifiable by their distinctive native dress. The image of the "Anglo-Fante" (upon which the playwright elaborates in Sekyi 1970) by contrast encapsulates urban coastal cosmopolitanism. These regionalist characterizations became a crucial way in which individuals on the coast thought about social identity.

Remaking Coastal Identity

At the same time that Fante assimilation was at its height, great societal shifts were taking place. In 1877, soon after the British declared the Gold Coast a colony, the British moved their capital from Cape Coast to Accra because it occupied a more central location along the coast of the newly formed Gold Coast colony (Graham 1994). While Cape Coasters had enjoyed a privileged position vis à vis Europeans because of the status of Cape Coast as the center of British activity, with this move, they faced the rapid decline of their political significance. Coastal residents expected nonetheless to maintain their status during the colonial era by serving as intermediaries between the colonial state and the local population.

During this period, however, along with political reforms, the colonial government no longer recognized coastal elites as a distinct social group. Instead of embracing these assimilated men and women, under the system of indirect rule, political power was vested instead in traditional rulers who the colonial government believed better represented the native population. As Kwaku Korang notes, while it designated coastal elites as natives, they were "not native enough" for political enfranchisement (2003, 45). Coastal elites' assimilation had become a handicap as they were viewed as improper colonial subjects. Africans who were most connected to their "traditional" beliefs and practices were celebrated as the proper colonial subjects, while those who attempted to assimilate into British culture were castigated and abhorred. Ray Jenkins notes that this shift represented an embrace of a "settled view" of colonialism, which he describes as "a strong preference for the rural and the traditional; the masculine, the athletic and the pristine, rather than the urban and the modern; the weak, the clever, the tainted and the hybrid" (1985, 145). In other words, the British would no longer cultivate coastal elites' assimilation.

Coastal elites were dealt a double blow. Not only did they face their class-specific disenfranchisement, they also had to grapple with a more general racial exclusion. Under colonial policy, colonial subjects without exception were grouped together as natives in their incontrovertible difference from whites. The rise of racial classifications and hierarchies in European and American science during this time period (see Baker 1998) provided further logic for this shift. At the same time then that traditional authorities were placed in particular positions of limited authority, all Africans were racially excluded from most sites of real political power. Thus, in contrast to the situation in 1883 when seven out of fifteen district commissioners were African, in the 1890s, nearly all of the Africans holding top posts were dismissed (Tenkorang 1973, 69). By this time, medical advances in the prevention of malaria meant that more Europeans could live and work on the coast. As a result, positions that had previously been held by Africans were given instead to Europeans.

Racial exclusion extended to social life as well. Whereas previously Europeans and African elites had fraternized together at social clubs on the coast, in the 1890s, racial segregation was introduced. Signs declaring "Dogs and Niggers Not Admitted" began appearing on doors of clubs that had previously had racially mixed memberships (Tenkorang 1973). Thus, by the end of the nineteenth century, Europeans had dashed the hopes of local African elites for recognition as equals.[16]

The logic for this shift was provided by a mix of references to the supposed biological differences between Africans and Europeans and the definition of the distinctive historical trajectory of Africans. With regard to the latter, European historians and observers were engaged in projects to define simultaneously the historical identities of specific ethnic groups and of Africans as a newly relevant undifferentiated group.

Within these historicizing projects, European historians discussed the degeneration of local residents, whom they by now referred to as Fantes. Europeans on the coast began to use the phrase "gone Fante" to describe Fante degeneracy. In an 1885 editorial in the *Spectator,* a local newspaper, the writer asks of Fantes, "Why, then, have they never risen, never learned that permanent obedience to a code which enables men to aggregate themselves into mighty, and up to a certain point improving, communities? Why—for this appears to be the truth—has their point of arrest arrived so quickly that they have been unable to remain at it, and have time after time fallen back into the jungle way of life, have apparently 'gone Fantee' as the whites of the West Coast phrase it, in huge masses?" (quoted in Sarbah 1968b, xvii).

Even some African coastal elites adopted this discourse. In 1882, James Hutton Brew wrote an editorial that appeared in the *Gold Coast Times* critiquing Europeans for their introduction of the slave trade to Africa but also noting its severe effects on Fantes. He explains, "We have shown how the white man not being content with the immense profit he was reaping, introduced trans-Atlantic slavery and by cajolery, bribery, deceit and wicked promise at last succeeded in subverting the nature of the Fantee and managed to bring him even lower than the beast in the field" (June 24, 1882, no. 49).

Such arguments supported the disenfranchisement of coastal elites who were viewed to be incapable of ruling themselves. In order to combat their political disenfranchisement then, early Fante nationalists had to attack this logic. In 1889, several prominent African elites in Cape Coast founded a political organization, which they named *Mfantsi Amanbuhu Fékuw*, or the Fante Political Society, which later became the Aborigines Rights Protection Society, to protest the highly unpopular Lands Rights Bill. Many of its members also began to defend their indigenous political and social institutions.

In 1897, one of its most prominent members, John Mensah Sarbah, wrote *Fanti Customary Laws*, followed in 1906 by *Fanti National Constitution*. In these two books, he defines a traditional Fante political culture and makes his claim for its legitimacy and thereby argues for its implementation as the basis of colonial law. He wrote of the need to challenge "the idea that aboriginal administration is hopelessly saturated with cruelty and inextricably permeated with corruption, and therefore should be destroyed" (quoted in Kimble 1963, 523). In the preface to *Fanti National Constitution*, he notes specifically that perceptions of the slave trade as "Africa's greatest curse" had led to notions of Fante degeneracy, encapsulated in the phrase "gone Fante." He, on the contrary, seeks to change the phrase's tone. Fante society had not been destroyed by the slave trade, he argues. Fantes' failure to completely assimilate to European norms, their going Fante, does not demonstrate their "curse"; on the contrary, it marks their free embrace of an alternative culture as the first step in the development of a national consciousness (1968b, xvii; see Korang 2003, 128).[17] If the former discourse plotted the descent of Fantes from a middling status into savagery over the course of the slave trade, Sarbah traced their ascension to a future self-rule.

Within this trajectory, Sarbah argues that the era of the slave trade saw neither their collapse into anarchy nor their handing of authority over to Europeans. To support his argument, Sarbah tells the story of Kwamena Ansa, a tale that is today thought of as the origin story of the Fante-European encounter. Sarbah explains that the Portuguese had been trading in Elmina since 1452, going onshore for brief periods and returning to their ships with the goods they had acquired. When John II ascended the throne of Portugal in 1481, he decided to build a permanent settlement on the coast as the base of Portugal's trading activities. He sent a fleet to Elmina, under the command of Don Diego d'Azambuja. The fleet arrived in 1482 and immediately went to meet with the chief, Kwamena Ansa.[18] The captain and his men dressed in their most formal attire to impress the chief and, communicating through a translator, asked the chief for permission to build a fort on the shore. The chief responded with the following speech,[19] which I include here in its entirety,

> "I am not insensible," replied Ansa, "to the high honour which your great master the Chief of Portugal has this day conferred upon me. His friendship I have always endeavored to merit by strictness of my dealings with the Portuguese, and by my constant exertions to procure an immediate lading for their vessels. But never until this day did I observe such a difference in the appearance of his subjects: they have hitherto been meanly attired, were easily contented with the commodities they received; and, so far from wishing to continue in this country, were never happy until they could complete their lading and return. Now I remark a strange difference. A great number are richly dressed, are anxious to be allowed to build houses, and to continue among us. Men of such eminence, conducted by a commander who from his own account seems to have descended from the God who made day and night, can never bring themselves to endure the hardships of this climate; nor would they here be able to procure any of the luxuries that abound in their own country. The passions that are common to us all men will therefore inevitably bring on disputes. And it is far preferable that both our nations should continue on the same footing they have hitherto done, allowing your ships to come and go as usual; the desire of seeing each other occasionally will preserve peace between us. The sea and land being always neighbors are continually at variance, and contending who shall give way; the sea with great violence attempting to subdue the land, and the land with equal obstinacy resolving to oppose the sea." (Sarbah 1968b, 60–61)

Ansa displays great skepticism with regards to the intentions of the Portuguese, who have displayed "a strange difference" in their sudden change in attire intended to impress him and their desire to build a permanent settlement. Presented as a master diplomat, he lavishes compliments on the Portuguese captain at the same time that he denies his request, foreseeing that it will "inevitably bring disputes." His use of metaphor and flattery is characteristic of Fante speech, in which, some have noted, direct refusals of requests are rare.[20] D'Azambuja was disconcerted by what he perceived to be the evasiveness of Ansa's answer and reiterated his request, insisting "that surely, had they any sinister design, they would not venture their lives and property in a strange country, and at such a distance from their own, from which they could get no assistance" (Sarbah 1968b, 61). After continued persuasion, Ansa finally gave his consent for the fort to be built. The next day, the Portuguese crew, equipped with all of the necessary building materials that they brought with them from Portugal, began building Elmina Castle.

Sarbah tells this story in order to stress that this encounter was not one of a violent imposition of European will; on the contrary, it was one of diplomacy. The Portuguese recognized the legitimacy of Kwamena Ansa's authority over the Elmina state, and asked permission to settle in Elmina. Although Ansa was reluctant, Sarbah argues that he was "coaxed," not forced, into giving his permission. Throughout his description of the era of the slave trade that follows, Sarbah gives examples of Fantes exercising agency in opposing the Europeans in their midst. In this way, he insists that they retained their autonomy throughout this period.

Sarbah can then contrast this era to the time of his writing, in which the imposition of colonialism represented a major shift. He explains this objective in the preface to *Fanti National Constitution*, in which he writes, "In these pages I have not hesitated to mention, frankly and openly, but as briefly as possible, a few defects of Crown Colony rule from the standpoint of the African, who feels that he has no legitimate opportunity to exercise his undoubted powers in the right direction; that once he has received a fair English education, no chance has he to rise from a condition of mere passive subjugation to a capacity for the discharge of one's legitimate responsibilities, public or municipal" (1968b, xii). In focusing on the inequities of colonialism, Sarbah demonstrates that harping on the horrors of the slave trade did not serve the interests of coastal elites.

Making National Identity

As I noted above, colonial historians wrote histories of both particular African groups and of Africa as a whole. With regard to the latter, the slave trade was also a pertinent topic of discussion. Many European observers suggested that enslavement was an accepted practice among *all* Africans, or as one individual wrote, "the consequence of the natural law of Africa" (quoted in Austen and Smith 1969, 77). Rather than depicting one community enslaving another, they popularized the much more damning image of Africans enslaving their fellow Africans. In this way, the notion of a corporate African identity was intimately tied to the stigmatization of Africans as brutal slave dealers willing to sell their own kind. This construction of a degenerate African culture furthermore provided a strong argument for European colonialism (see Austen and Smith 1969; and Curtin 1975). Accounts by European explorers like David Livingstone provided images of African brutality in the conduct of the slave trade and, as Austen and Smith (1969) note, then argued that African societies were so unruly and barbaric as a result that they required European guidance to become civilized. Thus, a critique of slavery was intimately tied to the racist, paternalistic logic of colonialism.

The production of such discourses continued throughout the colonial period and was a subject of debate during the nationalist movement. Many of these debates concerned European histories written for Gold Coast schools. Several of the developments in both education and nationalism took place outside of Cape Coast and Elmina and were concentrated after the first quarter of the twentieth century instead in Accra and specifically at Achimota College. In 1934, one of the instructors at Achimota College, a British historian named Ward, published a history textbook for use in Ghanaian schools entitled *Africa before the White Man Came* that covered the history of Africa from ancient Egypt through the sixteenth century. Having been intimately involved in the planning of the school, Ward was appointed history master in 1932. The concluding chapter of his textbook addresses the fall of the great West African kingdoms and the beginnings of the trans-Saharan slave trade, of which the author writes, "These old civilised countries were gone; in their place were Morocco and the Turkish empire, which had no use for the Negro race except as slaves" (1934, 56). He then discusses how Africans began capturing slaves to feed the Saharan trade, leading to the complete devastation of West Africa. He concludes the chapter and the book with the sentence, "the old roads by which civilization had come to Africa were closed; instead of peace, and trade, there were war, and plunder; and Africa became a Dark Continent" (1934, 57).

Ward's depiction of Africa recalls earlier abolitionist writings that first formulated the notion of African degeneration as a result of the slave trade. While many Fante nationalists rejected this argument, for Ward it functions quite usefully to demonstrate British superiority and to convince Africans therefore of the benefits of British rule. He writes elsewhere, "The study of biography or of constitutional and economic history helps the African to feel that he is coming near an answer to the great question which is always at the back of his mind: why is the European so much 'wiser' and stronger than himself, and can the secret of his wisdom and strength be acquired?" (quoted in Zachernuk 1998, 490). By painting an image of a savage Africa, Ward can celebrate colonial rule as the savior of Africa, a strategy that had become common among colonial governments. Undoubtedly, part of the colonial project is the creation of histories in which the colonist always plays the leading role. Frantz Fanon describes colonial histories in this manner, stating, "The settler makes history; his life is an epoch, and Odyssey. He is the absolute beginning: 'This land was created by us'; he is the unceasing cause: 'If we leave, all is lost, and the country will go back to the Middle Ages.' Over against him torpid creatures, wasted by fevers, obsessed by ancestral customs, form an almost inorganic background for the innovating dynamism of colonial mercantilism" (1963, 51; quoted in Sharp 2002, 106).

After its publication, Ward's text was heavily criticized by the leading nationalists in West Africa through a negative press campaign. William Ofori Atta, a former student of Ward and a member of the Accra Clubs Union, wrote a letter to the editor of *West Africa*, a local newspaper, in which he complained, "From first to last the book aims to prove two amazing facts: first, that the only place Africans, especially those living in West Africa, have occupied in history is that of slaves; secondly, that Africans have never made any original contribution to world civilization" (quoted in Jenkins 1994, 175). He and other nationalists fought to have Ward's text removed from schools on these and other grounds. The attack on Ward demonstrates that by the 1930s, nationalists had witnessed the ways in which descriptions of Africa as the Dark Continent, even when its "backwardness" was attributed to the slave trade and outside forces including European influences, had been used to bolster the case for colonialism.[21]

Not only did coastal elites seek to distance themselves from slavery, but as nationalist fervor began to grow in Ghana, they also sought to extend their vision of a respectable past to the entire nation. They therefore stressed Africa's past glory and resisted fatalistic descriptions of any period of its history. J. B. Danquah, in particular, heralded the study of the relationship between the contemporary Akan and ancient West African empires. Through his historical research, he argued that there is a connection between the ancient kingdom of Ghana and the Akan and called for the change of the name Gold Coast to Ghana (see Korang 2003). His attempt to associate Gold Coast Africans with ancient kings and queens contrasts sharply with Ward's depiction of them as members of a race of slaves.

The Ward episode reveals the extent to which Ghanaian nationalists viewed the slave trade (whether it be the Saharan or the Atlantic) as a foil to

their struggle for independence. Despite coastal residents' careful constructions of their special relationship with Europeans, in one sentence Ward
erases this special status and lumps all Africans together under a blanket
of stigma. It is no wonder that nationalists objected to Ward's historical interpretation. The story of the slave trade might appear to provide the perfect
grounds for the indictment of Europeans and therefore make an attractive
subject for nationalist arguments. However, given the paradoxical argument
that nonetheless held sway in many circles, namely, that the introduction of
the slave trade by Europeans had made Africa into a savage continent that
therefore needed European guidance to emerge from this dark past, this
history could not serve the interests of the nationalist struggle. Ward uses
the savagery of Africans as a whole as a justification for colonialism. It is for
this reason that he and others put forth slavery as the history of all Africans,
in contrast to earlier histories that had differentiated among different areas
of the continent as slave-supplying or non-slave-supplying regions.

In 1935, colonial officials released the new history syllabus for the West
African colonies, which was written by Sir Reginald Coupland and D. C.
Sommerwell, and in 1939, T. R. Batten wrote *Tropical Africa in World History* according to this syllabus (Jenkins 1994). In his textbook, Batten also
stresses the role of Africans in the slave trade. He writes, "The European
traders did not catch the slaves themselves. They did not send armed slave
raiders inland. The coastal natives were glad to sell slaves to the Europeans,
and made every effort to collect as many for them as possible" (1953, 2:86).
No doubt because of the influence of Coupland's 1933 book, *The British Anti-
Slavery Movement*, which champions the role of the British humanitarian
movement in the abolition of the slave trade, Batten's text not only discusses
the slave trade, but emphasizes its negative effects on the African continent. Batten writes, "[D]uring a slave raid, whole villages were frequently
destroyed. The young men and women were carried off as slaves, the old
people and young children were killed without mercy, the houses burned,
and the crops stolen or destroyed. From this cause between the sixteenth
and nineteenth century large districts of Africa became waste and empty
land" (1953, 2:87).

He also describes the journey to the coast to illustrate the horrors of
the slave trade of which he writes, "The slaves had good reason to fear the
journey to the coast. Besides the natural fear of going to a distant and unknown country, they suffered terrible hardships. Heavily loaded, forced to
march from sunrise to sunset, often without food, water, or a midday rest,
the weaker slaves sometimes had not enough strength to go on. In such

cases they were beaten, and if they still failed to get up they were killed or left in the bush to die" (1953, 2:88). In this portrait of the brutality of Africans (and not, importantly, of Europeans) during the slave trade, Batten was directly influenced by Livingstone's abolitionist writings and even includes an artist's rendering taken from his journal entitled "Fettered slaves left to die." Batten in this way also made use of the degeneration theory. By writing about African backwardness, he could then describe British rule as Africa's salvation, thereby supporting the colonial project. In a section of his textbook entitled "Prevention of tribal war and bad government," Batten describes the impact of colonial rule as follows:

> At one time war between African tribes was very common, and this meant the burning of villages, the killing of old people and children, and the enslavement of young men and women . . . Even strong tribes, which had little to fear in war, sometimes had cause to fear their own rulers. Evil chiefs might use their power to tax their subjects unmercifully and punish their enemies cruelly. Ritual murder was not uncommon in Africa. The ordinary people in some parts of Africa lived very unhappy lives, for they had no safety either for themselves or their property. Also, most of them were very poor indeed. Europeans, by stopping tribal war and instances of evil government in the territories under their rule, very greatly increased the happiness of their inhabitants. (1953, 3:121)

In this way, Batten rehearses popular arguments of that day that described colonial rule as Africa's salvation. It is within this context then that the notion of a "native" Gold Coast identity, which was always closely linked to a savage African identity, emerged. It is within this context also that the notion of a national identity emerged to contest it.

Because of the damaging implications of the history of the slave trade, nationalist leaders like the Fante cultural nationalists before them argued for its minimization. Kwame Nkrumah, who became president when Ghana gained Independence in 1957, recognized the need for a change in the focus of history instruction. He encouraged a project of Africanization, which entailed "affirming the history and culture of Africa disparaged by colonial rule and colonialism" (Quist 1999, 174). In 1959, a battle ensued between Nkrumah and the staff of the University of Ghana at Legon over the use of a new textbook written by John Fage (see chapter 5). Nkrumah's critiques were reminiscent of the critiques of Ward's book twenty-five years earlier and included its overemphasis on outside influences on the historical development of West Africa, the lack of information regarding the early kingdoms of West Africa, and its failure to address early nationalist attempts such as the Aborigines Rights Protection Society. Nkrumah describes the importance of the writing of history,

> The history of Africa, as presented by European scholars, has been encumbered with malicious myths. It was even denied that we were historical people. It was said that whereas other continents had shaped history, and determined its course, Africa had stood still, held down by inertia; that Africa was only propelled into history by European contact. . . . When the slave trade and slavery became illegal, the experts on Africa yielded to the new winds of change, and now began to present African culture and society as being so rudimentary and primitive that colonialism was a duty of Christianity and civilization. (1970, 62)

He continues,

> Africa cannot be validly treated merely as the space in which Europe swelled up. If African history is interpreted in terms of the interests of European merchandise and capital, missionaries and administrators, it is no wonder that African nationalism is in the forms it takes regarded as a perversion and neo-colonialism as a virtue. In the new African Renaissance, we place great emphasis on the presentation of history. Our history needs to be written as the history of our society, not as the story of European adventurers. African society must be treated as enjoying its own integrity; its history must be a mirror of that society, and the European contact must find its place in this history only as an African experience, even if as a crucial one. That is to say, the European contact needs to be assessed and judged from the point of view of the harmony and progress of this society. (1970, 63)

Nkrumah recognized that the slave trade had been used as part of an argument for African inferiority and called instead for histories of African agency and autonomy. National identity, as he saw it, would be based on histories of past glory. In this effort, he chose the name Ghana, as Danquah had suggested, recalling the famous ancient empire and thereby recalling a history that he viewed to be of greater utility to the nation than that of the slave trade. As I discuss in chapter 5, when I pick up this story, his vindicationist agenda continues to affect constructions of national history.

In this chapter, I have outlined the ways in which notions of family, coastal identity, and nationhood took shape over the course of the Atlantic and colonial eras and the ways in which their construction involved various types of negotiation of the experience and history of the slave trade. In all three cases, the slave trade was carefully, and I argue purposefully, excised from these group identities. In the following chapters, I explore the impact of these early excisions on contemporary identity formations.

2 » *Conundrums of Kinship*

SEQUESTERING SLAVERY, RECALLING KIN

Auntie Akua is an elderly resident of Elmina.[1] Her home, an impressive and ancient-looking merchant house surrounded by a walled courtyard, seems to stand as a sort of monument to the past, recalling the days of the Atlantic trade. The day that I visited her, upon entering the courtyard, I encountered a young woman preparing food. She greeted me warmly and led me up the stairs to the main living quarters. Auntie Akua and her brother, Uncle Kojo, invited me into the living room, which was filled with European furniture, including several straight back chairs, obviously of European origin and purchased generations earlier, and a quite formal portrait of the grandfather, the family head, over the mantel, invoking again the sense of a glorious though now tarnished past. After our introductions, I began to ask them about their family history, and they happily told me about their grandfather who was a wealthy merchant during the nineteenth century. I had previously learned from their niece, a friend of mine, that their grandfather had also owned many slaves. Foolishly, I decided to broach this topic directly and asked them if they could tell me about these slaves. Uncle Kojo immediately became tight-lipped and said dismissively, "There was never anything like that going on here!" Noting his discomfort with the topic of slavery, I quickly dropped the subject and moved on to something else.

My investigation into narratives about domestic slavery began, as I discuss in the Introduction, as a result of the fact that when inquiring into the Atlantic slave trade, people often thought I was asking about domestic slavery, a misinterpretation that would immediately bring conversation to a halt. Again and again I was told, "People don't talk about that" or "No one remembers anything about that." One particular acquaintance, upon hearing that I wanted to ask people about the slave trade, vehemently stated, "The ones who witnessed it are all dead, and they did not tell their children, so you will not be able to find out anything on that topic!" As a result of these responses, I spent a good deal of time puzzling over the reluctance and at times refusal of people in Cape Coast and Elmina to discuss slavery, which by extension, affects their reluctance to discuss the Atlantic slave trade. In contrast to what some suggested, it seemed, the history of domestic slavery is not forgotten, but neither is it openly discussed in conversations about family histories with those who are not kin.

One day, while I was discussing this problem with a friend, he quoted me the proverb, "Do not look into the eye of a dead person, or you might find a maggot." Slavery functions like a maggot on a corpse, I learned, or in other words, a blemish on history because, as I argue in this chapter, of the problematic nature of both slave ownership and slave status from a contemporary perspective. Coastal residents' reticence to discuss slavery arises then both from their desire to protect their families from being associated with slave ownership as well as from their reluctance to reveal past radical status distinctions within families: distinctions between slaves and freepersons. While they are reluctant to discuss past slave ownership, other aspects of the lives of the local trading elites are the basis of some of the most popular historical accounts in both Cape Coast and Elmina. Indeed, most public family histories concern prominent ancestors. Many of these stories are, however, undergirded by the memories of slavery in that an elite identity was constructed in direct opposition to slaves. Invocations of past elite status serve importantly as declarations of nonslave status. The categories of slave and free rely on each other for their meaning, each one serving as a looking glass that reflects back an image of the other. Thus, by remembering local elites, coastal residents remember those who were enslaved.

Within these narratives, however, elite ancestors' ownership of slaves is strictly sequestered from discourse. In the case of Cape Coast and Elmina, I argue then that the practice of silence arose as a result of the social divisions engendered on the coast during the era of the Atlantic trade that saw not only an emerging class of local merchant elites but also their increasing ownership of slaves and an attendant need to protect the coherence of these new families on the Atlantic littoral. In addition, laws requiring the incorporation of former slaves and forbidding any talk of slave ancestry as I discussed in chapter 1 mean that individuals must sequester these histories from discourse in order to present themselves as members of "modern" families, in other words, families in accordance with colonial and postcolonial law as well as international definitions of human rights. Today, descendants of slaves and descendants of slave owners live together, oftentimes within the same households. The sequestering of domestic slavery from public discourse is necessary to protect both.

While some scholars have focused on alternative narratives that attempt to reconcile domestic slavery with local notions of morality by attending to the debt it created (see Rosenthal 1998), I address the ways in which dominant narratives are oriented not only toward strengthening notions of local community but also toward recasting coastal residents as global citizens. Within family histories, nevertheless, the slave trade lurks in shadows of discourse, often in fact emerging within conversational contexts. This constant reemergence, in spite of assertions of permanent submersion, demonstrates that slavery haunts coastal residents with its ability to mark societal inequalities that they have yet to exorcize.[2]

Impeccable Ancestry

Because of the difficulty of asking individuals directly about slavery, when I decided to explore the issue of domestic slavery, I began by asking individuals about their family histories. These histories, and in particular their constructions of elite identities, however, turned out to be useful routes of remembrance of slavery. Within Auntie Akua and Uncle Kojo's family story, with which I began this chapter, the history of slavery, I argue, shapes not only their initial refusal to discuss former slaves in the family but also the ways in which they discuss the family's most prominent members. Our conversation began with a discussion of their grandfather, whom they told me was a successful trader who traveled back and forth to England regularly and often had British traders visiting him. In addition to his trading activities, Auntie Akua also added that he had been approached to become ɔmanhene, or chief of Elmina, stating, "He's a man who can become the ɔmanhene of this town." This reference to his status is a crucial part of her representation of her ancestry. By stating that her grandfather was eligible to become ɔmanhene, Auntie Akua sought to establish that he was a true descendent of the family's original lineage and not a slave or slave descendant.[3] As noted in chapter 1, descendants of slaves are not eligible for chieftaincy; thus, Auntie Akua's statement established her grandfather's status as both free and elite, demonstrating the great significance of indigenous status today. In addition, their large house and European furniture provide an illustration of coastal elites' past employment of a strategy of assimilation in order to distance themselves as much as possible from the *nnɔnkɔfo*. Similarly, these markers of European assimilation serve his descendants by placing them above suspicion of slave ancestry, a fact that they actively mobilized in my presence.

While many descendants of indigenous elites stress their family's status, in large part to distance themselves from the taint of slave ancestry, descendants of local women who married European men carry an extra burden when recounting the lives of these "grandmothers" because of the frequency with which European men purchased slaves to be wives or mistresses. Kwame's family history demonstrated well this burden. Kwame is also a resident of Elmina whom I interviewed because of his elite ancestry as the descendant of a local woman who was married to a Dutch merchant. When I asked about his family history, he described it as follows:

> I believe my great-great-grandmother who was an indigenous stool [a member of an indigenous family] of Edina happened to meet this man . . . So one of these merchants met my great-great-grandmother. She was so beautiful, of course, that's why a white man would fall in love with her. I am not a direct descendant, but you can see, I've not been in America before but look [pointing to the lightness of his skin color, relative to most Ghanaians without any European ancestry], yes! So this man met our great-grandmother, . . . And he built this house, lived in it with his wife, so they gave birth to children. Already, his wife had money, gold. It was kept in pots, in vessels, it was kept away, and then they brought them out once in a while and dried them on the corridor out there, polished them and the rest. So the woman was rich and then she got married to a rich Dutch merchant. So when they gave birth to a child, a daughter, I understand she was so beautiful, so they built this house for her. I can't say much but I know that we have come down from this woman.

Kwame's telling of this story reflects an added anxiety surrounding the status of African wives of European men. By mentioning that his "great-great-grandmother" came from an indigenous royal lineage, he seeks to establish that she was not a foreign slave brought to Elmina but rather the proper wife of the Dutch merchant. Mention of her wealth performs the same function. Kwame is concerned then with demonstrating his ancestor's indigenous status, which for him is a task made more difficult given that many European men took enslaved women as concubines. Her relationship with a European man gives the family prestige, but it also holds the potential to undermine this prestige unless he makes clear that she was not a slave or a concubine, but was rather a true wife, with wealth and status in her own right. Instead of a picture of European and male domination and enslavement of local women, Kwame reverses this image by representing his grandmother as a woman whose relationship with a European man served to increase her status. In this narrative, as in the lives of many women in Elmina in the eighteenth and nineteenth centuries, power and prestige lay in feminine charm. This conjuring of an elite past must be understood, as I have argued throughout this section, in the context of a society in which many individuals were indeed enslaved.

Owning Slaves

While these individuals stress their ancestors' elite status, they do not discuss their ownership of slaves, and even, as I point out above, at times vehemently deny such accusations. These denials result in part from indigenous notions of the moral dilemma posed by slave ownership. Indeed, some scholars have shown that past slave ownership is considered to be so problematic as to require ritual redress (see Rosenthal 1998). But in addition to their inculcation into this system of morality, in Cape Coast and Elmina, descendants of coastal elites have inherited a legal maneuvering from their ancestors who would have become quite skilled at denying that they owned slaves. Given the legal codification of the right of slaves to incorporation into the families of their owners, after the 1874 Emancipation Ordinance, slave owners by law had to insist that all of the members of their households were their kin. These laws no doubt encouraged many to construct such a discourse whether or not they had actually freed their slaves.

The British were not proactive in implementing the Emancipation Ordinance in the Gold Coast for fear that it would be too disruptive, giving instead lip-service to emancipation in order to satisfy the abolitionist lobby. Following the ordinance, courts did not seek out slave owners; rather, only when slaves came forward were slave owners prosecuted. Slave owners had simply to keep the members of the households quiet, to act as though their slaves had been freed and incorporated as kin, to evade the attention of the court system. When cases were brought against slave owners, they often continued to deny that they owned slaves, claiming instead that the slaves were either their wives or adopted children (Getz 2004, 116). Indeed, the line between free and enslaved dependants was often blurred, confounding colonial courts. In this way, local residents' refusals to discuss slave owner-ship emerged at least in part from their involvement in a conversation with colonial officials regarding an emerging definition of legal families.

Even more than the long-ago structure of prosecutions under the Eman-cipation Ordinance, denying past ownership of slaves also serves individuals by distancing their families from much-publicized contemporary instances of enslavement that have drawn a great deal of national and international attention. The year that I lived in Ghana was the same year of the infamous case of the *MV Etireno*, a ship that was found off the coast of Benin carrying children that were victims of a child-trafficking scheme. The story became front-page news in Ghana and around the world, drawing the attention of UNICEF and other child-welfare organizations, and leading to the publica-tion of staggering figures related to slavery in West Africa, including Ghana. The *New York Times* told its horrified Western readers that "[d]espite inter-national efforts to curb the trade, child slavery persists in West and Central Africa, from where European slave traders shipped millions of people to the Americas from the 16th to 19th centuries" (April 16, 2001, p. 6), seem-ingly feeding into all too familiar notions of African savagery. This article is also a prime example of the way in which contemporary forms of slavery in Africa are often tied to its earlier forms. In addition to this continental stigma, which I explore more fully in chapter 5, the history of domestic slavery as one of these earlier forms of slavery, particularly slave ownership by prominent families, opens up the possibility of the stigmatization of specific contemporary individuals who are members of the same families. The existence of present-day forms of slavery continues to make relevant slavery's illegality as an explanation for individuals' reluctance to discuss their families' past ownership of slaves. They do so, I argue, as a result of their engagement with local norms, legal proscriptions, and international discourses on human rights.

What is most striking about this reluctance is that it occurs in the context of vivid stories about past slave ownership. These stories are the province of private, family settings, not public discourse. While, as noted above, they are quite difficult for researchers to access, I stumbled across such discourses in my discussion with both Auntie Akua and Kwame. As I mentioned, I first learned that Auntie Akua's family had owned slaves from her niece, Miss Mensah. Miss Mensah is a teacher at a nearby senior secondary school, and I sat in on many of her classes (see chapter 5). During a lecture on the slave trade, she shared with the class the fact that her grandfather had owned slaves. This occasion was the only time that I heard an unprompted disclosure of a history of slave ownership. Because the history of the slave trade is primarily an academic discourse in Ghana, the classroom is the most common site of its disclosure. Within this space of academic inquiry, otherwise unspeakable personal histories can be voiced. As Miss Mensah constructed a social narrative of slavery for her students, her personal narrative became interwoven.[4] But the utterance of her personal narrative outside of the confines of the classroom remained problematic. Indeed, after observing the class in which she made this disclosure, I asked Miss Mensah to tell me more about her family history. She answered that she really did not know much about it, seeming uncomfortable with the topic now that we had left the classroom setting. Still, recognizing that my interest was academic and for the purposes of my research, she said that I should speak to her aunt and uncle.

In contrast to Miss Mensah's movement from the merely academic to the personal, in my conversations about slavery, I found that most individuals moved in the opposite direction, attempting to guide conversation away from the personal toward more anonymous, academic discussions. Uncle Kojo certainly followed this path when, after vehemently refusing to discuss his family's past ownership of slaves, he told me that he knew of a book that would be of great use to me and immediately got up and left the house to try to track it down from a friend to whom he had lent it. Feeling that I had established a rapport with the aunt, I tried once more to question her about slavery within her family. To my surprise, this time Auntie Akua admitted that yes, her grandfather had owned slaves. She also told me that the descendants of those slaves were still part of the family and that in fact the woman who brought me up from the courtyard was one of the descendants, in this way actually revealing the slave ancestry of one of the members of her household.

The difference between Uncle Kojo and Auntie Akua's levels of candor may result from their respective genders. In this region, women are most often responsible for passing down family histories to subsequent generations.[5] Thus, Auntie Akua, as an elder female in the family, is the appropriate person to share her family's history with me. Her initiation of this discussion then permitted Uncle Kojo to divulge aspects of it as well. Indeed, when he returned to the house, Auntie Akua told him, "I have told her about the slaves in the family." Uncle Kojo appeared to unquestioningly follow her lead. His previous rancor instantly evaporating, he simply nodded, suggesting that he too was well aware of this part of his family's history.

Kwame presented a similar situation. Because of his openness and our rapport, I decided to ask him whether his family had owned slaves. To my surprise, given my previous experiences, he was willing to discuss this issue. With unexpected candor, he told me how he learned about his grandfather's experience growing up in a house that owned slaves:

> I came to meet one very old man, just before he died, but I was so little. He sat us down most evenings and told us the history of this house. And that man never walked to school on his own two feet. Can you imagine how he went to school? He went on someone's back. Remember I told you originally that this house was a rich house, so they had a lot of, they had people serving them . . . So this house was so rich that it even at that time got filled with those people . . . Yes, so that's why this woman, my mother . . . she's not too old, but it's because of that that she cannot do anything for herself, do you understand? Everything was done for her . . . now she's got to find her own feet, and she can't do that properly, do you understand?

Kwame goes to great lengths to avoid using the word "slaves" in his discussion. He stumbles through some of his sentences with awkward phrases ("they had a lot of, they had people serving them") and refers to slaves as "those people." At the same time, he relates a rather vivid picture of slavery, of his grandfather being carried on someone's back to school. These examples suggest that the descendants of slave owners are told stories of the past slaves in the family, while at the same time they inherit proscriptions against publicly discussing them.

Family Ties

Few scholars have examined processes of sequestering slavery from discourse as a response to discourses emerging from colonial courts and the international press that pathologize families that have owned slaves. They have instead tended to focus on another reason, to which I turn to below, namely, the fact that individuals also seek to protect the members of their families who are descendants of slaves from the stigma of enslavement and fear that bringing up their ancestry might upset relationships within the family (see, for example, Greene 2003). The predicament posed by slave ancestry became quite apparent in my conversations with Auntie Akua and Uncle Kojo as well as with Kwame. After agreeing to discuss the slaves in the family, the first thing that Uncle Kojo said to me was, "Now they are part and parcel of the family." Auntie Akua explained that everyone in the family knows about the descendants of slaves in the family, including the descendants themselves, but no one discusses it; she stated, "No, anyway they know it themselves because today we don't discuss anything about slavery in this country, so we are all one, but they know it. Their grandfather or grandmother, they are not descendants of this man [her grandfather and the head of the family]. We are all one because today if you say something about it to somebody, that as for you, you are a slave—no, you don't say slave, because if you tell anybody that, if you say slave—we've stopped that." Auntie Akua's forthrightness allowed me to learn about the slave descendants in her family, but she also asserted a strange paradox: that everyone knows whose ancestors were slaves but no one discusses it. Indeed, Uncle Kojo's original vehement denial of the existence of slavery in their family attests to the necessity of silence. Her insistence that now "we are all one" conveyed her concern to stress the incorporation of the descendants into the family and the fact that no distinction is made between them and other members of the family.

At the same time, in attempting to explain why people do not talk about slavery, Auntie Akua pauses and stutters, demonstrating the strength of the wall of silence that surrounds the fact of the continuing subordination and stigmatization of slave descendants. Thus, even in admitting to the existence of slavery, she refuses to address the inequalities that it produced, such as the fact that the woman identified as the descendant of a slave appeared to me to have the status of a servant in the household. Auntie Akua clearly views slavery as a history with the capacity to dismember her family through the revelation of carefully concealed inequalities. Silence stitches over deep fissures that are constantly threatening to erupt.

Kwame discussed the slaves in his family in a similar manner, stressing that his grandfather was very kind to the slaves in his house and that their descendants have been incorporated into the family: "He built houses for them so they went to live there. In any case, they are still part of this family. Today we are one, do you understand? Today they come from here and they come from this house. *So today we are one, nothing like that ever happened, that is what we tell*" (my emphasis). Kwame articulates the obligation to keep silent and even to deny outright that slavery occurred, even in the face of astounding memories that continue to be passed down. He therefore insists that slave ancestry does not affect intrafamily relations.

These constructions of family history are shaped by the larger social narrative of incorporation. According to Halbwachs's notion of collective memory, individual memories can only be interpreted within the social context, which allows them to be narrated (1980). Also, memory, as Lambek (1996) notes, is a form of moral practice. Indeed, in Elmina and Cape Coast, what is recalled as well as that which is sequestered from discourse serve to secure relationships within the family. The phrase "we are all one" used by both Kwame and Auntie Akua is reminiscent of nationalist discourse, but it also reflects an ideal of egalitarianism that existed long before the nationalist movement. The importance of the notion of family unity is expressed in the Akan phrase *abusua baako, mogya baako*, or "one family, one blood" (Hagan 1993, 26). As a result, details of enslavement are sometimes kept even from family members to protect the notion of family unity. Some families have even sworn oaths not to discuss slavery (Perbi 2004, 11).

In her discussion of colonialism in Madagascar, Cole (1998; 2001) plays on the double meaning of remembering: to recall the past as well as to re-member or to re-constitute in order to discuss the ways in which memories may serve to reconstruct societies whose coherence has been threatened by tragic events. She notes that re-membering often involves "deliberate forgetting" (1998, 621), a process by which groups remember one set of relationships by forgetting another. In Cape Coast and Elmina, by forgetting distinctions between slaves and free persons, individuals hope to re-member their families, renouncing the existence of division and embracing instead an ideal of filial equality.

Forgetting these distinctions, however, responds not only to local notions of morality. It responds as well to legal standards. Like proscriptions against mentioning slave ownership, this practice is not simply a matter of local norms; it is also a legal requirement. Slave ancestry is so stigmatized that to claim that someone has slave ancestry without proof was categorized as defamation of character in traditional courts and upheld under colonial law. In many cases, slave descendants have successfully argued that the mention of their slave ancestry, even if factual, constitutes an insulting and offensive language that should be legally sanctioned. Akosua Perbi (1996) notes that in one such case in Kyebi, the defendant had said to the plaintiffs, "Slaves who were brought here by my grandfather Anafi Kwadwo now give me no respect. A freeborn person who sleeps in a thatched roof is worth more than a slave who sleeps in that room." Atakora, one of the plaintiffs, replied that because of abolition, "we are all equal." The native court agreed and fined the defendant for making those remarks. In a similar case in the Brong Ahafo region, Perbi reports that when a man had asked for a drink while Kwasi Krah and his wife were drinking, Krah replied, "Your grandfather was a slave and you have the impudence to join elders when they are drinking." The court fined Krah twenty pounds sterling for the use of offensive language (1996, 87). Indeed, the classification of the appellation "slave" as slander regardless of historical accuracy is spelled out in the 1960 case of *Ampong v. Aboraa* in which Justice Smith declared that "the epithet 'slave' constitutes slander in native law and is actionable in native law without proof of special damage" (Ghana Law Reports 1960, 29–31, quoted in Perbi 1996, 88).

The taboo nature of mentioning slave ancestry has been noted by numerous scholars. In his 1954 study of the Fante, Christensen writes, "Some slaves continue to work for families that, except for emancipation, would have owned them, though this varies from giving a third or half of their crop to a few days of labor a year for clearing new land or planting. One informant states slaves worked two days a week for their master, but he added significantly, 'you can't call them slaves or they will leave you'" (1954, 41; see also Greene 2003).

Because of the illegality of mentioning slave ancestry, domestic slavery is unspoken under normal circumstances. The sanctions against revealing someone's slave ancestry support the myth of incorporation of slaves. But the ideology of slavery is that slave ancestry is not only unspoken, it is erased, a notion that is expressed in the Fante proverb, "He who washes his hands clean may eat with the elders." This proverb suggests that slave ancestry is a stain that can be washed away, qualifying a person to be in the highest ranks of the family (Christensen 1954, 41). In reality, slave ancestry is not so easily discarded, and the social stratification wrought by slavery is extremely problematic. Under certain circumstances, slave ancestry can and must be revealed, particularly in land and chieftaincy disputes because descendants of slaves do not have the same rights with regard to land and the office of chief. The necessity of these revelations supports a competing myth that slave status is eternal. The latter myth suggests that slave ancestry is a stigma in Ghana. This stigma developed as a result of the intensification of domestic slavery that arose alongside the transatlantic slave trade. Thus, Rattray's characterization of slavery as simply one end of a spectrum of servitude in which "every one around him was in a sense 'the slave' of some one" (1969, 42) does not fully account for the persistence of this stigma today. Indeed, the contradictory beliefs regarding slavery, that slaves become incorporated into families and that slave status is eternal, create a difficult situation in which slavery is the insult that cannot be uttered.

While the silence that surrounds slave ancestry certainly protects the descendants of slaves and slave owners within the context of the larger society, *within* families, not only are many individuals quite verbal about ancestral distinctions, they also may be quite open about the consequences of such distinctions. My conversations with descendants of slave owners suggest that the grandchildren of those who grew up with slaves in the household were actually explicitly told about these slaves so that they would understand from an early age their own privileged status. Thus, the necessity of denial coexists not only with memories of slavery but also with the reality of the legacy of the status differentials that it created, as in, for instance, the case of the woman of slave descent in Auntie Akua's household. Kwame was quite open about the discrimination faced by descendants of slaves within his family. He explained that he learned about the distinctions within the family at a very young age,

> KWAME: I got to know about [domestic slavery] before I learned about it [in school]. When I was young, right, those who really come from this house, they discriminated a lot against those who didn't actually come from here . . . It is our generation that is going to bring the family together. But before my generation, those who came before me, they discriminated a lot.
>
> B.H.: What did they do?
>
> KWAME: They made you realize that you are a royal, this person is the descendant of a slave, you understand? You are from this house, this person is not from this house. Why is this person not from this house? Because they were brought and they came to serve us, but eventually they had to be freed and become independent, so they have become part of the family, but they discriminated a lot. So they made me aware long before I went to school.

These constructions of status then are passed down so that as they learn about their grandparents' pasts as slave owners, these descendants also learn the significance of the status that they have inherited. They learn that in fact within the family they are *not* all one. Clearly then, slavery is sequestered from public discourse, but it is discussed within private, family settings by both the descendants of slave owners and, as I discuss below, the descendants of slaves.[6] For the descendants of slave owners, the sharing of such information is a means of instilling in new generations a sense of their privileged status within the family.

Despite the problematic nature of these extreme status differentials and the resultant exclusion of slavery from public discourse, individuals still find

ways to establish their identities as descendants of free persons. They often do so through references to being "indigenous," "royal," or "from this
house." These terms imply that a given man or woman is a full member of
his or her family's lineage, in contrast to slaves, who were brought into the
family from other places and who do not have the same rights with regard
to that lineage.

Such techniques for defining difference without ever uttering the dreaded
word ɔdɔnkɔ allow the discrimination against slave descendants that Kwame
describes to continue. Nevertheless, the divulgence of slave ancestry outside
of the context of the family is a rare occurrence. Given the stigma attached
to slave ancestry and sanctions against its revelation, it should come as no
surprise that contemporary residents are reluctant to publicly discuss it. The
history of domestic slavery in Ghana exists as a public secret. Everyone not
only knows that it existed but often can identify people in the community if
not in their own families who are descendants of slaves. Despite this knowledge, the topic is strictly sequestered from public discourse. This careful
balance relies upon the maintenance of silence in public by the descendants
of slave owners. Erasure serves here to maintain the "imagined community"
(Anderson 1991) of "family" as a construct created through colonial, national, and international law. In addition to challenging the incorporation
of descendants of slaves, telling their secret would reveal their ancestors
as slave owners, the creators of the very inequalities that they denounce.
Indeed, memory implies accountability (Antz and Lambek 1996). Thus, the
descendants of those who kept slaves are, in many ways, the ones who are
held responsible by the social body for keeping quiet about the past divisions
in their families.

Debased Ancestry

Thus far, this chapter has addressed the ways in which the descendants of
slave owners construct the histories of their families through their reluctance to discuss their past ownership of slaves as well as their hesitancy to
reveal the contemporary distinctions within their families that it spawned.
But what about the descendants of slaves? Given its social consequences,
one might imagine that the descendants of slaves have an even greater
investment in concealing their slave ancestry than the descendants of slave
owners. Indeed, many scholars have noted examples of such concealment
by descendants of slaves throughout West Africa.[7] In 1948, Margaret Field
wrote that in Western Akim, a district slightly inland from the coast in the

then Gold Coast, where she suggests most people have some slave ancestry, residents refused to provide detailed information about their lineages. She writes, "I was puzzled at first to find that nearly every informant, after telling me cheerfully of his parents and grandparents, suddenly relapsed into sulky silence and would give no details of earlier ancestors. Sometimes an informant who had been courteous and interested would suddenly flare into anger and say 'What business is it of yours who was my grandmother's mother? I am too busy to tell you any more'" (1948, 19–20).

More recently, in her study of Sierra Leone, Mariane Ferme explains the reasons for the suppression of memories of domestic slavery, writing, "Their reticence was due in part to the perception that slavery was an institution frowned upon by outsiders like myself and to the fact that acknowledging it meant distinguishing masters from slaves. After all, who wants to be recognized as a descendant of slaves? Who is entirely free from suspicion of having slave ancestry?" (2001, 82).

Given the social sanctions against mentioning slave ancestry, identifying people with slave ancestry is a difficult proposition. As Christensen notes, sometimes aspects of an individual's personal history will suggest slave ancestry, such as when someone only reckons descent through one line rather than through both the maternal and the paternal lines. In this case, the individual most likely is providing the lineage of his master. Christensen notes the proverb, "One cannot point to his father's country with his left hand," that describes this occurrence, as it is customary to indicate the paternal line with the right hand (1954, 38). But even when individuals with slave ancestry are identified, broaching the topic of their ancestry is still problematic.

I was therefore astounded when, in the middle of a conversation with my friend Kwesi, he declared, "My grandmother was a slave." He was volunteering at the time as a tour guide at one of the castles. I spent countless hours at the castles and so had become quite familiar with many of the tour guides. It was a slow day, and no groups had arrived for tours, so Kwesi and I sat in the museum, where there was at least some relief from the glaring sun. I was telling Kwesi about my research when he made this unexpected admission. I asked him to tell me more.

When we were children, that lady was very, very old, even getting to eighty, ninety, or a hundred. But that woman was able to gather the children to tell them something about slave trade and slavery so many years ago so I can't remember most of it. According to her, she was not brought up in the South. She was from the North, even north of Ghana, other countries, North African countries. And in those days, there were even raiders. Some people raided villages in the night. She was able to name an African named Babatu and Samory. They raided villages in the night. They had guns, gunpowder, firearms. So they raided villages in the night and captured them. Others who were also just trading, they visited the various villages. Those who were poor, families in extreme poverty, they just sold some of their members, and she was also involved. The parents sold my grandmother and some other members of the family. They sold them to one of these raiders or these businessmen. And the man took them away in the night. They were brought in the night, so many miles.

So they traveled to a certain village, and the other members of the family were not aware that these people were sold (and you know in Africa you have extended family), and they did not approve of the sale. So they traced the route and came to where they had gone, to a certain village. They wanted to take back their relatives, but the owner also refused and that resulted in trouble between the two groups. And they were taken to the chief in the village. The man settled the case. According to the chief, since they were sold by their parents, the other family members should either pay the purchase price to the new owner so that they could take their sister (that's my grandmother) and other members of the family back, or the new owner should bring them down to the coast if they are not able to pay. And unfortunately, they didn't come with any money, so they could not settle that debt. So the chief ordered the businessman to take these people down to the coast. So that resulted in her and other members of the family being taken to the coast. So that's how my grandmother was transported to the coast. Instead of being taken to the castle, the man was rich, so the man kept my grandmother. Later she was given to somebody to marry. At that time, there were very few women along the coast, even in Africa, so getting somebody to marry was very, very difficult in those days. Some people traveled all the way to the North and bought some of these slaves and brought them down to marry them. So she was given to a son of that businessman to marry.

Kwesi's story tells us a great deal about the place of slavery within historical consciousness in Ghana. Not only does it exist within family histories of the descendants of slave owners as I discuss above; descendants of slaves also carry this lore, usually as part of a private family discourse. In his narrative, Kwesi describes a scene of an elderly relative relating stories of her past to the children of the family, who gather around her. Clearly, slavery, at least to some degree, among both slaves and slave owners is part of a family-based oral tradition passed down from generation to generation. But slavery is quickly disappearing from oral tradition. Kwesi later noted that children no longer hear stories about the slave trade because "people are forgetting them." As the generation that experienced slavery dies out, he suggests that their stories are no longer passed down but rather are forgotten.

His grandmother's story begins with the general atmosphere of fear that existed in the North that she herself experienced. Kwesi describes the prevalence of slave raiders, although some of this information may have been from his own knowledge of this time period rather than from his grandmother's recollections, given his familiarity with this history as a tour guide. He then describes the traders who visited the North to buy slaves, the selling of his grandmother, and the conflict that her selling caused within the extended family. His account of the conflict between the family members and the traders demonstrates that the practice of slavery was fraught with tension for all of those involved, and often, the families of the enslaved were relatively powerless to fight against it. By including this detail, the potential foil of her enslavement, Kwesi's grandmother was perhaps attempting to demonstrate her family's love and care for her. Rather than imparting the image that unfeeling families impassively cast their children into slavery, she creates an image of an extended family desperately wanting to keep her but finding themselves unable to do so. This incident also provides tension in the story as Kwesi's grandmother is almost saved from enslavement but ultimately must relent to being taken from her family.

Buying slaves to become wives in areas that did not have enough women to replenish the lineages was a common practice in West Africa during the eighteenth and nineteenth centuries. The fate of these slaves was somewhat different from that of male slaves. As wives, their incorporation into the families of their owners was automatic, and their children belonged to the lineage of their fathers rather than of their mothers. These descendants could then easily recreate their ancestry, by tying themselves to their father's matrilineage, and thereby gain the status of a full-fledged member of the family. In Kwesi's story, there is no mention of violence or maltreatment, either of his grandmother or of himself as her descendant; thus, it conforms to the myth of incorporation, which is a key narrative of slavery in Ghana.

This conformity necessitates an examination of the significance of Kwesi as the storyteller. As a tour guide at the castle, Kwesi is thoroughly familiar with the history of slavery. Telling this history was his temporary vocation; thus, while he is intimately acquainted with it, he retains an academic distance from it. It is this unique positionality with regard to the history of the slave trade that I would suggest made possible his disclosure of his family history. Just as Miss Mensah could mention her family's past ownership of slaves in the context of the classroom, Kwesi can disclose his grandmother's slave status inside of the castle and, perhaps more importantly, to me, both as a friend in whom he could confide and as an individual with an academic interest in the slave trade. Once again, personal biography and history as academic discourse merge into one category of memory. But in this merger, one must ask what has been forgotten (see Antz and Lambek 1996). Kwesi insisted that his grandmother was not badly treated and that buying slaves was a way to bring wives into the community, who were then treated like any other wives. The silence with regard to mistreatment conforms to the rules of exclusion that allow for the maintenance of family ties. Indeed, not only the descendants of slave owners but also the descendants of slaves must view memory as moral practice in order to maintain the cohesiveness of family (see Lambek 1996).

Despite these silences in his story, Kwesi does challenge the narrative of incorporation in another way, in the telling of the story itself. Within the myth of incorporation, the end result should be that eventually the true ancestry of a slave woman is disregarded and forgotten by both her descendants and the free members of her family. The passing down of the story of her enslavement suggests, however, that Kwesi's grandmother could not forget. Reciting the story to her grandchildren demonstrates furthermore her awareness that someone else might disclose their ancestry to them as a way of humiliating them. In this way, she recognizes that their ancestry is viewed as debased, at the same time that she attempts to diffuse its power as an epithet in the hands of others.

Thus, the passing down of her story emerges in part as a form of resistance to the discrimination faced by her and her descendants. Many theorists have claimed on the contrary that the slaves in West Africa aspired only to be more fully incorporated into the families of their owners (Klein 1989; Robertson 1983). Frederick Cooper makes a crucial intervention in this regard. He notes that "accepting new norms and behaviour patterns offered meaningful rewards where the odds of resisting were poor. And so the culture of the slave-owners became a crucial element of control. But culture could also be a crucial element of the slave's resistance. By remembering where they came from and asserting the value of the way of life of their homelands, slaves struggled *not* to be absorbed" (Cooper 1979, 124–25). In this way, he ties memory to resistance.

After Kwesi's surprising revelation, I attempted to find out more about the role of this history within his family. I found that the story of his grandmother is actively remembered and fairly liberally shared because her descendants have embraced their stranger status on the coast as the descendants of slaves and had attempted to regain their ties to their community of origin. Explaining their efforts, Kwesi told me,

> Actually that woman had a child, a child before she was even brought down. So it came to a point, one of my uncles decided to trace the family tree, so the man went north, to one of the towns in Mali. He visited a certain town and he went to the chief and told him my grandmother's story. The chief himself didn't know much about the story so he called some of the elders. They listened to the story, and some of them were able to tell him of a certain lady. . . . They invited her to join them, and this man told the woman the story, and she [confirmed that the events that he described had indeed taken place]. She even told more, how her mother was one night taken away . . . The woman who was very, very old at the time was one of the daughters, the first daughter that my grandmother gave birth to before she was transported. The woman was old, she was very, very sick at that time. . . . My uncle decided to bring the woman down, to visit the family, but because of her sickness, the woman could not come, and later we were informed that she died. And apart from that woman, most of them are no more, most of the members of the family in the North, they are no more. The grandmothers, brothers, uncles, and the rest, most of them are so old that, so many years have passed that most of them have died, so many years ago.

Not only does Kwesi's grandmother resist incorporation by relating the story of her enslavement, but the family continued her resistance by tracing her roots back North. The uncle's success in tracing his family back to a particular woman in a specific town in Mali is quite extraordinary, but equally remarkable is the fact that he attempted to do this at all. The search for their original family contradicts the notion so prevalent in discussions of African slavery that slaves became incorporated into new lineages and reckoned their descent through those families. When these ties are challenged, slaves then become kinless. Klein refers to slaves as "people without history" to highlight their lack of familial ties (1989, 212).

By telling the story of her selling, Kwesi's grandmother recalls her northern kin, and by searching for these kin, Kwesi's uncle rejects his "kinless" classification as a slave descendant and asserts that he does indeed have kin and therefore cannot be viewed as an inferior member of society. Although this form of resistance may not succeed in removing the stigma of slave ancestry that is imposed from the outside, it certainly is a vehicle toward self-respect. Numerous scholars have examined the benefit of a belief in incorporation among slaves and their descendants insofar as it helps them to attain self-respect regardless of whether or not others recognize the validity of their incorporation (see especially Robertson 1983). Likewise, rejection of the notion of incorporation may serve the same purpose of creating an internal vision of self regardless of society's categorizations. This story strongly suggests a form of resistance to the characterization of being kinless through the memory of kin and to the depiction of placelessness through the insistence that they too have a place to call home.[8]

The death of the old woman, the last link to their northern family, ultimately compromises the strength of their kinship claim, but the family's insistence on its validity remains an important form of resistance. Because the presence of resistance suggests the existence of domination (Foucault 1982; Abu-Lughod 1990), Kwesi's story also speaks to the treatment of himself and his kin within his southern family. His telling of this story illustrates the stigma that he and his kin must face. Despite the ideal of equality, difference remains, and in the face of stigma, the one source of power for those with slave ancestry is to give it voice. Whereas silence may be a source of empowerment in the context of the larger society, within the family, discourse remains a potent tool of empowerment.

While Kwesi's family may choose to remember their northern roots, the dominant narrative within families that "we are all one" attempts to distance all members of the society from the taint of slavery. Thus, while the stigma of slavery remains a source of division within families that may lead descendants of slaves to identify with their original homelands, the myth of incorporation provides slave descendants with a strong sense of belonging in the context of the larger society. In this process, the descendants of those individuals whose ancestors were slaves brought from the North are allowed to lay claim to indigeneity. In this way, they can separate themselves from inhabitants of the North who, as I discuss in the next chapter, retain the stigma of their association with past processes of enslavement. Within the process, histories of slavery and incorporation are erased from southern communities in theory, although they remain a lingering presence as family secrets.

3 » *Displacing the Past*

IMAGINED GEOGRAPHIES OF ENSLAVEMENT

I t is afternoon and I am sitting with the leader of one of the *asafo* companies in Elmina. We are discussing the history of the company and of European trade on the coast, when I decide to ask him if company histories include anything about the slave trade. "Yes, yes," he responds. "You know, actually, the people here were not sold into slavery. They were brought . . . the slaves were brought in from afar, from the North and other surrounding areas, and then this town was used as a sort of storage of those who were brought in." This was, apparently, the extent of what he could tell me on the subject. Similarly, on a separate occasion, another resident told me, "The people who were enslaved were not taken from here, they were taken from the North, kept here for a short while, and then taken away, so we never had any contact with them!" I repeatedly had similar conversations with men and women in Cape Coast and Elmina in which I found that my questions regarding the slave trade did not elicit stories about the coast. They did, however, elicit references to the North. While my questions regarding domestic slavery frequently were cut off when people insisted that such a thing had never occurred, my attempts to initiate conversations about coastal memories of the Atlantic slave trade then were often redirected. Coastal residents insisted that it was not part of their history; it was, rather, properly the history of the North as the source of slaves. These comments reveal that coastal residents seek to displace this history, suggesting instead that slaves came from the North and passed straight through their communities to the Americas. Within this narrative, they construct Cape Coast and

Elmina as mere transit points in the slave trade rather than places in which slaves either originated or remained.

While these towns may have been transit points from the perspective of powerful slave merchants who did not have much to fear, ordinary men and women in Cape Coast and Elmina were not immune from enslavement. They, along with other Akan speakers and northerners, were enslaved at different times over the course of the slave trade (see chapter 1). In contrast to this complex geography of enslavement, however, coastal residents' imagined geography names the North as the sole site of enslavement. This imagined geography reveals a key to our understanding of what it means for a society to remember the slave trade. Such memories recall not only the specific experiences of those vulnerable to enslavement including, as Opoku-Agyemang notes, residual hurt, memories of anger or danger, lingering knowledge of defeat, or a heritage of resistance (1992, 69), they also entail a recollection of a particular world order, a certain set of hierarchical relations among geographical locales. During the Atlantic era, just as slaves were stigmatized within families, regions most vulnerable to slave raiding were stigmatized within the country because, I argue, of notions of the brutality of slave raiders and the lack of sophistication of those whom they enslaved. They both became the cannibals in the interior, inhabitants of the savage bush. In describing northerners in this manner, this discourse tied the interior's remoteness from the European order to its lack of civilization.

For this reason, slavery is not just a concern within family histories; it is also a concern within community histories. Indeed, the term ɔdɔnkɔ (slave) came to mean "northerner" more generally and to be understood as a highly derogatory term that signals a stigmatized identity. It is this stigma that explains why residents of Cape Coast and Elmina not only insist that members of their communities were never enslaved but often do so vehemently. In contrast to domestic slavery, which they sequester from public discourse altogether, in the case of the slave trade, coastal residents can displace it onto the North and thereby avoid their own stigmatization.

Like family histories told in public, this narrative similarly hides divisions between the descendants of slaves and the descendants of freepersons on the coast. Instead, all coastal residents are united in their contrast to northerners. References to northern difference furthermore do not always require explicit references to enslavement. Note, for instance, my conversation with Kwabena, an educated older man from Elmina. To explain to me the difference between the North and the South, he said,

Now we were on the coast so we were the first point of contact when the Europeans came. As a result, we also became more enlightened than those in the interior. In fact, the first education in this country was in Elmina, Cape Coast, and other towns along the coast. So we became the elitest [*sic*] group. So they, so the people in the interior gave us due respect as people who were friends of the Europeans, who were educated. So just as the Europeans were more civilized than people in this country generally, people in Elmina were more civilized than people in the interior. So that gives us a sense of pride. So I would say we are proud in the sense that we saw the light earlier than those in the interior.

Given the dangers that northerners faced, both of enslavement as well as of their more general exclusion from any other type of engagement in the Atlantic order, coastal residents' regionalist sentiments are the result not, I argue, of their unthinking adoption of ideas of themselves and their neighbors introduced by Europeans but rather of the life and death consequences of the ideological system that they introduced. Discourses of the savage North persist, furthermore, because of the continuing dangers associated with remoteness from the global order. Since the economic downturn of the 1970s in Ghana, discourses of underdevelopment have dominated the public sphere. Within these, southern Ghana only fares well in comparison with the North, where an even more extreme lack of resources has led to many well-publicized violent conflicts among various groups that recall the violence between past communities of slave raiders and the communities they raided. From the perspective of coastal residents, it thus remains a landscape of terror. By invoking the different roles of North and South in the Atlantic economy as well as the different roles they now have in the global economy, coastal residents seek to displace the historical legacy turned contemporary reality of terror and perverse poverty.

In this chapter, I examine narratives about regional difference and argue that coastal residents often stress their difference from Ghana's North in order to distance themselves from its past and present terrors. By understanding that coastal residents' descriptions of the North as the savage bush result from their desires to displace images of remoteness onto the North and thereby avoid their own association with its supposed savagery rather than from some sort of primordial regionalist sentiment or blind following of Europeans (see Mamdani 1996 on this point), we can better understand the reasons for their partial and unstable nature.

To demonstrate this partiality, I begin with a discussion of alternative narratives about the North before turning to the ways in which coastal residents learn to invoke images of the savage bush. I explore specifically how public history forums teach them these narratives at the same time that they encourage them to disavow these unruly spaces. Ultimately, these narratives demonstrate contemporary concerns regarding the coast's place in the world.

The Cherished North

With regard to conceptualizations of the North (in Ghana and in its neighboring countries, which have a similar geographic divide), most scholars have focused on ideas encoded in ritual practices in the South. Through these practices, European discourses are completely inverted to create alternative images of northerners reimagined as beloved strangers. Rosenthal notes that within Mama Tchamba cults of the Ewe of southern Ghana and Togo, the spirits of northern slaves are worshipped as a form of repayment for the debt incurred through their creation of wealth for their owners. She notes the creation of a "romance of the north" (1998, 100) that contrasts sharply to notions of the savage North. The Mama Tchamba order thus allows descendant of slaves to transform their Northern slave origins from stigma to a source of pride (Rosenthal 1998, 105).

In addition to the worship of northerners in the South, the admiration for northern shrines has led to the development of a discourse that describes the superiority of northern ritual power in the South. After the abolition of slavery on the Gold Coast, many southern communities began to establish shrines to northern deities, usually to serve as antiwitchcraft shrines. Not only were the powerful deities of northern groups respected by slave raiders from centralized communities in the north (see chapter 1), these deities also became important presences in the South. The shrines were attractive to those in the South because the ritual resources needed to cure witchcraft had to come from outside of the realm of "human culture," leading many in the early twentieth century to begin to "draw on an increasingly exotic and other-worldly range of ritual powers that led ultimately to the cultural and ecological 'other' of the northern savannas" (Allman and Parker 2005, 127). This outside, however, was more specifically outside of the European colonial order. Indeed, some scholars have attributed southern interest in northern shrines explicitly to their resistance to incorporation into this order, noting that the antiwitchcraft movement in the Gold Coast Colony (what is now southern Ghana) originated in 1855, at the same time that government interference with native customs intensified (Debrunner 1959, 106). Around this time, northerners who had settled in the South reported that witchcraft was unknown in their communities of origin because of the power of their deities who protected them against it (Field 1948). The reported lack of witchcraft in the North is significant. Debrunner argues that "since they were the shrines of far off vigorous tribes not yet under the mental stress and conflicts arising from the culture contact in the South, they attracted the attention of the southerners who came there to get help from their troubles" (1959, 107). He suggests here that the lack of assimilation of northerners was admired by southerners whose own assimilation had led to spiritual trouble, thus providing an alternative to the view of northerners solely as uncivilized potential slaves.

Southern appropriations of northern ritual power led to a reimagination of the North. Rosenthal argues that the adoption of this ritual power "offered an aesthetics and ethics of north/south relationships in southern Ghana and Togo, including ways to interpret the history between northerners and southerners that broached the trauma of slavery" (2002, 322). Similarly, Fritz Kramer notes, "[T]he people of the grasslands appeared no longer primarily as uncivilized savages, whose enslavement the Asante saw as their unquestionable right, but rather as the vigorous tribes who successfully withstood the break-up of culture, along with the social conflicts and psychic burdens of modern existence" (1993, 44). The vigorousness attributed to northerners in these accounts suggests not only their ability to resist British cultural and political incursions but also their ability to resist destruction at the hands of slave raiders. The popularity of the Senyon Kupo shrine in particular, a northern shrine noted for its role in resisting slave raiders (see chapter 1), as an anti-witchcraft shrine in the South is suggestive in this regard (Field 1948).

Indeed, the celebration of resistance to slave raiders in many northern communities provides a wealth of material on which southerners can draw in order to create images of these "vigorous tribes." Goody, for instance, highlights an account of an incident in 1900 in which a group of European mounted soldiers traveled to a village in Gonja in order to collect taxes. As they passed through the village, they were attacked and pulled from their horses, which appeared to remind the villagers of slave raiders. The chief later sent a message, "saying that he was tired of 'the white man,' that he could not pay any money, and that if his soldiers came to or through his town he would kill them, that Samoury could not touch him, that therefore the white men could do nothing" (1971, 61). The chief's invocation of Samory, the infamous slave raider, in his discussion of British colonialism demonstrates that colonialism was often understood through memories of the slave trade.[1] Indeed, just as the Senyon Kupo shrine forbade horses from entering the village during the slave trade, it likewise forbade close relationships with Europeans during colonialism (Goody 1971, 62). For northerners, the slave trade and colonialism were similar engines of extraction that required parallel means of protection.

The history of their resistance has also become integrated into ritual domains of many contemporary northern communities. Among the Temne of Sierre Leone, houses and bodies are both ritually "closed" by medicines against attack by bush spirits and witches, recalling past modes of defense against slave raiders (Shaw 2002, 47–48). Symbols related to slave raiders were later appropriated by religious communities to recall their resistance. In the Tong Hills, "the use of horse-tail whisks in ritual dances represented an explicit and pithy commentary on the historical success of the Talensi in resisting mounted raiders" (Allman and Parker 2005, 62). In northern Togo, Charles Piot notes that a fertility ceremony uses a whisk supposedly made from the hair of the horse of a Samara warrior and argues that this invocation of the past serves as an attempt "to magically reappropriate the potency of the victory over Samasi and, in so doing, to revitalize the present" (1999, 144). Songs and festivals in the North provide other examples of a heritage of resistance to the slave trade. For example, in Nankani, an area in the North, its defeat of the slave raiders is remembered in a song that states, "Ayuli has fought the Kanbonga [raider] and has taken his gun from him" (Akantoe 1998, 6). In addition, in the Builsa area, an annual festival still celebrates the residents' victories over the slave raider Babatu (Der 1998).

Their histories of resistance in particular allow the slave trade to be recalled within these communities as a point of pride, particularly in the context of continued oppression in other guises, including colonialism and neoliberal capitalism. In the face of their ongoing struggle for security, political and economic, these communities recall their once active resistance to the destabilizing force of the slave raiders and celebrate the efficacy of their ritual powers in the effort. Southern ritual communities, furthermore, attempt to draw on this northern spirit of resistance to address their own spiritual needs. In order to do so, they often must atone for their role in the oppression of northerners. In contrast to narratives that described the northern savannahs as the savage bush, they construct an image of a cherished North.

Constructing the Bush

Despite these celebrations of resistance, northerners' vulnerability to enslavement also produced less celebratory narratives both in the North and on the coast. Many northern narratives describe simply the fear and helplessness faced by men and women during the slave trade era. Allman and Parker write of the Talensi in northern Ghana, "Present-day informants recall tales of the danger their parents faced in moving about the countryside due to the constant threat of kidnapping and sale to passing slave caravans. 'People were afraid to move from house to house,' explained the late Ba'an of Sipaat, one of the communities on the western flank of the Tong Hills. 'You would have to be well armed with bows, arrows and cutlasses, in case you met people stealing human beings'" (2005, 34–35). The same informant goes on to recount,

> At that time, people were eating grass and they were dying. The only solution they could find was to sell some of their children in order to cater for others. There was a slave trade at that time. Then they had to sell some of their children to people, who, in turn, would send them across the White Volta. They would tie them under a tree and the children would stand there and those who buy the slaves would come and look at them and get the ones they preferred and then buy them and send them far away to sell . . . If you wanted food and didn't have money, you would bring your children out. (2005, 35–37)

Similarly, Piot argues that the Kabre in northern Togo "still have vivid memories of this time of raiding. Elders can recall stories told by their parents and grandparents of raids by a group of fierce, mystically powerful warriors from northern Benin called Samasi (Bariba)" (1999, 31). More generalized fears of violence also reflect a history of slave raids. According to a man I met in Cape Coast who is originally from a village in the North, people there do not whistle at night because that was the signal that slave raiders used to coordinate their attacks, and therefore the sound of whistling at night still inspires fear.

Susan Drucker-Brown reports that in the 1960s, while she was in the former Mamprusi kingdom in northern Ghana, she was asked, "Haven't you seen those herds of sheep and goats going south to the Techiman market? Those are the people witches have caught and turned into animals. And the smoked bush-meat for sale in the Accra market? Have you not seen it? That too is people caught by witches" (1993, 539). She argues that these statements reflect memories of both the capture and transport of the Mamprusi as slaves during the Atlantic trade in which they were "consumed" by southerners as well as contemporary forms of economic exploitation by the South. Indeed, common portrayals of slave raiders as cannibals throughout West Africa support this conclusion (see, for example, Shaw 2002, 225–46). Such fears continue into the present in the form of suspicions of strangers as became apparent from an anecdote told to me by a friend in Cape Coast about his recent trip to a village in the North. He said that when he arrived in the village, he was surrounded by a crowd of curious children. He began handing candy out to them, until an elderly woman shouted to the children to leave, and all of the children immediately scattered. He later asked someone why the woman did not want the children to talk to him, to which the man responded, "She doesn't know if they will come back." This explanation reflects a history of disappearances that continues to be remembered and to instill a fear of strangers.

While northerners' retrenchment from outside influences, reflected in the old woman's attempt to keep the children away from strangers, was clearly a strategy to avoid danger, it was frequently read in the past by both Europeans and Africans in the South as the North's means of keeping its own dark secrets. Their shrines raised the greatest anxieties. European missionaries and their coastal converts portrayed these "bush" shrines not as strong resistors of slave raiders and colonial officials as other religious communities did but as fomenters of evil, in order to uphold Christianity as the only legitimate source of salvation. In the secluded hinterland of the North, and indeed in other places that were similarly shielded from the glare of European scrutiny, they imagined evil practices to sprout like mushrooms.

Many contemporary church discourses continue to tie remoteness to evil and danger in a similar fashion. The fact that the majority of coastal residents are Christian makes churches key sites of inquiry into the production of historical discourses. In particular, as I describe below, the Cape Coast Methodist Church's narrative of the destruction of a "traditional" shrine has contributed significantly to the popularization of notions of regional difference. This highly publicized narrative recalls the rural South's own savage past. However, because the story demonstrates that the "savagery" of the rural South was ultimately overcome, ideas culled from it about the nature of the bush are placed once more onto the North.

Wesley Chapel is located directly in front of Cape Coast Castle near the center of town. The area in front of the church, called Chapel Square, is a central gathering place, so the church's placement of a banner there in September 2001 announcing its latest program received a great deal of attention. The banner announced the launching of a two-day program of religious tourism entitled "Cherishing the Gains of the Past: The Role of Religious Tourism in Ghana Methodism." The church invited participants from every diocese of the Methodist Church in Ghana to tour local sites considered to be important to the history of Methodism in the country in order to educate them about the history of their church.[2] When the day of the event finally arrived, a group of about eighty participants gathered at the church, making it one of the larger public history events that I have witnessed in Cape Coast.

I was invited to tag along with the group on their tour, and I eagerly accepted, curious to see how the church would define "gains of the past" and what this might mean for local constructions of history. The highlight of the program was a trip to Mankessim, a town not far from Cape Coast, where we were told the story of the *Nananom Mpow*. This story has long been part of the history of the church.[3] It begins with the migration of the Fantes to the coast. The origin story of the Fante people states that they migrated from Techiman, a town in the hinterland, and settled in Mankessim. The three leaders of the Fantes died soon after their arrival and were buried in the spot that came to be known as the *Nananom Mpow*, or "grove of the great-grandfathers." Up until the middle of the nineteenth century when it was destroyed, this site was the center of spiritual power for the Fantes.

To reach the grove, we traveled forty-five minutes on dilapidated school buses that made the bumpy road almost unbearable. As we approached the site, a sign announced it as an important site for Methodist tourism. There was nothing else to mark the turnoff from the main road onto a dirt one that made no attempts to be navigable. Huge potholes sent us pitching forward in our seats as long grasses from the encroaching fields whipped the sides of the buses. Once we got off of the buses, we continued along a narrow footpath through a field that turned into a forest. In the forest, we came to a large tree in a clearing, with nothing to identify it, and were told that we had reached the *Nananom Mpow*.

John Crayner, a local historian who has written a book on the grove, then began to recount the story of how the Fante priests once held court there and tortured and killed many men and women. Words such as "fetish," "cult," and "black magic" were peppered throughout his talk and the ensuing discussion. The pamphlet put together for the program paints an especially negative picture of the shrine. It states, for example, "A lot of people went through these atrocities and were destroyed by these unscrupulous fetish priests."

For followers of the shrine priests, the shrine was a spiritually potent and morally superior space. It was set in a remote spot in the forest shaded by a thick canopy of leaves and vines, the perfect site to house powerful spirits. McCaskie notes that such shrines "were conceptualized as being part of that liminal zone or fringe area (*kurotia*) that separated the human society of the village (culture) from the unknown, anarchic and dangerous realm of the forest (nature)" (1990, 135). Not only did the grove encode a history of migration from the hinterland, it also embodied a similar otherworldliness as northern shrines. Indeed, before their turn toward northern shrines, southern antiwitchcraft movements also looked to the southern forest to provide the spiritual power that they required (Allman and Parker 2005, 127). Like its northern counterparts, the *Nananom Mpow* also maintained its autonomy from British power on the coast for quite a long time. Not surprisingly then, in contrast to the shrine followers' construction of the potency of the shrine, European missionaries defined this liminal space not as powerful but simply as immoral and dangerous. Their description of the shrine has become part of the history of the Methodist Church and as such is disseminated to contemporary coastal residents. What is most interesting about its portrayal, however, is that just like references to the cannibals in the interior discussed in chapter 1, it seemed to implicitly tie the priests of the shrine to practices of enslavement.

While we stood in the grove, Mr. Crayner pointed to a rock with faint grooves. He explained that those accused of crimes were made to pay a fine in gold dust that was measured using these grooves, which the priests had carved into the rock. If the accused did not have enough gold dust to fill a particular groove, they were often killed and their bodies were thrown into a nearby pond. In his book about the *Nananom Mpow*, which was offered for sale during the program, Crayner explains that the dangers of the grove arose from priests' need for blood to use in their rituals:

> In times of the need for blood . . . prisoners were slaughtered and the blood collected in the [blood] pot. To collect the blood the condemned prisoner was taken to "Akwa" pond. He was tied to a tree trunk with the legs tied to the tree branches high in the woods. His head was made to

hang above the pot to make it easy for the blood to drop into the blood pot when the prisoner was being slaughtered. The dead body was then pushed into the pond to feed the crocodiles. (1979, 20)

The brutality of the priests was directed not only at those who had committed crimes but also at times at unlucky passersby. Crayner explains: "Individuals who passed by the grove alone were caught and killed. If a man crossed the road with a wife or a child accompanying and following him, he would suddenly hear the companion crying in the bush but no longer following. When he asked from the gods of Nananom, he would be told that the companion had been caught by Nananom's Kite and that he should not have his wife or child following him when traveling" (1979, 19).

These kidnappings as well as the shrine's need for blood evoke the Atlantic slave trade's thirst for captives. So too does the fact that the accused could exchange their lives for gold. Indeed, the story of the shrine recalls the many dangers including enslavement that resulted from the generalized instability that ravaged near coastal areas in the first half of the nineteenth century.[4] During this time, a series of Asante incursions devastated southern communities and led to widespread poverty. Whereas previously the priests of the shrine had served to keep social order, they may have become involved in practices of banditry on rural roads and, as Crayner notes, prosecuted individuals in order to exact fines from them at their secluded shrine, no doubt to compensate for their decreasing wealth. They may have also sold those sentenced to death into the illegal slave trade, adding their own victims to the many Fante war captives who were disposed of in this manner during these dangerous years (Getz 2004, 31–32). Tales of such bush atrocities flourished after the peace treaty that temporarily secured the safety of coastal towns under British control. Europeans and urban coastal residents displaced their fears onto the surrounding countryside. To them, the rural South became like the North, not only in terms of its forms of spirituality, but also in terms of its danger.

In her Sierra Leone example, Shaw also notes that the association of the bush and the roads that run through it with danger reflects a history of kidnappings during the Atlantic trade. She describes roads as places of danger where bush spirits and witches attack unwary travelers. She recounts stories quite similar to the one quoted above about the dangers of being seized on the road, like the following told to her by an elder in a village in Sierra Leone that had a history of slave raiding: "If a child is born, and he follows this road, him alone, and meets a warrior, he (the warrior) will seize him (the child) and sell him. He will say, 'Pa Road, lend me this one.' He will seize him, ghap! The one who bore him, if he/she approaches there, he will cut his/her head off . . . The first world in the old days, it was an angry world" (2002, 64). This angry world, Shaw argues, was the world of the Atlantic slave trade.

While the story of the *Nananom Mpow* constructs a narrative of the savagery of the southern forest region lying as it did outside of the European order, it quickly turns to its incorporation. In this way, any hint of a history of enslavement is quickly superseded by a story of salvation. Indeed, the second half of the story we were told described how Reverend Thomas Freeman, a famous Methodist missionary who settled near Cape Coast in 1841, was a regular visitor to Obidan, a town neighboring the grove where he delivered sermons. As a result of his attendance at these sermons, Akweesi, a local gourd farmer, as well as many of the other residents of Obidan converted to Christianity. Then in 1851, Akweesi and his friends went into the grove and overheard the priests talking. They discovered that the priests were the source of the supposed supernatural occurrences that had been attributed to the oracle. Akweesi and his friends declared that from then on they would never seek guidance from anyone except their God. Soon afterward, Akweesi and his friends were chasing a deer through the woods and found themselves in the sacred grove. Akweesi decided to cut down some branches to use to repair his house, thereby desecrating this most sacred of places. The priests of the *Nananom Mpow* were furious. They already resented the establishment of a thriving Christian community in such close proximity to the shrine, a community that did not rely on their authority for its success and well-being. They thus had Akweesi and his companions arrested and ordered their beheadings. One of the men managed to escape and sought refuge at Anomabu Castle where Thomas Freeman was stationed.

Freeman immediately contacted British government officials at Cape Coast who ordered that the prisoners be released, but the priests refused, arguing that the *Nananom* god was angry and had caused the drought that they were experiencing as a result of the Christians' opposition to him. The chief, who had backed the priests, was taken to trial, during which some of the priests admitted that the supposed supernatural happenings at the *Nananom Mpow* were the priests' own doing and that many people had indeed been tortured and killed as a result. The chief was fined, and several of the priests were publicly flogged and sentenced to five years' imprisonment. The government then gave Akweesi an axe to cut down the trees and bushes surrounding the *Nananom Mpow*. The British court also gave the following order, which is still in the hands of Akweesi's descendants: "This is to certify that Akweesi of Obidan and his Fellow Christians suffered persecution from the worshippers of the fetish Nananom, and now have the full permission of the Government to return to their country and to the possession of their lands. All persons attempting to molest them are hereby given warning that these converts to Christianity are under the special protection of the Government" (Crayner 1979, 37). Akweesi became ordained a minister and continued to preach in Obidan for many years.

As this story describes, the bush shrine was brought into the European order through the cutting down of trees, which undermined its remoteness. Akweesi, furthermore, had taken on the attitude of a model coastal cosmopolitan, having embraced Christianity and relying on European authority. At the same time that the program participants learned of the dangers of the bush, they also learned that those dangers have been displaced as a result of the discrediting and destruction of the shrine. This representation ignores the fact that after a few years, many local residents in fact began to worship once again at the shrine (McCarthy 1983, 118). To the colonial government and European church officials, however, the story of the shrine's total destruction was quite attractive as it celebrates local residents' embrace of British authority over that of their own religious leaders. Indeed, Brodie Cruickshank, the acting judicial assessor who signed the order that granted Akweesi and his companions the protection of the British, noted that the shrine had become "entirely deserted" (1966 [1853], 2:331). The fact that this story is today commemorated by the Methodist Church demonstrates not only church members' celebration of Ghanaian Methodism but, along with it, their acceptance of colonial versions of their history.

Not only does this story imagine the South's complete incorporation into the European order, but in its illustration of that which lies outside this order, it also raises the specter of the North. For while the participants in the church program may celebrate that Christianity, and the European order more generally succeeded in spreading to the bush surrounding the coastal towns, they know that it did not spread to the North. The North in fact became even more dangerous at the turn of the century as a result of Babatu and Samory's slave raids. These raids procured slaves for domestic use during the last decades of the nineteenth century. It is in fact this time period and these raiders that are being recalled in many of the narratives of northern communities discussed above that describe past vulnerability and resistance to slave raiders.

Participants in this program might easily wonder, If the southern forest, which represented the liminal space between the known world and the dangerous realm beyond, possessed such dangers, how much more so the far hinterland? And while Christianity and the European order more generally may have succeeded in spreading to the former, what does this mean for the seemingly impenetrable North? In fact, as the following section demonstrates, many coastal residents who, through programs like this one, learn to invoke narratives of the dangerous bush, when speaking of the contemporary landscape, apply those narratives to the North. Following the European discourses that were discussed earlier, coastal residents attribute the North's impenetrability to an imagined hostility of its inhabitants toward civilization and not to the structure of the Atlantic order and later colonialism, both of which required an outside from which they could extract: in the case of the former, slaves for the Atlantic trade, and in the case of the latter, laborers for the colony. The North has, as a result, become the site upon which displaced notions of the dangerous bush are re-placed, and with a vengeance. Unlike the *Nananom Mpow*, the North's distance frees coastal residents to make explicit references to its past processes of enslavement. But more often, as I discuss below, they let its savagery speak for itself.

The Geopolitics of North and South

Mmaa Nkommo is a wildly popular television program, a sort of Ghanaian *Oprah Winfrey Show* that addresses social issues, usually through the format of a panel of guests and a highly vocal studio audience. One particular episode addressed the issue of clitoridectomy, or female genital mutilation, which continues to be practiced in parts of northern Ghana. During the show, a clitoridectomy was shown being performed on a very young girl who was being held down by what seemed to be a dozen people and screaming incessantly for her mother. Predictably, this show sparked many lively conversations and incited harsh condemnation from many viewers in Cape Coast and Elmina. I saw the show with a young woman who is a member of the family with whom I resided. She commented during the show, "People in the North do that. They are too hard. How can they do something so barbaric?" The next day, many people continued to discuss the program and similarly commented on the "barbarism" of the practice and at the same time were quick to say that only people in the North do such things; they do not.

In this way, these individuals attempted to "erect a moral cordon"[5] around the North. They argued that the North is the site of savagery in order to free their region from a similar designation. In the process, they describe clitoridectomy as if it were a blood pot ritual of the *Nananom Mpow*; it is a barbaric practice that only occurs in remote places, far removed from their own societies. The only difference between the grove and the North is that salvation has yet to reach the latter. It is, for this reason, the quintessential bush. This denigration occurs not only because most northerners are not Christian, as are most coastal residents, but also because they are seen largely to be poor and uneducated, and reside far from urban centers and are therefore viewed as unsophisticated and backward. In the above example, for instance, women's bodies are the objects of debate. They literally embody northern difference and, as such, become that which must be defended by those northerners who claim that clitoridectomy is part of their "tradition" or condemned by southerners as a sign of the inferiority of not only these women but of their entire region. While this debate draws upon contemporary discourses regarding universal human rights versus cultural relativism, it has deeper roots, I argue, in stories like that of the *Nananom Mpow* that describe the violence and danger that adhere to remote places. Indeed the vulnerability of northern women's bodies parallels the past vulnerability of the North as a whole to enslavement. The dangers of stigmatization furthermore are heightened by the contemporary popularization of development discourses that stress achievements in the spread of education and industry, not to mention church discourses that establish the importance of Christian beliefs.

Certainly, not all references to northerners that I heard were negative. They were, on occasion, cast is a kinder light. But quite often, coastal residents, alongside and in contrast to their self-portrayals as enlightened individuals, portray northerners as uncivilized heathens and the North as a space hostile to Christianity and other markers of "civilization." Unlike the southern forest, which was saved from its own barbarism, the North remains for them an unruly landscape. Such descriptions are, I want to suggest, part of the same long conversation with Europe about incorporation that was spawned by the slave trade and is continually reanimated through popular narratives like the story of the *Nananom Mpow*.

The North as a distinct geographic locale has continued to have many negative connotations since the days in which it was regarded as a pool of potential slaves. Indeed, not only the slave trade but also colonialism led to the marginalization and victimization of the North. When the British established the Gold Coast Colony in 1874, it included only the southern third of present-day Ghana. The Asante kingdom became part of the colony in 1901, and the Northern Territories became a protectorate the same year.

Not until 1951 did the North gain full membership in the Legislative Assembly (Saaka 2001, 146). Throughout the colonial era, the British viewed the Northern Territories as a labor reserve and enacted a policy of nondevelopment under which it did not invest in agriculture or other industries in the North, thereby forcing northerners to migrate south for work, continuing the tradition of travel down to the coast, only now not as prisoners of war, but as economic prisoners (see Kimble 1963, 533–36; Songsore et al. 2001). In the early 1900s, the gold mines began to actively recruit laborers from the Northern Territories, often paying chiefs for each man that they sent south. These workers faced a high death rate from infectious diseases and poor living conditions; for instance, an influenza epidemic in 1918–19 reportedly killed over 25,000 migrants from the North (Kimble 1963, 41–42). Others traveled south to find work farming or performing menial labor, further contributing to characterizations of their inferior status.

Today, "the North," though clearly more than a geographic construct, can be precisely mapped within the contemporary nation-state. Ghana is now divided into ten regions. The Northern, Upper East, and Upper West regions are commonly referred to as "the North." These regions are distinguished by ethnic group, language, climate, and terrain, and they have their own political representatives. But in common parlance, "the North" can extend into Burkina Faso, Ghana's northern neighbor, or refer to Hausa peoples or Muslims in general who are also associated with northern-ness (see also Rosenthal 2002). In his mapping of conceptions of ethnicity among residents of a neighborhood in Accra, Sanjek draws a primary division between northerners (a category that includes Dagomba/Dagbani, Tamale people, some Hausa, Dagarti, Frafra, Moshi/Mossi, Kusasi, Grunshi, Sisala, Lobi, Wala, Gonja, Konkamba, Busanga/Mosanga, and Bosu) and southern Ghanaians (including some Ewe/Ayigbe, Ga-Adangbe, and Akan, including Fantes; Sanjek 1977, 609).

Concerns about northern underdevelopment and exploitation led to the founding of the Northern People's Party in the 1950s. Since independence, northerners have occupied various political offices, including currently the vice presidential office, but the perception of northerners as "hewers of wood and carriers of water" (see Allman 1991; Hasty 2002) continues. The stigmatization of the North, which began during the slave trade with descriptions of northerners as "cannibals in the interior," has evidently continued since. In her study of notions of regional difference among schoolchildren in southern Ghana during the 1960s, Enid Schildkrout (1979) found that students associated northerners with a lower degree of civilization through claims of their engagement in practices such as cannibalism and human sacrifice. The derogatory nature of the term ɔdɔnkɔ neatly captures the relationship between the perceived inferiority of northerners and their past vulnerability to enslavement.

Today, debates over the significance of geographical space often occur in cyberspace. In particular, the crisis in Dagbon, a northern area, has been a major source of Internet invidiousness regarding regional identities. In 2002, political violence led to the death of the *Ya Naa*, or ruler, of Dagbon, sparking further violence in the months after the murder. A particularly vitriolic letter quoted on Ghanaweb.com in response to a request made by the members of Dagbon-net, an online community of people from the area, for government support to address the Dagbon crisis complained bitterly,

> My dear brother, Charity begins at home. You and your people should start the dialogue to live in peace before the Government can provide the security you are talking about. Your northern people are the cause of Ghana's problem. We provided free education since time immemorial while the rest of the people struggle to make [ends] meet to pay their school fees . . . If you people will kill yourself who cares. Your people need to take the initiative first. If you kill your brethren through guinue [*sic*] fowl misunderstanding, how much more can the Government do to bring the so called peace and security you are making noise about. You rather should grow up. We will not entertain that stupid thing again. If you want to kill, resort to that in your Northern part [of the country] for we know you people.[6]

This letter is brimming with disdain for northerners, whom it accuses of tribalism, a familiar charge levied at societies viewed to be overly traditional. It also recalls depictions of the North during the Atlantic era that described societies poised as enemies, one raiding the other for slaves. The writer argues that northerners are incapable of development, despite the provision of free education, and instead continue to kill each other over matters as trivial as guinea fowl, a reference to a commonly cited story that claims that a major conflict in the North that resulted in 15,000 deaths began as an altercation between two men in the market over a guinea fowl (see Talton 2003). The writer furthermore insists that the government cannot be held accountable for the inability of the North to "grow up."

In many ways, northerners are easy targets for stigmatization. The northern regions are the furthest distance from the capital (a full day's journey by bus), which is the location of the only international airport in the country. The North therefore has less access to international influences, information, and goods and is often viewed as a contemporary "out of the way place" (Tsing 1993). Northerners in the South, furthermore, continue to have associations with menial labor. Many coastal residents retain vivid memories of northerners who were hired in the past to empty waste buckets, an image that evokes the lowest depths of debasement. Indeed, when I asked men and women in Cape Coast and Elmina for their views of northerners, their occupation of this position was often the first thing they mentioned.

The nationalist movement recognized the problem of regionalism and tried to combat it by emphasizing the validity and equality of all cultural groups within the nation. The first president of the independent nation of Ghana, Kwame Nkrumah, sought to unite the different regions of the nation by celebrating all cultural groups. For instance, he wore a *fugu* or smock of northern origin as his battle dress and *kente* of the Asante on formal occasions (Hagan 1993, 16), thereby, significantly, including the North in his vision of the modern nation-state, and openly condemned all forms of regionalism. In a speech given on the occasion of the tenth anniversary of the Convention People's Party, he said, "[W]e insist that in Ghana in the higher reaches of our national life, there should be no reference to Fantis, Ashantis, Ewes, Gas, Dagombas, 'strangers,' and so forth, but that we should call ourselves Ghanaians—all brothers and sisters, members of the same community—the state of Ghana. For until we ourselves purge from our own minds this tribal chauvinism and prejudice of one against the other, we shall not be able to cultivate the wider spirit of brotherhood which our objective of Pan Africanism calls for" (Nkrumah 1976, 168). But despite the nationalist movement's rhetoric of unity, regionalism remains a deep-seated ideology in Ghana. This ideology is closely tied, in fact, to the government's rhetoric of modernization. In accepting the premise that Ghana needs to modernize along Western lines, political leaders have endorsed Western development discourses. These discourses, furthermore, have historically been heavily focused on regional disparities, thereby bringing such disparities to public attention.

As they had during the Atlantic era, throughout the colonial era and the first few decades of independence, European social scientists argued that Ghana was divided into two parts: the developed South and the underdeveloped North. One observer wrote that people in the North "lived on a diet of sorghum and yams supplemented by an inadequate supply of animal protein, occupied houses built of clay with grass-thatched roofs, possessed no furniture other than stools and a few chairs, were three-quarters of a mile from a water hole, two miles from a motor road, market, clinic or school (none of the children attended school), 47 miles from a doctor, and 340 miles from the railhead in Kumasi" (quoted in Rimmer 1992, 1). Such descriptions were part of a prevalent discourse of the "failure of the North." During the same period, observers described the South, in contrast, as an area of growing prosperity, in which people benefit from "plentiful food (though it contains too large a proportion of carbohydrates), adequate and often very beautiful cotton clothing, a fairly wide distribution of useful manufactures such as bicycles and sewing machines, and a sprinkling of luxuries, including tobacco for smokers and sweets for children" (Hancock 1943, 79). This rosy depiction attributes to southern Ghana a higher living standard than parts of southeastern Europe (1943, 79, and cited in Rimmer 1992, 2). Although such descriptions arose from observations of the prosperity of cocoa-growing regions to the east as Cape Coast and Elmina were already facing economic decline, they led to generalizations about "the South" that focused on its prosperity.

While disparities between the North and South remain, more recent studies have stressed the fact that not only have living conditions in the North not improved, but also the perception of southern prosperity has largely eroded. By the 1980s, not only were northerners poor, but so too were those individuals in the South who had been considered traditionally to be relatively well-off, including cocoa farmers, wage employees, urban residents, and even the upper salariat (Rimmer 1992, 4). In an article tellingly entitled "Things Fall Apart Again: Structural Adjustment Programmes in Sub-Saharan Africa," Riddell writes, "In the years following independence in Africa there was a feeling of hope and expectation among the citizens of the new nations and their leaders. The rewards of economic development and growth were about to be obtained and seemed just around the corner" (1992, 54). As a result of the economic decline of the 1970s, Ghana, and many would argue Africa as whole, has disappointed nationalists' dreams of progress. Riddell continues, "[T]oday there is a growing sense of failure throughout much of sub-Saharan Africa . . . The world has fallen apart for most of the continent's citizens, ranging from public servants in the growing urban centres to peasants in the often declining rural areas" (1992, 54).

For coastal residents, in many ways, the world has indeed fallen apart. Given their own distance from the goal of modernization, a distance of which they are constantly reminded by political figures and development agencies, regional identities are perhaps even more salient today, and in particular the stigmatization of the North continues unabated. Faced with the economic decline of their towns, many argue that they are still better off than northerners. They insist that while northerners have always been backward, their current situation does not reflect anything about their inherent character. They assert their special status as having proceeded further in the modernization project than northerners in an attempt, I argue, to evade assertions of an inability to develop (see chapter 4).

The images that coastal residents invoke of the northerner as, when not a savage being, at least a sort of country bumpkin is of course common in many contexts. But in Ghana, it does not represent simply the denigration of the Other from a position of privilege. It is tied rather to the desires of coastal residents to embrace an "imagined cosmopolitanism" (Schein 1999; see chapter 4), which is a far cry from actual access to global resources or respect. Richard Price describes Martiniquan constructions of difference in similar terms. He explains, "Martiniquans have been encouraged to situate themselves as thoroughly modern, bourgeois members of the First World (and Europe) and to look with benevolent condescension upon, say Haitians, Saint Lucians, or Brazilians as their disadvantaged, sometimes picturesque, but backward Third World neighbors. Yet despite all this, Martiniquans (most Martiniquans) do not feel fully French. Nor, of course, do most Frenchmen consider them to be" (1998, 181–82). Similarly, coastal residents, despite their claims to be "friends of the Europeans," are hardly such.

The e-mail quoted above is a prime example of the construction of a "North as failure" discourse that attempts to distance the rest of Ghana from the backwardness of this region. Despite the unifying ambition of nationalism, the highlighting of regional differences within development discourses has overwhelmed any efforts at national cohesion, particularly in the post-1980s era of economic decline. Thus, part of the characterization of northerners as backwards results from the marginalization of Ghana as a whole in the contemporary global economy, reflecting Ulf Hannerz's (1992) conceptualization of the bush in West Africa.

Hannerz argues that in the non-Western world, "metropolitan influence does not reach evenly into various regions of a country" (1992, 231). The world is not simply divided into core, semiperiphery, and periphery as Immanuel Wallerstein suggests (1987); the periphery has its own periphery, where "transnational cultural influences tend to reach in a more fragmented, and perhaps indirect manner" (Hannerz 1992, 230). Transnationalism operates through a "power geometry" to use Doreen Massey's

(1994) phrase, by which individuals have different levels of access and entry to the flows of global traffic.

Many scholars have noted the problematic nature of designating some individuals as existing outside of the global economy. In particular, Anna Tsing's (1993) reconceptualization of the notion of the out of the way place demonstrates that even the most remote places have ties to the global economy. Charles Piot (1999) similarly challenges the notion of the bush in West Africa as a region cut off from global traffic. Indeed, buses connect northern Ghana to Accra, and northerners can and do travel south. Even those who do not are integrated into national and international frameworks of commerce, development, and social life. But these factors do not negate the significance of the dichotomy between cosmopolitan sites and bush in many African imagined geographies. Hannerz argues in the Nigerian context that the characterization of bush "could be used descriptively but would ring in Nigerian ears especially as a denunciation hurled, in richly varying combinations, at adversaries and wrongdoers: an epithet for ignorance and rustic, unsophisticated, uncouth conduct. To be labeled bush in one way or other was to have one's rightful place in modern society put into question" (1992, 229). Hannerz aptly recognizes not only the realities of interconnections but also the myths of disconnection under which people operate that are so important to our understanding of globalization. The notion of the North as an utterly insular region is a popular national myth in Ghana, as the hinterland often is in many countries.

Although Hannerz mentions the significance of the early contact of coastal groups with Europeans in defining their contemporary cosmopolitanism, he focuses mostly on contemporary conditions, in particular, the development of large international cities in Africa and the travel of Africans to European metropoles. While this analysis is quite useful for conceptualizing contemporary globalization, in Ghana, the creation of notions of difference is not a result solely of this moment but also of a prior stage of globalization: the age of the transatlantic slave trade. With this historical background, their regionalism gains a terrible logic. Coastal residents' negative characterizations of northerners, which are at times accompanied by explicit references to their past vulnerability to enslavement, provide an ethnographic illustration of the dreadful depth of African historical interactions with Europe (see Wolf 1982).

Indeed, much of the distinction between coast and hinterland dates back to the precolonial European contact and specifically to the slave trade. Thus, what the above comments illustrate is a distinction based on historical links and not solely on contemporary ones. *Mmaa Nkommo* viewers mobilized an already existing discourse about the barbaric North versus the civilized South that hearkens back to eighteenth-century European conceptualizations of northerners (the cannibals in the interior) that served the purposes of the slave trade by describing those who could be enslaved and those who could not. The stereotypes that they articulate result from viewing the North during the Atlantic trade as a pool of potential slaves and the continued marginalization of northerners after the abolition of the slave trade. These stereotypes, furthermore, circulate in the context of coastal residents' own increasing poverty, a context in which Cape Coast and Elmina appear less and less as urban spaces and more like the terrifying and antithetical bush.

4 » *In Place of Slavery*

FASHIONING COASTAL IDENTITY

In April 2002, the Prince of Orange and Princess Máxima of the Netherlands traveled to Elmina as part of a state visit to commemorate three hundred years of diplomatic relations between the Netherlands and Ghana. The starting point they recognized was not the arrival of the Dutch on the coast, which had occurred a century earlier, but rather a Dutch expedition in 1701–1702 from Elmina to the Asante kingdom, which would become a major supplier of slaves. While this meeting marks a key moment in the development of the slave trade, in a speech he gave to mark the event, the prince described it as a meeting "to discuss peace and prosperity." He went on to note that much of the period of the Dutch presence on the coast was marked by the slave trade, but he ultimately marginalized its significance within a larger story of a peaceful, diplomatic relationship between the Dutch and what became Ghana. In fact, he turned quickly to another favorable interpretation of this presence by noting its beneficial effects on the town of Elmina itself. Before the assembled crowd, he remarked, "Throughout the Dutch presence on the Gold Coast, the relationship with the people of Elmina was close. The Dutch played an active part in the planning of this town and built a number of fortifications around it. The relationship is still visible in the monuments and sites in the town itself, in the Dutch family names many people from Elmina still bear and in the use of some Dutch words in the local language. We share an interest in our common past."[1] Through these words, he described the close relationship between the Dutch and Elmina in terms of Dutch influences on architecture, families, and language.

His narrative creates an image of the "cosmopolitan coast" that stands in stark contrast to narratives of the "savage bush" described in the previous chapter. But the prince not only constructed a cosmopolitan past, he also suggested that it could be recovered. His speech was made, after all, at the launching of a town consultation to discuss development plans for Elmina. For this reason, local residents welcomed the prince's visit, greeting him and the princess by cheering and waving Dutch flags.

Their enthusiastic response to the prince's visit reflects the dire state of Elmina's economy. Economic stagnation in the town is not only the result of the recent decline of the formerly prosperous South described in the previous chapter; Elmina's problems began long before. Its economy has in fact been in decline since the departure of the Dutch in 1872. After this time, Elmina's shipping industry remained small until its port was finally closed in 1921. Cape Coast has faced a similar situation. While it had the most important port at the turn of the century, it was soon dwarfed by Sekondi and Accra, which were connected by roads and railways to important agricultural areas (Kimble 1963).[2] Its port finally closed to international trade in 1962. In addition, in contrast to their former roles in the administration of the region, today Elmina and Cape Coast have little role in national politics. The basis of the nation's economy has also shifted to the production of cocoa, which takes place in other regions. There are few job opportunities in these towns and high unemployment rates. Coastal residents have thus lost their political power, economic prosperity, and cultural caché.

As a result, some of the men and women assembled to hear the prince's speech, in particular those who are familiar with the town's history, appreciated not only that he supported Elmina's economic development but also that he broached the topic of the town's past close relationship to the Dutch. Such references, they believe, provide proof to counterclaims of their town's inexorable marginalization. These claims, which are made through images of Africa as a dark continent and of Africans as "a race of slaves," deplete coastal residents' limited supplies of both symbolic and real capital.

Because these discourses, which were first produced by Europeans during the Atlantic and colonial eras, continue to circulate within national and international arenas today, keeping them at bay requires constant vigilance. For this reason, not only do they displace the slave trade and its attached images of savagery on to the North, many coastal residents also replace it with their own stories of their past incorporation into the Atlantic order on favorable terms. In other words, faced with their own increasing poverty, they argue that they were better off in the past than they are now, that they are in fact the heirs of a glorious past. Their past centrality within the "global ecumene" (Hannerz 1992) is in fact their rightful one, they maintain, and one that therefore must be recovered. Their contemporary marginalization, they insist, is not the result of an inherent racial inferiority that diminishes their ability to obtain political power and economic prosperity; their power and prosperity have been confiscated. Drawn in this fashion, their images of the Atlantic era become an indictment of the present.

While coastal residents mobilize narratives about their past incorporation into the Atlantic era in order to protest their exclusion from the contemporary global economy, such descriptions are not, it is important to note, a glorification of the slave dealing that took place on the coast and was in fact the basis of its prosperity for much of the period of European settlement. They are rather, I argue, a different view of the Atlantic era altogether. Indeed, even more so than the prince, coastal residents erase the slave trade from narratives of coastal cosmopolitanism. They do so, as I discuss in the following section, by veiling histories of slave dealing that took place on the coast. These histories are for many reasons troubling, a fact that their veiled accounts indicate. Once their narratives of the Atlantic era are stripped of explicit references to the slave trade, however, they are free to describe it as the golden age of the coast. Such narratives, which are the main focus of this chapter, are told then *in place* of narratives about the slave trade. These images function, furthermore, as a means of challenging arguments that naturalize their contemporary marginalization. They lend credence to their calls for greater inclusion in the global economy by providing them with a precedent.

Veiled Histories

In contrast to the arguments of some scholars regarding other West African regions (Akyeampong 2001; Law 2004), men and women in Cape Coast and Elmina do not commonly admit that their own ancestors were involved in slave dealing. This is after all the first step in making their case against their contemporary marginalization. Recall the comment discussed in the previous chapter: "The people who were enslaved were not taken from here, they were taken from the North, kept here for a short while, and then taken away, so we never had any contact with them!" Not only does the speaker stress that coastal residents were not enslaved, he also erases the history of the sale, imprisonment, and transport of slaves, all of which did indeed take place on the coast. These processes are removed from the provenance of coastal residents in order to exonerate them from the charge of witnessing or, worse yet, participating in such atrocities. Similarly, a man from Cape Coast explained to me, "The slave trade did not go on here; this was more or less a transit point. I cannot say that [none of the] people in this town . . . engaged themselves in the trade, probably the chiefs did, but not *the people* in this town. This was more or less a transit point." His insistence that "the slave trade did not go on here" erases the trade in its every manifestation, suggesting that Cape Coast was not a backdrop for any of the events related to the trade. Interestingly, the term "transit point," which many coastal residents use, is not meant to position Cape Coast and Elmina as key junctures in the trade; on the contrary, it is meant to point to the towns' marginal significance. But his other comment notes more specifically that local residents, apart from the chiefs, were not involved in the selling of slaves. The fact that coastal residents deny the past participation of people in their towns in slave dealing suggests that they judge not only the violent processes associated with the acquisition of slaves (which they displace onto the North) but also the "ordered" trade that took place on the coast to be highly immoral.[3] Indeed, stories that point to slave dealing in veiled ways further support this interpretation.

Auntie Amma provided an example of such veiled histories. She is the mother of Kwame (the descendant of a local woman who was married to a Dutch merchant introduced in chapter 2). In the course of a conversation we had about her family's past wealth, she constructed a fabulous tale of coastal prosperity. "When I came here," she said, "I heard, I did not see, I [heard of] vessels of gold . . . And they had special unique beads. These beads, in the morning, they put them on a mat like this, and by the end of the day, it would bring another one, it would give birth to another bead!"

How do we make sense of a story of beads that magically reproduce? Their historical significance provides many clues.[4] Beads were an important form of wealth that Europeans traded for slaves in Ghana during the era of Atlantic trade. The display of beads designated wealth and status along the coast of Ghana (Alpern 1995, 22). Maxine Kumekpor suggests that among the Ewe of southeastern Ghana, the ownership of beads denotes that the wearer belongs to "a home so wealthy that the ancestors bought and owned slaves" (1971, 104). Given the connection between wealth in beads and the slave trade, Auntie Amma's story points to her family's past involvement in slave dealing.

Indeed, not only did her Dutch merchant ancestor sell slaves, but his descendants likely did so as well. In failing to mention slave dealing as the reason for her family's wealth, some might say that Auntie Amma provides a false explanation. But perhaps her story does provide an accurate picture of the slave trade if one considers that African traders often received wealth in the form of credit with which to buy slaves. They then sold those slaves to European traders and received the balance of their price. As a result, they did not bear any of the costs of this trade (Cruickshank 1966; see also Miller 1988). Ian Baucom notes that this use of credit was one of the many types of speculative transactions that made the Atlantic era one of a repeating series of moments in which "capital seems to turn its back entirely on the thingly world, sets itself free from the material constraints of production and distribution, and revels in its pure capacity to breed money from money—as if by a sublime trick of the imagination" (Baucom 2005, 27). In this regard, Auntie Amma's comment might refer to the fact that the process of the transformation of credit into income earned during the slave trade was in fact one in which, sure enough, beads gave birth to more beads.

Such high-finance moments, Baucom notes, allow for great acts of violence as people themselves become currency. Auntie Amma likely understands this fact well. Rather than the immaculate conception that it seems to describe, her story must be read in conjunction with the observation made by various scholars that within many African societies, all types of wealth accumulation are viewed within a "zero-sum universe in which the amount of wealth in the world is limited. Anyone who gains riches is therefore suspected of having drawn them from the property and—more frightening—the vital energies of someone else" (Austen 2001, 238). Debrunner described perceptions of wealth in Ghana in 1961, which no doubt existed long before, stating, "How otherwise can a man become rich unless by neglecting his beloved ones, by meanness and avarice, in sharply anti-social means?" (quoted in Meyer 1995, 247).

There are numerous examples throughout West Africa that explicitly tie currencies during the Atlantic era to violence. One such story, which comes from an oral history in Benin, tells of cowry shells fished from the ocean using human corpses as bait that are sacrificed for this purpose (see Elwert 1989; Isichei 2002). Austen (2001) argues that this explanation of the origins of cowry shells, the main form of currency in parts of West Africa during the slave trade, links wealth to death, an understandable equation in the context of the slave trade, and this defines it as an immoral economy or one that relies on ill-gained wealth. In his explanation of the narrative told to him by elders of the Ayizo of Benin, Elwert (1989) writes that they explained that they had told him the story in order to express their disdain for the kings of Dahomey. Indeed, these kings, who were in full control of the local operation of the slave trade, were notorious for selling their own subjects into slavery. In this way, the story functions as a critique of extreme social stratification during the Atlantic trade (see also Baum 1999).

Another story from the other side of the Atlantic illustrates how trade goods could ensnare human beings. It describes Africans being lured onto slave ships with red cloth, a commodity that they apparently could not resist (Gomez 1998). These stories are often ways in which victim communities of the slave trade communicate the violence of slave captors that occurs through their reduction of human bodies to a means of wealth generation.

Such critiques occur at other high-finance moments as well. Comaroff and Comaroff refer to the "magicalities of modernity" to describe the ways in which magic is often entailed in African understandings of the influx of market economies and other foreign forces attendant on colonialism and its aftermath (1993). In particular, they discuss the ways that witchcraft accusations often coincide with immoral economies. As Shaw notes in her discussion of the connection between wealth and witchcraft in postcolonial Sierra Leone, "such tropes make a powerful moral commentary on a 'politics of the belly'. . . a commentary that is especially salient in the context of a succession of 'kleptocratic' regimes" (2002, 202).[5] In southern Ghana today, some individuals believe that those who become wealthy do so through a type of witchcraft called *sikadro*, and stories abound of those who have "gone in for *sikadro*" in Cape Coast and Elmina (see also Meyer 1995).

The family of Auntie Amma's merchant ancestor may have had little contact with the violence of the slave trade. Using the credit system, the slaves that local traders acquired were immediately handed over to their creditors. The time period during which they came into contact with slaves, in other words, when the trade took on flesh for them, was very short. The family could therefore pass down a story of beads begetting beads without deception or harm to anyone. And yet this process, I have argued, nonetheless encodes immorality. This encoding demonstrates a recognition that the way to wealth was simultaneously for others a "way of death" (Miller 1988). It relied on processes of violence and terror from which coastal residents, including the families of merchants, were largely shielded but of which they were, no doubt, aware. What Auntie Amma veils then is the before and after of the moment in which the beads, lying on a mat, produce more beads.

Because of this veiling, her story might easily be mistaken for simply a celebratory view of this wealth. She may well have believed that I would understand it in this way. In fact, I encountered many such descriptions of past wealth. The question then remains, Why do coastal residents veil their critiques of the Atlantic trade? Why do they present a seemingly positive image of the trade when they in fact harbor such ambivalence toward it? The answer, I suggest, is that they do so in order to preserve an image of the coast's reputable past. It is only with such an image in place that their complaints regarding their grim present gain traction.

Abjection and Atlantic Pasts

In his book, *Expectations of Modernity* (1999), James Ferguson employs the term "abjection" to refer to the experience of contemporary Copperbelt mineworkers. He explains,

> For many Zambians, then, as these details suggest, recent history has been experienced not—as the modernization plot led one to expect—as a process of moving forward or joining up with the world but as a process that has pushed them out of the place in the world that they once occupied. . . . *Abjection* refers to a process of being thrown aside, expelled, or discarded . . . This complex of meanings, sad to report, captures precisely the sense I found among the Copperbelt mine-workers—a sense that the promises of modernization had been betrayed, and that they were being thrown out of the circle of full humanity, thrown back into the ranks of the "second class," cast outward and downward into the world of rags and huts where the color bar had always told "Africans" they belonged. (1999, 236)

Ferguson stresses that these workers' experience of abjection was not an experience of being excluded but rather one of being expelled (1999, 237), of losing a status that they once enjoyed.

This description well describes the experience of today's coastal residents and particularly the experience of highly educated ones, whose contemporary conditions also challenge the modernization plot. While during the Atlantic era level of education was a better marker of economic success, today there are few professional jobs for the large percentage of educated men and women in Cape Coast and Elmina. As a result, they no longer have as great an economic advantage. Because education is one of the few fields in the region that has not declined in significance, teachers make up a large a percentage of the educated class (and therefore a large percentage of those mentioned in this chapter). With their modest salaries, they illustrate the educated class's loss of economic status with the collapse of the economies of their towns. These men and women are thus uniquely positioned to critique the barriers to their social mobility. Because they are also well acquainted with the histories of their towns, many of these individuals do so by contrasting their contemporary conditions to the incorporation of coastal elites into the global order during the Atlantic era.

In many cultural contexts, groups "seek the identity of place by laying claim to some particular moment/location in time-space when the definition of the area and the social relations dominant within it were to the advantage of that particular claimant group" (Massey 1994, 169). Coastal residents' constructions of the past, however, define the privileged lives of past coastal elites to be the heritage of their entire towns, thereby painting over past internal distinctions including those between slaves and freepersons and between Fantes and members of groups who settled later on the coast. Within this construction of an undifferentiated coastal population, past forms of oppression are effectively silenced. In addition, all contemporary coastal residents are allowed to lay claim to this past. Their creation of a shared coastal heritage occurs in the context of a leveling of class differences, which has made the grounds upon which the educated elite have traditionally asserted their class superiority increasingly shaky.

So what do their town histories look like? In Elmina, many residents often stress the fact that it was the site of the first European building in sub-Saharan Africa and one of the first places in which Europeans settled. In referencing the earliest moment of the Portuguese trade, they avoid discussion of the slave trade altogether. A young teacher in Elmina readily recited to me the following narrative of his town's past:

> It happened that when the whites first came to Africa, or let me say West Africa, they landed here first and Elmina was on its own, it was a state, it was flying its own flag and those of the indigenous [people] who were here met some of the whites. These whites who came initially came as merchants, traders, they were trading over in front of the castle. Then there was no castle there, but the indigenous people of the town were already trading there, so these people also came, brought their items . . . All the Fantes were also traders. They brought the items, sold them out. There was a lot of gold here, gold, proper gold! A friend even said that he believes so much that the whites came here with that purpose, the purpose of taking the gold away, so they brought enticing items, we bought them with our precious gold, so that made this place the center of trading.

Not only does he stress that "the whites" landed in Elmina first but also that it was already an independent state. He then notes that it became a "center of trading," focusing on the gold trade that preceded the trade in slaves. In stating that the Europeans came in search of gold, he seemed in fact to be intentionally deemphasizing the significance of the trade in slaves that followed. In this way, he celebrates the early encounter between Europeans and men and women in Elmina as a trade in legitimate goods between sovereign states.

In a discussion I had with the *supi* or leader of one of the Asafo companies in Elmina about the town's history, he also discussed the Portuguese presence and, in particular, the story of the meeting between Kwamena Ansa and Don Diego D'Azambuja mentioned in chapter 1. He said of this time period, "During that time, there were interactions between the people but at first, King Kwamena Ansa of Elmina did not like the Portuguese to come and stay. He told them to watch the waves of the sea; the waves come to the seashore, bank on the seashore and go back. You must also come, trade, and go. So upon persistent request for a place to build the area of the castle was shown to them."

This story stresses that initially Ansa opposed the establishment of a permanent Portuguese presence on the coast. The *supi*, however, went on to talk about this presence in glowing terms. The purpose of bringing up this story then was not to point out Ansa's coercion. On the contrary, he sought to demonstrate Ansa's incredible agency. He had the power to say no to the Portuguese captain and to make him plead his case. This was clearly a time in which, compared with the present, coastal residents had a remarkable relationship with Europeans in which their opinions mattered, their voices were heard, and their approval sought.

In this way, Sarbah's agenda in his telling of the story to demonstrate Elmina's recognition by Europeans as a sovereign state, a context in which coastal residents could "talk back" to Europeans and even refuse their requests, operates in the *supi*'s telling, and this is no accident. Many residents of Elmina are in fact familiar with the story of Kwamena Ansa as a result of its publication by local historian J. Sylvanus Wartemberg, who drew heavily on earlier texts that trace back ultimately to Sarbah's text. Indeed, many oral histories on the coast derive from written histories. This story, as some scholars have noted, illustrates the process of feedback in oral tradition. Feedback, which refers to the incorporation of nonoral sources into the oral tradition, is a common occurrence in this region because of the high degree of literacy among its residents and the availability of written histories by local historians (Henige 1973). Oral tradition then is not parallel to the written tradition; the two are quite enmeshed. Note, for instance, the use of poetic metaphor in the *supi*'s story. His comparison of Europeans to the waves of the sea that should "come to the seashore, bank on the seashore, and go back" in particular recalls Sarbah's construction of Ansa's language: "The Sea and Land being always neighbors are continually at variance, and contending who shall give way; the Sea with great violence attempting to subdue the Land, and the Land with equal obstinacy resolving to oppose the Sea" (1968b, 61). It suggests a great deal of overlap between popular contemporary oral histories and turn-of-the-century written histories. This overlap reflects the fact that conjuring images of a time in which Europeans viewed coastal residents as their equals not only served Sarbah in the context of the imposition of colonization, it also serves the *supi* in the context of neoliberal structural adjustment policies.

A similar agenda was apparent in Mrs. Yeboah's use of the story. A seventy-two-year-old teacher in Elmina, Mrs. Yeboah brought up the story in response to my question as to what she thinks is the most important part of history for people in her town. She immediately responded, "How the white man came to see them." She then explained, "They asked for the land to build the castle, that's very important because they [the Europeans] knew that this was theirs [the local people's]. They came to the chief and the chief gave them the land to build the castle." Her assertion that Europeans viewed the people of Elmina as citizens of a sovereign state contrasts sharply to narratives about northerners that suggest that Europeans saw them as nothing more than potential slaves. In this context, Mrs. Yeboah's statement carries the subtext that the white man *did not* view coastal residents as slaves but rather as equals. But in addition to contrasting her ancestors to slaves, she also contrasts them to contemporary residents. By stating that this event marks the most important moment in their history, Mrs. Yeboah suggests that such recognition by Europeans was not forthcoming at later ones.

Residents of Cape Coast produce similar town histories of the European presence, both orally and in print. Because interactions with Europeans in Cape Coast began with the slave trade, and there is no earlier period in this encounter to which they can refer, its residents often simply marginalize this aspect of that relationship. In 1994, J. Erskine Graham, Jr., a teacher at Ghana National College and a local assembly member, published a book entitled *Cape Coast in History* that traces historical developments in the town. In his description of the effects of contact with Europeans, he only briefly mentions the slave trade while he lists many positive effects, including the growth of the town. He quotes a Danish visitor who described Cape Coast in 1836 as "a little heaven, worthy to be reputed the most attractive citadel of the whole African coast" (1994, 23). He then writes, "Cape Coast, therefore, hitherto unimportant town, became a powerful flourishing trading centre and soon assumed a cosmopolitan outlook" (1994, 23).

In addition to constructing a glorious past, many individuals explicitly contrast it to a present decline. In an article about the history of Cape Coast, Nkunu Akyea, head of the Central Regional Development Commission, describes the desolation that has become a popular theme within accounts of both Cape Coast and Elmina: "As far back as 1911, S.R.B. Attoh Ahuma observed . . . 'Cape Coast is dull and monotonous enough in all conscience.' Almost a century later, the settlement presents an outward image of rusted corrugated iron-roofs with cracked and crumbling facades of the once huge clay-built imposing merchant and family homes . . . Undoubtedly, Cape Coast has aged: she is wrinkled, has a stooped gait with shuffling feet for steps, dim eyes and ears hard of hearing and crackling voice" (2001, 38). He explains that this decline is due to the fact that "there are no viable commercial and industrial activities in Cape Coast and its immediate environs to write home about. The town and most of the Central Region has, for about a century now, been losing its population (out-migration) to other economically more attractive adjoining areas" (2001, 38). He claims, however, that the town was not that way in the past, quoting another writer who insists, "Cape Coast has not always looked like this. The careful observer can soon see that behind, its forlorn and dilapidated appearance there are indications of what was once a much more flourishing past" (2001, 38). More than a simple lament for the passing of a better time, in other words, expressions of nostalgia, these statements are highly political. They seek to provide a precedent for the coast's incorporation into the global order.

Finally, to return to my conversation with Auntie Amma, not only did she veil the trade in slaves in her story of magically reproducing beads in order to create an image of fabulous wealth, but later in the same conversation, she noted the present decline of Elmina. It began when my companion, after hearing her description of her family's past wealth, asked her, "Then you were rich, but now you are poor. Why?" The question had been on my mind as well. Sitting in the courtyard in front of Auntie Amma's house, the poverty that she and her family face is undeniable. Her house, once grand, has fallen into disrepair, and the lack of job opportunities in Elmina has clearly hit her family hard. Her family's poor economic condition was made all the more startling in comparison with her description of the family's past

6 Posuban shrine of number 5 *asafo* company, Elmina, depicting a Dutch boat

wealth. She summed up the contrast between her family's past wealth and their present poverty saying, "*Kanka hɛn apa Edinaman ho,*" or "The Dutch boat has left Elmina."

This statement is a common saying in Elmina that is used to comment on the town's economic decline. Its original reference may be lost on members of the younger generation,[6] but it continues to function as a metaphor, like the saying "that ship has sailed" for lost opportunity. By invoking this proverb, Auntie Amma not only noted her family's situation but also tied it into the experience of all of the residents of Elmina and cited more generally the town's expulsion from the global economy since the departure of the Dutch and the British takeover. As Elmina's longtime enemies, the British neglected the town's economy, thereby marking a significant shift from the era of the Dutch presence. That residents trace their current underdevelopment to the departure of the Dutch demonstrates then their sense of abjection rather than simply a celebration of Dutch trade.

The latter reading easily leads to an interpretation of a blind attachment to Europeans (see Ferguson 1999, 2002), which is the diagnosis that many Ghanaians from other regions indeed provide. An extremely harsh characterization of coastal residents and Fantes in particular appeared in an editorial in December 2004 after the reelection of President Kufuor. In response to a previous editorial that had questioned why Fantes had not supported Atta-Mills, a fellow Fante, in his bid for the presidency, the writer argues that Fantes have no sense of ethnic solidarity; rather, "the first person the Fanti owes his allegiance to is the white man." She further writes,

> If one studies the history of colonial rule and the slave trade (though other coastal tribes were involved, but I will only focus on the Fante tribe), it can be said that the fantes [*sic*] "sold their soul to the devil" for unimportant worldly things without pausing to think of the consequences. That was the beginning of their "curse." They allowed the "white" people to plunder our gold, rape our women for pitiful remunerations such as alcohol, sweets and the chance to climb abord [*sic*] a ship and listen and dance to music, which was foreign to our culture. They did not stop there; they actually supplied slaves to the white men . . . Fantes feel superior to the other tribes because of their affiliation with the white man. Their language is even inter-laced with the English language. They were taught to speak, eat, dress and behave like the white man.[7]

This passage demonstrates that their involvement in slave dealing is used against Fantes by others in order to vilify them. The writer also explicitly critiques coastal residents' celebration of their past affiliation with Europeans and their assimilation to European cultural practices, recalling the popular image parodied by Sekyi (see chapter 1), but with much less humor. This characterization invokes Frantz Fanon's analysis of African practices of assimilation under colonialism (1967). However, while Fanon attributes this phenomenon to the effects of colonial rule on the mentality of the colonized, the writer here suggests that Fante mentalities have been altered by their own greed. They chose to be traitors and have thus lost their souls.

In contrast to both interpretations, I argue not only that their practices of assimilation protected them from enslavement in the past (see chapter 1) but also that today, coastal residents do not articulate Eurocentric discourses unwittingly or unwillingly; rather, they do so out of a conscious "will to be modern" (Gable 1995) and with the intention of highlighting a fundamental contradiction, namely, that despite their past favored position, flows of wealth and power today largely bypass them. The editorialist quoted above ignores the fact that the desire for an affiliation with the white man stems from a recognition of gross global inequalities and not simply from psychological damage. Her critique of this past affiliation overlooks the reality that for some, the horrors of late capitalism make the Atlantic era appear in fact desirable.

Comments like Auntie Amma's should be read, I suggest, again following Ferguson (1998; 2002), not as evidence of a colonized mentality, but rather as attempts to transform an image of the coast's intrinsic outside status to an image of its past belonging followed by its unfair and unfortunate expulsion. Instead of being merely a celebration of the Atlantic era, it is actually a critique of the colonial and postcolonial eras that followed.

"The Romance of Elmina"

Despite its oversimplification of the historical consciousness of coastal residents, interpretations of a colonized mentality are somewhat understandable. After all, many contemporary European discourses do indeed glorify the past European presence on the coast. While most contemporary popular Western histories are notorious for their lack of distinction among the different regions of the African continent, much less the distinctions between different regions of the same country, lesser known historical traditions, like the one upon which the Prince of Orange drew, have singled out the special history of Ghana's coast. In doing so, they have recreated a precolonial European tradition that produced images of the coast as less a part of the Dark Continent of Africa than as an extension of European modernity (see chapter 1). These narratives, in their uncritical embrace of a notion of a glorious past, reveal a European nostalgia for the Atlantic trade, which contrasts to coastal residents' critical use of the past.[8]

Many Dutch writers in particular are devoted to remembering the history of Elmina and its relationship to the Netherlands. The Save Elmina Association, which functions to disseminate Dutch representations of the history of their imperial presence throughout Elmina and the Netherlands, is a key example of this agenda. Founded in 1990 by a group of Dutch nationals living in Ghana together with a handful of Elmina citizens, Save Elmina is an organization committed to the preservation of Elmina's Dutch heritage. Many Dutch businesses that operate in Ghana contribute to Save Elmina as part of the Ghana-Netherlands Business Club including Vermeer Ghana and Interbeton, both construction companies; Dizengoff Ghana Limited, a chemicals company; and the Volta Aluminum Company (VALCO), an aluminum smelting company. Through their involvement with Save Elmina, these companies, like the Dutch imperialists before them, have spread their influence from the realm of economic production to the arena of the cultural and social life of Ghana. They undertake various conservation projects to restore Dutch buildings that are currently in a state of decay, in the hopes of not only preserving this history but also of engendering a sense of pride in Elminans who share this heritage. In addition to its conservation efforts, the Save Elmina Association publishes occasional journals that include articles on the history of Elmina by Dutch and Ghanaian scholars.

In the preface to the second volume of their journal, J. V. L. Phillips, the chairman of VALCO and a trustee of the Save Elmina Association writes,

> The texts [in this volume] will endeavor to interpret Elmina's life and traditions, to open windows on its vanished generations, seek insights into the life once led behind the then elegant façades of Liverpool Street and Buitenrust Lane, or in the ancient court of its Rulers, or behind the closed ramparts of the great fortress, and to reveal their link—for often there was a link—with those greater events which now and then reverberate throughout the entire country. Such is the romance of Elmina lurking behind the now pathetic exterior. Let us hope that the chance of a facelift and a repolish will make a powerful appeal to all those, be they in Ghana or in the Netherlands, or elsewhere, who know that their ancestors or countrymen created that distinctive culture, to all those who love to rescue the beautiful and valuable from ruin and destruction, and last, but not least, to all who take a just pride in their descent from Elmina. (1995, 4)

Phillips represents the European presence as an unproblematic, positive force, and in fact, he suggests that Elmina's ruin stems from the conclusion of what might be summed up as the good old days of Dutch trade. This statement represents a particular construction of locality that evokes a sense of elegance and national and international importance and hints at wealth and European tradition, while it disavows any notion of discord, violence, or inequality. In contrast to "the romance of the North" narrative that celebrates the North's resistance to European incursions, the "romance of Elmina" narrative celebrates the European presence as the main contributor to Elmina's cosmopolitan environment.

The object of the Save Elmina Association, to preserve Elmina's Dutch heritage, provides a startling contrast to the object of those within the tourism industry who have fought to bring the history of the slave trade to light in Elmina. Phillips virtually obscures the history of the slave trade, making only a passing reference to it in an earlier passage when he states that Elmina Castle "acts as a powerful magnet on the ever-increasing numbers who are either fascinated by its long and often sombre history, or drawn by the romantic associations of its past" (Phillips 1995, 3). Here he suggests that visitors are as readily drawn to the castle's romantic past as to the somber history of the slave trade. He calls for the preservation of historic sites in Elmina, not because of their connection to the brutal history of slavery, but because they are "elegant" and "beautiful" and because they were created by a "distinctive culture." Finally, he appeals to all Africans and Dutch whose ancestors were part of that culture, as well as people "elsewhere" (although he makes no reference to the tie between Elmina and the African diaspora), to take "just pride" in their descent from Elmina. This writer and the Save Elmina Association more generally paint a romantic picture of Elmina, while outright ignoring the operations of the slave trade that not only occurred during the time that they describe but that was the foundation for the very culture they celebrate.

The Save Elmina publications provide astonishing insight into the construction of a discourse of nostalgia that links Elmina and the Netherlands. The article topics include the role of Elmina in the popularization of Dutch wax prints in Ghana, town culture in nineteenth-century Elmina, and prominent Euro-Africans. All of these articles focus on sites of assimilation and the impact of Dutch culture on Elmina. The tone of nostalgia is not subtle; the author of the article on town culture writes, "Even though the growth of this town and others has not kept abreast with modern times, and the plantations have disappeared, the visitor may still feel its antiquity, and with a sense of nostalgia, particularly when its historic role with the advent of the white man on the west coast is discussed" (Van Dyck 1996, 28). In an article in the same volume discussing the government garden in Elmina, the author writes, "People with a European way of living enjoyed a walk in the green surroundings, in their best dresses on a Sunday afternoon. As such the Government Garden formed part of the Enlightened European life style" (van den Nieuwenhof 1996, 32). Save Elmina's unambiguous message is that the Dutch presence in Elmina was a positive force and worthy of remembrance. The last passage's reference to "Enlightened European life style" in particular celebrates the development of a European cultural style and its spread to places like Elmina, which are viewed as its fortunate recipients.

"Black and Proud"

Texts like those of the Save Elmina Association provide coastal residents with narratives about their past that many readily embrace. In adopting these narratives, however, I have argued that they do not simply celebrate the European presence but rather use them to critique the present.[9] At the same time, many recognize that invocations of a glorious past are not enough to transform the conditions in which they live. This recognition reveals their skepticism with regard to the conduct of those like the prince and members of the Save Elmina Association as to whether they, despite their offers of aid, are truly committed to transforming this system of exclusion or rather are operating in bad faith.

Kwame, for instance, expressed bitterness over the failure of the Dutch to do more for Elmina. While speaking of the Dutch, he said, "I know because the whites do a lot of research, I know that they would be aware that they have family members over here. I wish that we could unite, but you know these whites." In this way, he delivers a critique of the Dutch, suggesting that despite their awareness of their historical ties to Elmina, they have not come to its aid. The explanation for this failure, furthermore, should be obvious to me, another black person, who must "know these whites." Indeed, this statement functions on both sides of the Atlantic as a reference to anti-black racism. What he and I both know is that Elmina's marginalization is tied to the racialized nature of global exclusions in which white nations and institutions have not historically shared their wealth with others.

This critique could include the early Dutch traders as well. If they never intended that their relationship with the town be a permanent one, it is no wonder that they easily pulled up anchor when the tides turned out of their favor, leaving Elmina to its fiery fate at the hands of the British. In this context, the saying "The Dutch boat has left Elmina" takes on new meaning, alluding not only to the decline of Elmina after the Dutch departure but also to the bad faith of the Dutch throughout their occupation of Elmina. This more probing reading posits local residents' recognition that the Dutch never considered their forebears as their partners in an economic order; they rather viewed them as their pawns.

Given his critique of the Dutch, I wondered how Kwame felt about his own Dutch ancestry. A question I posed to this effect prompted the following exchange:

KWAME: I don't feel so much Dutch at this time, no I don't feel so much Dutch, though I think that I am a Ghanaian, not that I think, I am Ghanaian, I have no Dutch blood, I don't think that at all.

AUNTIE AMMA: I am proud.

KWAME: She is proud because she knows she is an indigenous Elminan—

AUNTIE AMMA: I am black and proud!

B.H. So even though your great-grandfather was Dutch—

KWAME: No, we are black.

As this exchange demonstrates, while coastal residents highlight their past interactions with Europeans, they do not seek to be white; rather, their fundamental identity remains that of black people. Their desires are for an inclusion in the global order that they enjoyed in the past, not for whiteness. Indeed, Auntie Amma's exclamation, "I'm black and proud" is strong evidence that she takes pride in an African identity. In making this assertion, she draws on a transnational discourse of black pride in which James Brown's 1968 anthem becomes key. Indeed, while she had been speaking primarily in Fante throughout our conversation, her sudden declaration, "I'm black and proud" was made in perfect English. Hearing this statement, Auntie Amma, an elderly woman without formal education, demonstrated to me just how wide the circulation of this transnational black discourse is in Ghana.

Black pride emerges not only because of the bad faith of the Dutch but also because of the dismantling of "mixed-" race privilege on the coast. In the past, while Euro-Africans were granted a special status, they retained their African identities to a large extent because of the strength of the matrilineal descent system and the persistent function of families and their larger communities as the main source of identity for local residents. Their embrace of a notion of a separate Euro-African identity was because of its social and economic advantages more than because of a belief in their fundamental difference. With the evaporation of those advantages, being of Dutch descent has little if any meaning in Elmina today. Indeed, one can hardly speak of an "ethnoscape," to use Appadurai's term (1996), connecting Elmina and the Netherlands.

When I asked one Elmina resident if people with Dutch ancestry have any special status, he replied, "No, before they had it, but today, no. People don't respect them, especially if you don't go to school and you don't gain the wealth. Today in Elmina we know some who are illiterate, they have not been to school before, they can't say anything, but they come from [one of the Dutch families in Elmina]."

The decline of Elmina and Cape Coast more generally indicates that sites of necessary advantage have shifted geographically away from the Central Region, placing all coastal residents in the same boat. Another long-time resident of Elmina responded to my question about whether people ever talk about their Dutch ancestry, "No, they don't talk about it, they are superior? No, no, no, in fact they don't boast." As these comments demonstrate, coastal residents are less committed to claiming Dutch ancestry on an individual basis, to creating, in other words, a shared ethnoscape with European nations, than they are to reestablishing "financescapes" (Appadurai 1996) with them.

In this context, it becomes clear that coastal residents' favorable constructions of the Atlantic order do not represent a colonized mentality. On the contrary, they serve to critique the global orders that followed by demonstrating that things have not always been this way. In addition, their constructions of the past often contain veiled critiques of the Atlantic order itself, serving as further evidence for the strategic use of affirmative accounts of the past. By reading statements about coastal superiority due to their proximity to Europeans as largely strategic practices, we can see Werbner's (1996) wink in play (see the introduction). In other words, coastal residents' seeming collusion with Europeans in their celebration of their past inclusion within a Western modernity begins to reveal their experience of abjection.

In the face of contemporary national and global economies within which they occupy a marginalized position, constructing narratives about a prosperous past allows coastal residents to refute conceptualizations of their intrinsic inferiority. A notion of coastal cosmopolitanism then is an attempt to stake a claim to social and economic empowerment. Coastal residents mobilize memories of their past favored status in hopes of converting it into present symbolic capital. They submit this precedent in making their contemporary claims on state and global political economies for greater opportunities for an improved standard of living. Their narratives are similar to Sarbah's turn-of-the-century critique of colonialism as the disenfranchisement of Fantes, who had previously enjoyed a level playing field with Europeans. To stress that the Dutch boat has left Elmina is to call for an improved position within the global economy, to call, in other words, for its return. Their positive construction of the Atlantic era, furthermore, does not preclude their simultaneous critique of this era. Their relationship to the past remains, in this way, one riddled with ambivalence.

5 » *E-Race-ing History*

SCHOOLING AND NATIONAL IDENTITY

In his controversial PBS documentary, *Wonders of the African World with Henry Louis Gates Jr.* (1999), Gates, upon visiting Cape Coast and other sites of embarkation for the slave trade, is deeply troubled by the issue of African participation in the trade. He later wrote, "[O]thers have wondered and I am thinking here of Yambo Ouologuem's great novel *Bound to Violence* (1971) if Africa was cursed because of the apparent willingness of so many African societies to participate in the slave trade, bartering what, to us here appear to be their sisters and brothers, for a mess of pottage" (2001, 3; also quoted in Diouf 2003, xv). His comments reflect a popular perception of a corporate African identity that transforms the involvement of some Africans in slave dealing into an act of their selling "their sisters and brothers." This notion contrasts sharply to West African realities in which, as I have argued, regional differences became increasingly important as a result of the slave trade, leading coastal residents to define themselves as wholly different from northerners, who were those who could be enslaved.[1] Nonetheless, Gates's formulation coincides not only with popular perception but also with many academic historical treatments in which the Atlantic slave trade has been used not to discuss regional differences within West Africa, but rather to construct a continental African identity, which is at the same time stigmatized.

Gates's conceptualization of Africans selling other Africans, or what Sylviane Diouf (2003) refers to as the "black betrayal model," dates back to the very origins of the European notion of a corporate African identity. As I discuss in chapter 1, when this notion first emerged in Europe, it reduced

Africans to slave raiders, describing them as if they were all engaged in practices of kidnapping, raiding, and warfare, in order to paint an image of African savagery and thereby make an argument for European intervention. Within these narratives, the slave trade represents an age of African ignorance and immorality, while the coming of colonialism heralds the triumph of European civilization. Indeed, when Ward wrote in 1934 that Africans are a "race of slaves," arguing that as a result of the Saharan and Atlantic slave trades Africans had no other role in the global order,[2] he constructed a disgraceful history of the continent that prefigures European salvation. Not only their enslavement but also their participation in the enslavement of others became the pivot upon which this disgrace turned for him and his contemporaries. Thus, European academic histories have long used the slave trade as a key history to define the African/European divide. Attending to the history of Ghana and the African continent as a whole led them to describe African-ness as a debased racial identity, in contrast to the popular European histories discussed in the previous chapter that focus on the "enlightened" inhabitants of specific towns like Cape Coast and Elmina. As a result, even today among Western historians of the slave trade in Africa, there has been an undue focus on African participation in practices of enslavement to the detriment of analyses of those strategies against the slave trade in which so many Africans were engaged (Diouf 2003). As a result of this historiographic tradition, not only do Ghanaians have to address the effects of the history of the slave trade on constructions of family and regional identity, they also have to contend with its effects on notions of their racial identity. Not surprisingly given this context, in Ghana, the slave trade is not a popular choice for constructions of national history.

As I discuss in this chapter, school textbooks are a prime example of how the slave trade is minimized as an element of national history. Schools are central arenas for the creation of histories of the nation as a whole. As a result of the creation of a national standardized history syllabus in Ghana, they not only create histories *of* the entire nation, they also disseminate them *to* the entire nation. The story of the nation that they tell focuses primarily on the history of colonialism and the independence struggle, reflecting an attempt to mimic the histories of European nations. European histories have long focused on great nations and in fact view the nation-state as the natural end of a universal teleology. Many of them have suggested that the African continent occupies an earlier stage in this teleology as an amalgamation of "tribes." In this context, postcolonial histories that highlight Ghana's achievement of nationhood serve to vindicate its citizens and place them squarely in a universalized teleology with nationhood as its endpoint. Within these histories, the achievement of independence is narrated as a romantic story of the immorality of colonialism and the ultimate triumph of nationalism. Kwame Nkrumah himself popularized this version of history. Within his own history of the nation, he paints independence as Ghana's destiny, and, as such, its achievement marks the end of the story, erasing of course his personal downfall as well as the tumbling of the nation from its place on the pedestal of African optimism (Nkrumah 1971; see Korang 2003). Fifty years later, in school textbooks, independence continues to be the end of the story.

With regard to their relationship to the slave trade, academic histories present a unique case because, unlike family histories and narratives of coastal cosmopolitanism, textbooks do not completely remove the slave trade from explicit public references; rather, they marginalize it. The slave trade thus maintains a presence, albeit a deeply troubled one, within these histories. In the small spaces in which it does appear, furthermore, the slave trade is often discussed in ways that stress its inappropriateness to national history and therefore attempt to explain why it does not command greater attention. In this way, these narratives are similar to coastal residents' discussions of the North's slave-raiding past. These discussions raise the history of the slave trade for the sole purpose of displacing it. Academic discourses are thus another arena in which Ghanaians seek to distance themselves from the slave trade in order to combat the stigma that it produces.

I begin my discussion with a description of the dominant national history, that of colonialism/independence, and point to its construction within a romantic mode. I then discuss constructions of the slave trade since the mid-twentieth century that have influenced the representation, albeit brief, of the slave trade within Ghanaian textbooks. While there are other histories that might provide promising alternatives to the use of the slave trade as evidence of African savagery at the same time that they address postcolonial problems, those histories, as I note, have not entered into school textbooks. Finally, I turn to contemporary textbooks and the teachers who continue to view the slave trade as a foil to their stories of the nation and therefore produce arguments for its marginalization.

National History

Most Ghanaian students gain the bulk of their historical knowledge in junior secondary school (JSS), the equivalent of junior high school in the United

States. In primary school (the elementary school equivalent), there is no separate class for history instruction. In senior secondary school (sss, the high school equivalent), history is an elective subject. In addition to required courses in English, math, science, and social studies, students choose from among general arts, general science, agriculture, business, vocational skills, and visual arts tracks in which to take additional courses. Only students in the general arts track have the option of taking history. On top of this fact, only about a third of all youth in Ghana attend sss to begin with.

In contrast to this small figure, well over half of children attend jss, ideally between the ages of twelve and fifteen, where they all study history under the rubric of social studies (unlike social studies in sss, which does not include history).³ The jss social studies book then is largely responsible for the construction of history for children.⁴ The social studies curriculum resulted from the Accelerated Development Plan in 1987 and combines what were previously separate courses in history, geography, and civics. The goal of this plan was not only to provide students with a basic education but also to teach them about their cultural heritage as well as the needs of the modern nation-state, or in other words, to create proper citizens. For this reason, history remains in the curriculum, but jss have also made room for the introduction of technical and vocational skills. Thus, the actual time allotted to history is less than one year out of three, during the second year of jss. In the second-year social studies textbook, the main focus is the history of colonialism and independence. This history, furthermore, is presented in the mode of a romance story. In his discussion of narratives structured as romances, Scott argues that they "move in sequential and processional form, moving steadily and rhythmically (one might even say, teleologically) in the direction of an end already in some sense known in advance. It has the shape of 'a quest': the protagonists (invariably associated with the new, with light, with order) undertake a perilous journey; there are encounters with antagonists or enemies (invariably associated with the old, with darkness, with disorder); the inevitable conflict ensues between these irreconcilable principles. There are heightened moments when darkness seems poised to vanquish light, and finally the victorious deliverance or overcoming from bondage, from evil, comes" (2005, 70).

The jss textbook certainly presents independence as the natural end of a teleology. It presents Ghana's entire history, moreover, as leading up to this struggle and to a large extent, as its background. In addition, there is a protagonist, Nkrumah; an enemy, the colonial state; and an ultimate victory, independence. The simplicity of this story may function well for its target audience of children, but it nonetheless glosses over many of the complexities of actual historical events that do not conform to it in order to maintain the integrity of the story. It also ignores the postcolonial critiques of nationalism's failures. Below I discuss the various chapters of its central narrative.

PRECOLONIAL TIMES

Not surprisingly, given the young age of students (ideally between thirteen and fourteen), during the second year of JSS, the JSS textbook paints a one-dimensional picture of European trade and colonialism. The first section of part I, which covers preindependence history, is entitled "Our People Ruled Themselves Well." As the title suggests, it provides a romanticized view of precolonial Ghana. The learning objective of this section is made clear in the second sentence, which states, "The British did not become rulers in Ghana because the people could not rule themselves" (1988, 1). In order to dispel this myth, the text begins by insisting that the people of Ghana had their own forms of government before the arrival of the Europeans based on communal living. It presents a picture of cooperation devoid of any conflict. It describes village life, stating, "Each family helped the other families. They rejoiced with the other families and also felt sad for any family that had any problems" (1988, 1). The institution of the chieftaincy is described in a similarly idealized fashion: "Everybody respected the chief. They did whatever he asked them to do" (1988, 1). Precolonial African life is stripped of any notion of its internal dynamics to provide a corrective to common assumptions that African life was dominated by war and strife prior to European contact. To efface this stereotype, the textbook goes to the opposite extreme by presenting an idyllic golden age, in a similar fashion to coastal histories' construction of the Atlantic era. In addition, precolonial African life is not a major area of concentration in the syllabus. The textbook devotes only two pages to this topic. In such a small space, a complex analysis is hardly feasible.

BRITISH RULE

Next, the text turns to the arrival of Europeans in Ghana. This section begins with an intriguing critique of European rule: "The British came as traders. The people of Ghana did not know at first that the British wanted to rule them. The British *tricked* them in some cases. For example, the British told them that they wanted to make friends with the various states. They also said that they wanted to protect some of these states. But they soon became their rulers" (emphasis in the original; 1988, 3). Despite this suggestion of the bad faith of Europeans in Ghana, the text goes on to present European rule as a largely benevolent force. European leaders are presented in a heroic manner. For instance, the text describes Governor George Maclean, who became governor of the Gold Coast in 1830 and is widely considered to be one of the champions of African people in Ghana, in glowing terms: "He was a very clever leader. He was very good at persuading people. He was a peace lover and did not like war. He also believed in justice" (1988, 4). Similarly, the authors write of European governor Sir Gordon Guggisberg, "Guggisberg wanted to make our people very happy. He had many difficulties but he did his best for Ghana" (1988, 12). The positive representation of British rule is in part a legacy of the colonial educational system. Additionally, the colonial government's economic successes with the cocoa industry and small-holder farming have led to less severe critiques of colonialism within many public arenas in Ghana than one might find in other former colonies.

KWAME NKRUMAH AND INDEPENDENCE

The central story within the construction of children's history is the story of Kwame Nkrumah and the independence struggle. Despite the social studies textbook's construction of European rule as largely benevolent, its discussion of the nationalist movement celebrates African opposition to colonial rule, as in the following passage: "By 1950, it became clear that the British did not want to allow the chiefs and their elders to rule their people the way they liked. The British always wanted to tell the chiefs how they should rule their people. The people were not happy. They therefore waited for a chance to let the British know their feelings" (1988, 15). This passage seeks to rationalize nationalist sentiments, but nationalism is described in very specific terms. Nationalism does not entail a critique of the operation of colonial power but only the placement of that power in the hands of the British rather than the hands of Ghanaian elites, like the chiefs and elders to which the above passage refers. Thus, representations of the story of independence need not demonize the British. Colonial benevolence and nationalist opposition can exist side by side (see Fanon 1963).

The text then describes the formation of nationalist organizations such as the Fante Confederation and the Aborigines' Rights Protection Society, but the story of the struggle against colonialism is primarily the story of Kwame Nkrumah. The text provides a biography of his life, in the middle of which it reminds students, "As children, we must always try to learn from great men. This will help make us become very important and useful to our country, like Nkrumah" (1988, 21). In national contexts, history is often constructed as the story of individual, usually male actors. Within the romance narrative structure of JSS presentations of history, the presence of a protagonist is crucial. The protagonist as an individual actor is much more compelling in this context than representations of collective action, which was in fact the driving force of the nationalist movement in Ghana. Thus, through school socialization, children learn to view Nkrumah as their national icon and the embodiment of the nationalist struggle.

The celebration of Nkrumah and independence extends outside of schools; it forms part of the government's agenda as well. The celebration of Independence Day in Ghana is, not surprisingly, the most important historical commemoration of the Ghanaian government. Ghana's status as the first sub-Saharan country to obtain independence and Nkrumah's Pan-African vision make Ghanaian independence also a crucial event for the entire continent of Africa as well as for Africans in the diaspora. Indeed, because Ghanaian independence was such a milestone in the history of Africa, Kwame Nkrumah is perhaps one of the best-known African historical figures in the West.

In Accra, the capital of Ghana, Independence Square stands as a perpetual memorial to this past. Every March 6, Independence Day, a parade and program of speakers are held at the square. In 2001, while I was living in Cape Coast, I watched the parade on television, as did most of the Ghanaians around the country who had access to television. That independence day parades form part of not only a commemoration of the past but also of an affirmation of the power of states was quite clear in this case.

The parade, like examples that could be drawn from many other postcolonial contexts, had a strikingly military character, including members of the armed forces and a brass band marching in a circuit around the square, which was surrounded by thousands of onlookers. They were followed by groups of schoolchildren, marching with the same military precision. The air force performed a flyby of military planes and helicopters, and a folkloric cultural group performed a dance in front of the president, who sat on a raised dais. A student orator and a student drummer then welcomed the president, the drummer drumming the message and the orator translating from drumspeak. Finally, the president took center stage to deliver his address. He commented on the loss of importance ascribed to the celebration of Independence Day and said that he hopes that "it will now be returned to its proper place as the premiere holiday in the nation," adding that it deserves "the full pomp and pageantry of the state."

The participation of schoolchildren in the parade is significant. Youth are often the targets of constructions of nation and history.[5] It is as children that individuals learn the meaning of patriotism, by reciting the national anthem, singing national songs, and parading in Independence Day celebrations. These activities certainly form part of the process of the socialization of children into Ghanaian citizens. In addition, youth are appropriate subjects in the remembrance of independence because youth played a large role in the nationalist struggle. The centrality of independence in the construction of children's history and the active role that children play in its celebration are then attempts by the state to inculcate youth with pride in nation, a sense of collective belonging, and a strong sense of African agency in the victory over oppression. Many Ghanaians, of course, challenge this romantic portrait of the nation. As the previous chapter demonstrates, coastal residents readily discuss postcolonial challenges. In venerating the nationalist triumph, however, one might say that textbooks are out of touch with many of the sentiments of abjection on the ground.

In the context of the story of colonialism and independence, the history of the slave trade cannot find footing. The JSS textbook makes an oblique reference to European trade that preceded formal colonization but does not describe the nature of this trade. It also mentions the forts and castles that European companies built but asks students to identify only the years in which they were built and the European nations that erected them. Thus, the history of the slave trade is largely ignored in order to maintain the coherence of the story of colonialism and independence. Indeed, given the fact, as I discuss in chapter 1, that histories of the slave trade in Ghana have focused on African brutality, inserting this history within a story of a precontact golden age and following it with colonialism would break the momentum of a story that has African independence as its climax. The slave trade, however, has not disappeared entirely from the textbook; rather, it appears briefly in a separate section. The representation of the slave trade found here has been heavily influenced by debates in the Ghanaian academy over the past half-century. For this reason, in the following section, I discuss these debates before returning to an analysis of the textbook.

The Problem of the Slave Trade

In 1948, the University College of the Gold Coast was established.[6] This event marked the beginning of a new era in West African historiography.[7] Soon afterwards, the West African Examinations Council was established to administer the school certificate examinations in Nigeria, Sierra Leone, and the Gold Coast. This council was an attempt to Africanize educational standards. In 1955, John D. Fage, a British history instructor at the University College, published *An Introduction to the History of West Africa* to respond to the need for African histories demanded by the Africanization platform. As a key player in the professionalization of African history, Fage sought to provide a sophisticated analysis of Gold Coast history and, in fact, published a more nuanced account than most European histories previously written.

Fage sought to challenge descriptions of African degeneracy that dominated European histories of Africa by arguing instead that African history had unfolded according to rational principles. He did so not by ignoring the slave trade, as many African leaders were doing at the time (see chapter 1), but rather by reinterpreting it. In his construction of the slave trade, to which he devotes a chapter, he sought to contest the demoralizing story of Africans participating in their own destruction by replacing it with a narrative of their careful calculation of a cost-benefit ratio. But his attempt to combat the image of Africans as a "race of slaves" would also prove to be problematic.

Fage's interpretation of the slave trade has three major components that have become central to the representation of the history of the slave trade within Ghanaian schools. The first point addresses African participation in the slave trade. Like earlier colonial historians, Fage stresses that Africans did indeed sell other Africans, but Fage seeks to rationalize African participation in the slave trade by stressing that slavery already existed in African societies prior to the arrival of Europeans. In this way, he contests the idea that Africans participated in the slave trade because of the degeneration of their morality. He writes, "When Europeans first began to ask for slaves in return for the goods they brought to West Africa, [Africans] were not repulsed . . . The presence of a slave class among the coastal peoples meant that there was already a class of human beings who could be sold to the Europeans if there was an incentive to do so, and an economic incentive existed in the form of the growing African demand for European imports" (1955, 78). Fage argues that those African elites who participated in the slave trade acted in accordance with a well-established rational economic system, thereby contesting the notion that the slave trade sparked an unprecedented level of greed within Africans and in this way providing a solution of sorts to what is often considered to be a fundamental problem that plagues the study of the slave trade in Africa.

Descriptions of African degeneration attempt to respond to the question, Why would Africans contribute to their own destruction? This question, of course, relies on a notion of a unitary "African" history involving a single group that both participated in the slave trade and was harmed by it. In the context of this image of the irrationality of African conduct, Fage argues that the slave trade did not harm African societies. Their participation in it was therefore rational. To this end, he presents his second major point, a controversial analysis for which he is perhaps best known outside of Ghana. He argues that while one might assume that the slave trade would greatly impinge upon African development, those areas of the continent most affected by the slave trade are today the most advanced and densely populated areas. He concludes, "There is evidence that the trade with Europeans, even, in certain circumstances, the trade in slaves, acted as a stimulus to the growth of population and the development of political institutions" (1955, 85). Furthermore, he argues that the slave trade led to the development of the major West African kingdoms. His oft-quoted passage on this point reads, "[T]he rise of Benin, Dahomey, and Ashanti is closely connected with the European demand for slaves, while the slave trade was also an element of some importance in the expansion of Oyo" (1955, 87).[8] Here he combats the notion that the slave trade led to the degeneration of African political and economic structures.

Many have viewed Fage's construction of the slave trade as a politically vacuous narrative. It undermines the argument that Africans participated in their own destruction by denying that such destruction ever took place, but by the same token it renders the slave trade an ineffectual object for the critique of European viciousness, thereby introducing a new problem to the study of the slave trade. Walter Rodney (1966) later critiqued Fage in an article published in the *Journal of African History* for claiming that the Atlantic trade was merely an extension of domestic slavery and thereby, one might say, blaming Africans for it. He argued instead that the institution of slavery was not an indigenous institution on the Upper Guinea coast, the westward coastline from the Gold Coast, and therefore could not have been the basis of the Atlantic slave trade. He insists rather that domestic slavery developed as a result of the export slave trade and suggests that the same might hold true for other parts of Africa. By establishing that Africans were attempting to forge responses to something utterly new to them, something that Europeans had introduced, he can then safely argue that the Atlantic slave trade led to major transformations in Africa without laying blame on Africans themselves.

To further nuance African participation in the slave trade, Rodney argues elsewhere, with regard specifically to the Gold Coast, that Asante centralization provided a "policy of insurance against the ill effects of the Atlantic slave trade" (1969, 25) and relates this to their own slave-raiding activities. He explains, "Ashante was in this process using its strength to insulate itself from the worst consequences of slaving, for those consequences were transferred beyond its own boundaries" (1969, 25). In other words, by forbidding the enslavement of its own citizens and establishing a strong military to enforce this rule, the Asante kingdom insulated itself from the dangers of enslavement. At the same time, the development of its military strength led to its ability to enslave outsiders. Rodney suggests then that the European introduction of the Atlantic trade created the necessity of centralization and the development of strong militaries. Only then did new opportunities arise for such strong states to exploit decentralized communities. As he explains, "[T]he ruling class joined hands with the Europeans in exploiting the African masses—a not unfamiliar situation on the African continent today" (1966, 434). In contrast to Fage's assertion that the slave trade caused no harm, he argues that powerful states benefited from the slave trade to the clear detriment of others. What had been a mere class distinction between the ruling nobility and the commoners became, as the result of European influence, a distinction between enslavers and those they enslaved.

Rodney places the blame back onto Europeans for encouraging Africans to sell slaves, something that they had not done previously. But he also notes the degeneration of the morality of African elites marked by their willingness to exploit the masses. The class specificity of his argument, however, as I discuss below, has largely been overlooked within Ghanaian history textbooks. Because the textbook writers are charged with writing the history of the nation as a whole, they participate in the construction of a corporate African identity just as colonial officials did in the past. Rodney's argument also serves to challenge Fage's contestation of the scope of the slave trade's negative effects in that Rodney argues rather that the Atlantic trade had many damaging consequences, including violence and the reduction of the adult male population (1969).[9]

The Fage/Rodney debate continued with Fage issuing a response in the same journal in which he reiterated his argument for the Gold Coast (1969).

Rodney's analyses have influenced many historians who have stressed the unequal power relations between Europeans and Africans during the trade, and have therefore suggested that European demand provided the stimulus for both African slave owning and dealing.[10] Within Ghanaian public history venues, and schools in particular, however, many of Fage's arguments continue to hold sway and have indeed achieved the status of orthodoxy.

One of the effects of his argument that the slave trade benefited some African individuals and communities is that Fage provides no motivation for Africans to end the slave trade. Indeed, Fage's third major point is that abolition was the result of the triumph of European morality. In this argument, he was heavily influenced by Sir Reginald Coupland, the author *The British Anti-Slavery Movement*, a text often credited with popularizing the idea that abolition resulted from the humanitarian nature of British abolitionists. By the time Fage wrote *History of West Africa* Eric Williams had already published his seminal work on the slave trade, *Capitalism and Slavery* (1944), in direct response to Coupland (among others; see Williams 1944, 178), that stresses the economic motives for abolition over and above the humanitarian motive. Fage nonetheless continued to believe in the decisive role of British humanitarianism. Indeed, he expresses his continued support for Coupland in the Coupland/Williams debate in his preface to the second edition of Coupland's book in which he writes, "[T]here would seem to be more in the humanitarian argument than he [Eric Williams] was prepared to allow" (1964, xx).

Fage further argues that the development of legitimate trade also grew out of humanitarian concerns. While noting that the establishment of such a trade served to provide an alternative source of wealth for British merchants in West Africa, he writes, "[M]ore generally the positive policy was at first advocated by the abolitionists principally because they wanted to right the wrong which had been done to West Africa by the European trade in slaves to America" (1955, 105). He thus privileges the morality of Europeans in the story of abolition, thereby constructing a romantic ending to a story that otherwise lacks a plot and therefore, as many would argue, political efficacy.

Nkrumah himself critiqued Fage's book (see chapter 1). Whereas he sought histories of positive agency as part of his vindicationist agenda, Fage not only omitted many of these, but the arena in which he assigned Africans the greatest agency was the slave trade. Faculty at the University of Ghana, however, considered it to be the best work on West Africa to date, while noting the dearth of scholarship in this field and thus the lack of alternatives (Quist 1999, 178–79). As a result, schools continued to teach Fage's work for several years until a new crop of Ghanaian historians arose. In particular, the publication of Adu Boahen's school textbook entitled *Topics in West African History* in 1966 marked an important moment in the incorporation of Ghanaian scholars into the writing of history textbooks.

"AN UNMITIGATED MISERY"

Adu Boahen, a Ghanaian scholar who is often considered to be the father of Ghanaian history, also focused on the slave trade within his textbook, and in doing so, like Rodney, provides many critiques of Fage. But like Fage's narrative of the slave trade, his story begins with the fact that Africans sold slaves. He writes, "African scholars and politicians today must be honest and admit that the enslavement and sale of the Africans from the seventeenth century onwards were done by the Africans themselves, especially the coastal kings and their elders, and that very few Europeans actually ever marched inland and captured slaves themselves" (1966, 110). Despite his reference here to "coastal kings and their elders," Boahen later describes unspecified African gangs who raided villages for slaves. By excluding regional or ethnic markers, he participates in the making of a shared African history, but one that he recognizes many will not be happy with. Boahen further suggests that the introduction of the Atlantic trade led to a great increase in African participation in wars to acquire slaves and argues that in contrast to the period before the advent of the Atlantic trade, "fighting was motivated by greed not by self-preservation nor imperial ambitions" (1966, 112).

In this way, Boahen reduces the reasons for Africans to raid for slaves to their greedy desires for European goods, thereby feeding into theories of the degeneration of their morality. Furthermore, Boahen argues that the slave trade had devastating effects on the material conditions of African societies. With Fage clearly in mind, he writes, "Curiously, some European historians say that the slave trade did have some good as well as some bad effects" (1966, 111), noting in particular the argument that the slave trade led to the development of the major West African kingdoms. Boahen counters that Benin rose well before the slave trade and that Asante expansion continued after the slave trade, which suggests that the trade was not the impetus for its growth. Finally, Boahen argues that the expansion of Dahomey was an attempt on the part of its kings to stop the slave trade. After debunking Fage's arguments, he concludes, "The slave trade did not confer benefits of any kind on West Africa. On the contrary, it was, to use the words of one historian of the 1890's, 'an unmitigated misery—a crime unredeemed by one extenuating circumstance'" (1966, 112).

By suggesting that Africans participated solely out of greed and that their actions did not ultimately benefit any Africans, Boahen, like others before him, renders African participation in the trade amazingly shortsighted. Without a regional or class analysis, the history of the slave trade becomes one of Africans participating in their own destruction. His reluctant assertion that scholars and politicians "must be honest" demonstrates his conviction that a recognition that Africans, not Europeans, were responsible for the actual procurement of slaves leads to the unavoidable conclusion that they are, at least in part, to blame for the negative effects of the trade. By addressing not only scholars but also politicians, Boahen furthermore points to the political efficacy for Africans in the context of the global arena of a story of the slave trade that lays the blame fully onto Europeans and, by contrast, the ruinous nature of one that lays some of the blame onto Africans themselves. While this conclusion attempts to move away from Fage's diminishment of the significance of the slave trade, by attributing African involvement in the trade to greed and stressing the destruction wrought by the trade, he recalls theories of the degeneration of both the morality and the material conditions of African societies.

On the question of abolition, Boahen argues for a compromise between Coupland and Williams, suggesting that it resulted from both humanitarian and economic concerns. He argues that by 1792 when the British House of Commons passed a motion calling for the gradual abolition of the slave trade, most of its members had been convinced of the immorality of the slave trade, but their concern that abolition would lead to financial ruin led them to hold off the abolition of the trade in slaves until 1807. He then summarizes Williams's argument linking abolition to the Industrial Revolution. Without the glorification of abolition, Boahen's narrative resists the romantic register, but it provides no alternative plot structure. It remains a partial, unresolved story of downfall through ignorance and rescue through greed, providing no protagonist and as such is as politically vacuous as Fage's assertion that the slave trade did not lead to the destruction of African societies. It thus demonstrates that the problem presented by the slave trade remained unresolved.

THE TRAGEDY OF SLAVERY

In contrast to the construction of the slave trade as alternately a story of African participation as a rational economic choice resulting in long-term benefits for Africa as a whole or as simply a bad choice resulting from simple greed with no calculation of its costs, there is another option, that of focusing not solely on African agency but rather on the conditions under which this agency took shape. Scott calls for a similar type of analysis with regard to African agency under colonialism. He writes, "What is at issue is not *whether* the colonized accommodated or resisted. What *is* at issue is how (colonial) power altered the terrain on which accommodation/resistance was *possible* in the first place. Attention has now to be turned, therefore, to a description of that terrain" (1999, 16, original emphasis). We might similarly turn our attention to how European mercantile power altered the terrain on which African rulers and merchants operated during the slave trade.

Other historians have noted that Africans involved in the trade did calculate the costs and found that trading in slaves had benefits *given that there were few other options*. These benefits included the ability to maintain their own freedom. In a recent edited volume, Joseph Inikori (2003) notes, for instance, that not only did many West African kingdoms including Asante consolidate in order to protect their members from enslavement (as Rodney and others have noted) but that furthermore, maintaining their power required military materials that they could only acquire from Europeans, and the only way to acquire those materials was through the selling of slaves. They sold slaves then not simply because elites were provided with an opportunity to increase their wealth (although this motivation cannot be dismissed), but because they often in fact had to do so in order to maintain their own strength and therefore their own freedom. Similarly, as I discuss in chapter 1, for coastal residents, by supporting the logic behind the enslavement of northerners, they ensured their own freedom. Moreover, by selling slaves, coastal merchants gained control over who did and did not enter the Atlantic trade. Some in fact subverted European plans by covertly freeing slaves bound for export.

African rulers and merchants were thus important players in this game, often quite savvy players, but not unrestrained ones. For the fact remains that they might have been better off if the slave trade had never developed at all. Longstanding wealth in West Africa resulted not from the slave trade but rather from the legitimate trade that followed, and the elite classes would no doubt have accumulated more wealth in the trade with Europe had it always involved goods instead of people (Inikori 2003, 193). For this reason, Joseph Inikori insists that on the African continent, not only those enslaved, but "even the political and economic entrepreneurs were ultimate losers" (2003, 193).

For those attempting to write a history of Africa (or West Africa or Ghana) as a whole, this analysis provides a view of a shared African tragedy. In describing tragedy, Scott explains that "sometimes we can *only* choose badly even as we are obliged to choose. We may be essentially good people, have good characters, but acting in the world necessarily presents us with situations that are anomalous or that make conflicting and incommensurable demands on us. Tragedy is a meditation on the nature and consequences of action in such circumstances" (2004, 185). Using this framework, he describes Toussaint Louverture, of Haitian revolution fame, as a "conscript of modernity." He explains that "[h]e was a man who had come up in a world that had been coercively reorganized by the material and epistemic violence of a modern regime of power and forcibly inserted into a global order in a state of subordination and dependence" (2004, 129). In this way, he shifts the popular perception of Louverture away from an image of him as one of history's victors. A similar interpretation of the varying levels of constraint that the slave trade placed on differently positioned Africans can forestall a generalized condemnation of Africans. As I discussed earlier, such condemnations have been tied to larger political projects of domination. It also avoids dividing Africans into simply good and bad, victims and perpetrators, a strategy that has clearly been rejected by textbook writers because it works against the construction of a national history. Tragic histories point not toward individuals or groups but rather toward a *system* of oppression.

For this reason, tragedy might provide a way to think about the inescapable nature of the Atlantic order in which African rulers and merchants were its conscripts. This reading challenges the insistence within nationalist narratives of a romantic triumph over oppression. It instead suggests the deep embeddedness of oppression that is not so easily overcome and points to the continuing effects of this oppression. In this way, as Scott notes, "the mode of emplotment of tragedy comports better with a time of postcolonial crisis in which old horizons have collapsed or evaporated and new ones have yet to take shape" (2004, 168). This time is one in which the optimism of the nationalist era has waned, leading to postnationalist outlooks (Appiah 1992). Interpreting the slave trade as a tragedy, indeed a key tragedy in the formation of contemporary African states, would be an effective postnationalist narrative and, as such, a viable protest narrative. The mode of emplotment of protest narratives, by which I mean narratives that tie past oppression to present suffering, contrasts sharply to the happy endings of romantic narratives of nationalism. These narratives call for continued struggle at the same time that they call into question the possibility of victory.[11] Rodney's later work entitled *How Europe Underdeveloped Africa*, for which he is best known, does just this by indicting Europe for the slave trade and arguing that its effects are partially responsible for contemporary inequalities between Africa and Europe.

Such an interpretation can also point us toward histories that place Africa and its diaspora under the same rubric as places in which struggles against the slave trade have been carried out. As I discuss in part 2, black Atlantic histories have begun to circulate in Ghana as a result of diaspora tourism, and these histories do at times construct narratives of tragedy. Rather than explore the possibilities of tragedy, however, schools have continued to present histories that are a product of the optimism of the independence moment. Within these histories, the story of the slave trade remains a partial, morally problematic narrative that is therefore marginalized within the public domain. As a result, the shift from Fage's to Boahen's text has not resolved debates regarding the slave trade, which continue in history classrooms today.

Representing the Slave Trade in Schools

Given the available academic historical interpretations of the slave trade, it is little surprise that it has been deemphasized in schools. Indeed, the presentation of the slave trade that remains within the JSS textbook presents it in such a way that one can easily understand why its authors would assign to it such a marginalized position, virtually hidden in the last section of the JSS textbook, entitled "The West African Community." This section begins by addressing a wide range of topics including the geography of West Africa, the ancient empires of Ghana, Mali, and Songhai, the coming of foreigners, colonialism, independence movements, and economic developments throughout Africa. This section is somewhat of a hodgepodge of the geography, ecology, sociology, and history of West Africa as a whole. The topic of the slave trade arises in two portions of the text, "The Effects of the Coming of Foreigners" and "New Homes for Freed Slaves." The same three themes stand out in the presentation of the history of the slave trade here that have been the subject of the debates outlined above and explain in part its lack of visibility in Ghanaian society.

First, it attributes African participation in the slave trade to a corporate African immorality in even stronger terms that Boahen, recalling colonial histories like T. R. Batten's. The text reads, "The African slave dealers made a lot of profit. This made them fail to see that the very people who should develop West Africa were the young people who were being sold into slavery. Do you not agree that these African slave dealers were very selfish? They were greedy, and so *they sold their own people*. People who wish to be respected in society should never use their neighbors to make themselves rich" (1988, 88, emphasis added). There is no discussion of the complexities of participation itself that would modify characterizations of African greed and brutality. Instead, the social studies textbook suggests that Africans sold each other, thereby making all Africans culpable for a decision that furthermore was made solely out of greed.

Second, the slave trade is presented as having had both positive and negative effects. Three paragraphs are devoted to the negative effects of the slave trade, including the loss of freedom for enslaved individuals, the depopulation of Africa, and the economic decline as a result of fear and instability in some communities, after which, four paragraphs are devoted to the positive effects of European contact, including the introduction of foreign crops, formal education, and Christianity. In addition, the text accepts Fage's argument that the slave trade led to the development of centralized governments. The authors write,

> It is important to admit . . . that foreign contact also helped promote the development of state systems . . . It was also the trade with foreigners which made the empires rich. Also, most of the states of the forest region became powerful because of the guns and gunpowder which they got from the Europeans. Weaker ethnic groups were brought under the control of stronger ones. Moreover, new towns grew along the coast because of the trading activities. (1988, 89)

Here, Fage's arguments win out over Boahen's. The authors' seeming reluctance to "admit" these purportedly positive influences, like Boahen's reluctance to discuss African participation in the trade, demonstrates the hegemony of Fage's arguments that historians have found difficult to refute, even when they strongly desired to do so. While Africans may be greedy, it suggests, the outcome for their material conditions has been mixed, leading away from narratives that describe the devastation of the continent. At the end of the chapter, students are asked to state five bad effects of the coming of foreigners to West Africa and then to mention four things that West Africa has gained from contact with foreigners. The juxtaposition of these questions as well as the structure of the chapter in general places the positive and negative effects of the European presence in equilibrium. It suggests that the slave trade had a negative impact, for which African traders are to a large extent responsible, but that Africans simultaneously benefited in many other ways as well.

The third issue, the description of abolition, departs somewhat from Fage. The textbook describes abolition: "The Europeans eventually, abolished and stopped the slave trade. Not because they felt for the Africans, however. It was mainly because they no longer needed many slaves. They needed more raw materials for their new industries. Europeans always make sure that they do only what benefits them. For this reason, Africans must always think carefully about anything Europeans propose, before they accept it" (1988, 88). Here, the influence of Williams's refutation (via Boahen) of Coupland's emphasis on the role of British humanitarianism (via Fage) is apparent. As in many previous examples, the authors feel free to provide commentary on the historical events that they present. In this case, they render a harsh critique of Europeans' motivations and suggest that Africans retain a stance of skepticism with regard to them. But ultimately, this critique is tempered by the similar critique quoted above of African slave dealers. There are no protagonists in this story, only villains.

Together, these factors almost ensure the marginalization of the slave trade within national histories. Unlike the history of independence, which conforms to the standard structure of romance in which there are clear opponents (the British on the one hand and the Ghanaian people on the other, symbolized by Nkrumah, the story's protagonist), a struggle between the two sides, and the ultimate victory of the protagonist, with the moral of the story being that good ultimately triumphs over evil, the story of the slave trade is an impoverished tale. There are no clear opponents, as Africans are presented as both perpetrators and victims of enslavement. There is no real obstacle to be overcome, as the slave trade has positive and negative effects, and there is no ultimate victory, as abolition was a result of European design. The only moral that students can draw from this story is that Africans are greedy and Europeans are selfish, hardly an edifying lesson. As a result of this construction of the history of the slave trade, it has been marginalized within schools.

NOT A STORY TO DWELL ON

For most students, what they learn in JSS represents the extent of their exposure to the slave trade as an academic subject. Many of those who study history in SSS do not gain much more depth of knowledge about the trade. The SSS history textbook in use at the time of this research (Fynn and Addo-Fenning 1991) addresses the slave trade, but its emphasis is still marginal in comparison with its attention to colonialism and independence. The SSS textbook also gives a great deal of attention to the ancient African kingdoms, following nationalist desires to create a glorious past for the nation. With these dual agendas, the slave trade remains a minor subject. Ultimately, however, the amount of knowledge that students gain depends, as this final section demonstrates, on their teachers.

Miss Mensah is a native of Elmina who teaches history at one of the area's elite all-girl sss. Its atmosphere resembles that of elite private schools in the United States. It enrolls some of the brightest students in Ghana, most of whom plan to attend university after graduation. The campus has a formal atmosphere. Students wear uniforms, and teachers are quick to reprimand any student whose clothes are not perfectly arranged. The girls address teachers with the utmost respect and deference, replying to every request with a curtsey and a "Yes ma'am." Despite the fact that the curriculum no longer privileges the domestic arts over academics as a result of the creation of gender parity in schools, its continuing mission to create proper young ladies is evident.

Miss Mensah's third-year class included approximately thirty students. She is a dynamic and outspoken teacher who is truly invested in her students' learning. She graciously allowed me to observe several classes over the course of two weeks, during which time she addressed the slave trade. Her presentation of the slave trade included many of the features of its depiction in the jsss, particularly: an emphasis on African participation in the slave trade and on the benefits of the European presence. In raising these issues, she argued that slavery is not a subject that students should dwell on. This message arose from her coastal origins and more specifically, her family history, which came into play within the classroom.

Classroom instruction is particularly important in the discussion of ssss because it is this factor that makes for such huge disparities among them. Philip Foster explains that "[t]heoretically all public secondary schools [in Ghana] enjoy 'parity of esteem'; they are all highly selective, follow the same general curricula, and their students enter for identical public examinations. In reality however, the schools do not enjoy parity in terms of the occupational and educational opportunities of their students or in public repute . . . so far as pupils are concerned, the particular secondary school that one attends is just as important as obtaining a secondary school education *per se*" (1963, 156). I describe Miss Mensah's classroom then not in order to provide a picture of an average class in Ghana, but, on the contrary, in order to illustrate the lessons that take place at its pinnacle.

During the first class that I observed, Miss Mensah addressed the topic of the "Effects of the European Presence in Ghana." The effects covered included the rise of forts and castles, coastal towns, and merchant princes. After addressing these effects, Miss Mensah explained that the slave trade was another effect of the European presence but was quick to add that it should be treated as a major topic on its own. She expressed her belief in the inadequacy of the SSS history syllabus in that she said it does not classify the slave trade as one of its major topics. She in fact spent several days covering the slave trade, more time, apparently, than the syllabus suggests. It soon became clear, however, that she did so in order to allow herself enough time to present all of the reasons why the students should dismiss this history. She refused to paper over the history of slave trade; she intended to dig it a very deep grave.

The class was a combination of lectures during which the teacher dictated notes for students to write down in her exact words and discussion in which the teacher asked questions and students were encouraged to discuss what they had learned from the readings as well as share their opinions. Students had read the relevant sections of the textbook beforehand; thus, they were able to respond to Miss Mensah's questions with information gathered from their readings. Miss Mensah often added her own opinion on the material she covered, particularly regarding the culpability of Europeans for the slave trade. She opened the discussion of the slave trade by asking the students, "Did slavery exist in the African community before the advent of the transatlantic slave trade?" Students then replied with various examples of the ways in which individuals became domestic slaves in the past including pawning, or *panyarring* (which is the seizure of a debtor in lieu of the debt) and capture. Miss Mensah then spelled out her point stating, "It wasn't the white man who brought slavery, slavery existed before the transatlantic slave trade was introduced." In this way, she stressed Fage's argument that the Atlantic slave trade was an outgrowth of domestic slavery in Ghana.

Next, students engaged in a discussion in which they drew connections between history and contemporary conditions in Ghana. The timing of this lecture was highly significant. Not only had Emancipation Day and PANAFEST recently ended, but earlier that year, the Ghanaian government had decided to join the Highly Indebted Poor Countries (HIPC) Initiative, essentially a national declaration of bankruptcy in return for some alleviation of debt to European nations. One student noted that because of HIPC, Ghanaians are still enslaved (see chapter 7). Miss Mensah's response to this discussion belied her opinion of the tourism industry's emphasis on the slave trade. She told the students, "We should put it behind us and not dwell on it.

Now we have Emancipation Day, we were emancipated a long time ago. We should move ahead. When we were taken into slavery, they brought Christianity and education, so there have been mitigations. I think we should get on with our lives and not think about slavery and what Europe can do for us." In stating "we were taken into slavery," Miss Mensah suggests that within national history, in contrast to regional histories, enslavement becomes the inheritance of the entire nation. In this context, she suggests that Ghanaians not think about the slave trade. Whereas coastal residents might displace it onto the North, in the context of the construction of a national identity in which all citizens inherit a shared past, the enslavement of some cannot be displaced; to be avoided it must be ignored.

But in addition to the danger of being seen as the victims of the slave trade, Miss Mensah also attempts to demonstrate what she believes is the impossibility of using the slave trade as the basis of a protest narrative. Within her construction, Africans are responsible for the trade, for "it wasn't the white man who brought slavery." For her, the slave trade makes a poor candidate for the basis of a critique of global inequalities.

She also presents another logic for exclusion that arises from the extenuating circumstances. Miss Mensah stated this logic explicitly when she said, "When we were taken into slavery, they brought Christianity and education, so there have been mitigations."[12] Her emphasis on Christianity and education is not surprising given the school's roots in mission education. The syllabus follows the topic of the slave trade with the social impact of the European presence. Although some negative features are mentioned, including the introduction of alcohol, the impact is presented as largely positive, including the introduction of new crops, the establishment of Christian missions, and the development of Western-style education. The insistence on the positive influence of the European presence in Ghana in both JSSS and SSSS illustrates the continuing effects of the logic of colonialism, which suggests that Europeans civilized Africans by bringing them Western education and Christianity. Even in the face of one of the worst atrocities in human history, the transatlantic slave trade, Europeans remain somewhat sheltered from critique.

Following Miss Mensah's speech, another student again brought up Ghana's economic woes and suggested the need for more development aid. Again, Miss Mensah expressed her disdain for the idea of compensation, stating emphatically, "Why should we always think we should be compensated? Africans should put slavery behind us. Are you still a slave? You can be enslaved in the mind. Are you enslaved in the mind? What are you? An emancipated individual!" Her question, "Are you still a slave?" suggests that wanting compensation implies a relationship of dependence similar to slavery, except that Africans are now enslaved in the mind, providing yet another Fanonian analysis. Indeed, Miss Mensah actively sought to make her students into what she deems are "emancipated individuals" by teaching them to put slavery behind them.

During the next class period, the lesson turned to the beginnings of the transatlantic slave trade. Miss Mensah asked how slaves were acquired. One student responded that they were captured by "the natives," to Miss Mensah's great approval. Another student noted that in a play that they had seen at the Center for National Culture, Europeans were shown kidnapping Africans. Miss Mensah immediately dismissed that portrayal saying, "I think that was a big lie. I didn't like it," emphasizing again that Africans were responsible for the actual acquisition of captives for the slave trade, not Europeans. The students continued to list the ways in which Africans acquired slaves including kidnappings, wars, and slave markets. Miss Mensah then asked the students, "So the whites didn't go there to capture them, so why do we blame them?" She rhetorically extended her argument that Africans are responsible for the slave trade by not only arguing that domestic slavery preceded the Atlantic trade but also by noting that the latter depended on African agency.

In response to her question, one student proposed, "We don't want to accept the blame so we blame them." Another commented on the inhumanity of Africans with regard to their involvement in the slave trade. A third student added that she had heard that the father of Philip Quaque, the famous African minister, sold slaves.

What happened next clearly demonstrated the problematic nature of the history of the slave trade in Ghana. To everyone's surprise, Miss Mensah announced, "My great-grandfather was a slave dealer. We have an ancestral home in Elmina. We have pictures of slaves, and we have descendants of slaves living in the house. My great-grandfather benefited. I come from a family where slavery was accepted. We have slave quarters." A buzz went around the room as students expressed their astonishment at Miss Mensah's candor with regard to slave owning and dealing, which, as I discuss earlier, is quite rare. Intent on demonstrating African agency in the slave trade, she offered up her own great-grandfather as an example. She then added, "I'm not proud of it," thereby explaining that her intention was not to suggest that African agency in the trade is something to be celebrated. On the contrary, she brought up her own family in order to demonstrate the dangers of discussing the slave trade. Such conversations, she showed, inevitably come back to damn Africans for their participation.

In this way, Miss Mensah's own elite coastal origins explain her approach to the history of the slave trade. The politics of silence surrounding the domestic slave trade and slave dealing complicate her attempt to narrate the history of the transatlantic slave trade. Miss Mensah, as a native of Elmina and the descendant of a slave owner and dealer, downplays the significance of the slave trade to her students, thereby seeking to free her own family from condemnation. Clearly then, the presentation of the slave trade as part of national history is shaped in part by concerns regarding the construction of local history.

In the construction of the slave trade in this classroom, many of the same themes found in the JSS textbook arise. African participation is once again a major theme. Students could hardly miss the significance that Miss Mensah attributed to this fact. She stated emphatically in class that Europeans are not to blame for the slave trade. Clearly, she insisted, the slave trade is not a simple story of European oppression. In addition, Miss Mensah emphasized the benefits of the European presence and argued that they mitigate the damage done by the slave trade. During one class discussion, Miss Mensah allowed the students to ask me questions, several of which revolved around the perceptions of the slave trade in the United States. To my shock and dismay, one student asked whether or not I thought the slave trade was "a good thing." This question was not an isolated occurrence. The benefits of the European presence and even of the slave trade itself are regularly emphasized in secondary-school discussions. A common exercise that teachers give students is to address the question, "Was the slave trade a blessing for Africa?" (Perbi 1999), clearly drawing on Fage's arguments with regard to the growth of kingdoms as a result of the slave trade.

Finally, in contrast to her attention to African participation and the effects of the slave trade, abolition was not a major concern. She did, however, use the idea of emancipation to further her argument that the slave trade is not a story to dwell on. Her students, she insisted, must free their minds from this history.

In Miss Mensah's presentation of the slave trade, as in history textbooks, the complexities of African participation are absent. Instead, the story of the slave trade is a story of simple defeat, the physical defeat of those enslaved and the moral defeat of those who enslaved them, from which there can be no redemption. Miss Mensah urged the students to put slavery behind them for this reason. For her, to remember the slave trade is to remember a defeat from which Africans could not escape but which Africans themselves caused. To ask for reparations is even worse because it is an admission that Africans continue to occupy a defeated position from which they alone cannot extricate themselves. Thus, for Miss Mensah, the slave trade is not an edifying part of history.

In spite of her insistence on its unimportance in many respects, Miss Mensah stressed the inhuman nature of *European* ideas about and treatment of slaves, which stand in stark contrast to African ones. These two categories are finally fully separated at the moment in which slaves became the warehoused goods within slave dungeons and the cargo of ships. During one class period, she discussed the fact that children made up a large percentage of those cramped in the holds of slave ships. She read a quote from a letter of instructions for the governor at Cape Coast Castle that was written in 1622 and quoted in Boahen's school text (1966, 112); it included a request for "good merchantable Negroes . . . six-sevenths of each cargo to be about 16 to 30 years of age and upon no account to exceed 30, one-seventh boys and girls of which none should be under the age of ten." She added, "It was tragic, they took the young ones, sometimes they even took ones under ten!"

She also stressed the appalling conditions on slave ships and the harsh treatment of slaves by Europeans. In this, Miss Mensah's presentation of the slave trade is unique. Neither the history syllabus nor the national textbook provides information on this subject. The sss textbook provides a dispassionate description of the slave trade. It allots two sentences to the cruelty of slavery that read, "It was not uncommon for brutal Europeans to give a slave a hundred strokes of the whip for breaking an ordinary plate, or flog him ruthlessly for falling into a trance. Some of the Danish planters succeeded in arranging with chiefs in the neighborhood of their plantations to kill runaway slaves" (1991, 213). In addition to this scant information, Miss Mensah told students about the conditions of the Middle Passage, including how slaves were often stripped naked and packed like sardines in the holds of ships, forced to lie in their own waste. She also told them about what is often viewed as one of the worst horrors of the slave trade, that when slaves died aboard ships, their bodies were thrown overboard. Through such descriptions, Miss Mensah distinguished between European and African conduct. In contrast to domestic slavery, an already existing system through which captives were also acquired for the Atlantic slave trade, which she discussed dispassionately, she presented vivid images of the brutalities of European slavery. Her emphasis on these horrors is the beginning of another story of the creation of an alternative vision of the significance of the slave trade and of the resultant radicalization of some of her students. The telling of this story, however, must await some further contextualization that is provided by the following chapter. It is positioned therefore in the last chapter of this text and in many ways as its culmination.

With regard to the more general picture of the academic treatment of the slave trade, because of the scant nature of the presentation of the slave trade in JSSS, most students come to SSS knowing that the slave trade existed but lacking any knowledge of its severity or the atrocities that it entailed. For those who do not enroll in history as well as for those whose teachers do not take the initiative to stress these aspects of the history, their naivety continues. Even Miss Mensah, who focused on some of its horrors, argued quite stridently that her students should forget the slave trade. She insisted that it is not a strong basis for a critique of Europeans. Not only, according to her, do Africans bear a great deal of responsibility for it, but Europeans have made many positive contributions to Ghana. After dismissing the slave trade in this way, Miss Mensah could then proceed with the rest of the lesson plan, which moved quickly to (what else?) colonialism and independence.

Many of her students followed Miss Mensah's directive to forget the slave trade. As I discuss in chapter 7, they agreed with their teacher that it is not a story to dwell on. When asked to talk about national history, on the contrary, they could certainly readily recite the story of the independence struggle. This history, however, did not seem to move them the way that textbooks and the celebration of Independence Day suggest it should. Indeed, regional histories are invoked more often than histories of the nation. Coastal residents tend to view national histories as the province of schools, while they locate regional histories within most other realms including, as we have seen, churches, development discourses, oral histories, and popular written histories. They lack enthusiasm for the romantic plot of national histories because it does not allow them to express their sense of abjection. Even teachers, who, as the last chapter demonstrated, are quite enthusiastic about regional histories, often seem uninterested in the idea of national history outside of the classroom.

In addition to turning to subnational histories of different regions, as I discuss in chapter 7, some men and women have turned to transnational histories of the black Atlantic, further demonstrating the problems inherent in national history. While the history of the slave trade has long been a subject of debate between European and Ghanaian historians, as I discuss in the following section, the interest of African Americans in this debate has led to the expansion of this debate outside of the academy. It has also led to a shift in the status of the history of the slave trade as well as the available functions that it can serve, which now include a function within the formation of protest narratives. This shift reveals the failures of the romantic narrative of nationalism in the context of postcolonial despair and the need for a reorientation toward history that includes a meditation on the slave trade.

PART II »

Centering the Slave Trade

6 » *Slavery and the Making of Black Atlantic History*

In 1997, former Ghanaian president Jerry Rawlings traveled to Jamaica on a state visit. While there, he observed the celebration of Emancipation Day.[1] Aware of the fact that many of those enslaved in Jamaica and elsewhere passed through the castles on Ghana's shore, he decided to inaugurate a similar celebration in Ghana. In doing so, he hoped to attract tourists from the African dispora. He therefore called on the Ministry of Tourism to design the event, and on August 1, 1998, Emancipation Day was celebrated in Ghana, a commemoration of the emancipation of the slaves in the British colonies on the same day in 1834.

As a result of this event and the larger diaspora tourism industry in which it is situated, tourism represents one arena in which the slave trade is a central part of a very public discourse in Ghana. In this way, it contrasts sharply to the arenas discussed in part 1, in which the slave trade is sequestered. Clearly then, these arenas are largely undisturbed by diaspora tourism. Many local residents in fact dismiss diaspora tourism as something designed for tourists, not for them. Given their awareness of the ways in which the history of the slave trade has been used to discuss and denounce African families' ownership of slaves as well as rampant slave raiding as a feature of particular regions and of the nation as a whole, they are understandably wary of attempts at its commemoration.

Some local residents however, do tour the castles and participate in tourist events. For them, their constructions of history are forever altered by the castles, which either strengthen their resolve to forget the slave trade or provide them with a new vision of history. For these reasons, diaspora tourism demands attention within the discussion of constructions of history on the coast. In this chapter, I explore the forces that led to the development of diaspora tourism out of a long conversation between Africa and the diaspora. I examine in particular the structure of its historical narratives in the castle museums, in tourist events, and on castles tours. This chapter provides a background for a discussion in the following chapter of the ways in which both African Americans and Ghanaians have interpreted these narratives by alternately confirming and combating the dominant discourses in place on the coast.

Making a Black Atlantic Discourse

The development of diaspora tourism has been the outcome of an extended conversation between Ghana and segments of the African diaspora, particularly African Americans. It is the product, in other words, of a black Atlantic conversation. I use the term black Atlantic here to refer to the *back and forth* traffic between Africa and the diaspora, similar to what J. Lorand Matory calls "Afro-Atlantic dialogues," which "highlight the ways in which the mutual gaze between Africans and African Americans, multidirectional travel and migration between two hemispheres, the movement of publications, commerce and so forth have shaped African and African-American cultures in tandem, over time, and at the same time" (2005, 291). In this way, Matory departs somewhat from Paul Gilroy's discussion of the black Atlantic. Gilroy uses this framework to discuss the deep engagement of black subjects with Western modernity. As the first part of this book has demonstrated, coastal residents are certainly part of Gilroy's black Atlantic. Such an engagement, however, often takes particular routes, routes that link black subjects on different continents to each other. It is these routes that part 2 explores.

Unlike Ghana's long conversation with Europe, which has often been about incongruity, or, in other words, the ways in which Africans are *not* like Europeans, its conversation with the African diaspora, like most Afro-Atlantic dialogues, is one in which various notions of connection are regularly mobilized. The relationship between Africa and the diaspora is usually viewed from the point of view of the latter. A growing body of literature has addressed the ways in which the African diaspora is a community and tradition that are "discursively constituted principally (though not exhaustively) in and through the mobilization of a common possession, namely, the historically constituted figures of 'Africa' and 'Slavery'" (Scott 1999,

124). Kamari Clarke (2004) and Paulla Ebron (2002), for instance, provide examples of diasporic creations of an "African homeland imaginary." Other scholars have noted the significance of one diasporic group, namely, African Americans, to another (see Brown 2005; Neptune 2003, 2007). Few scholars, however, have placed Africans at the center of such discussions. In doing so, we might begin to think about how African actors, as a result of conversations with diasporic ones, have come to mobilize the history of the slave trade.

In Ghana, conversations with the African diaspora have a long history. At earlier moments, as I discuss below, such mobilizations involved appeals to similar cultural frameworks or political agendas. In this way, the development of diaspora tourism represents a shift in black Atlantic discourse in that many Ghanaians now mobilize notions of the diaspora through discussions of the slave trade. As I argue below, these earlier invocations of the diaspora, however, set the stage for diaspora tourism's construction of an international black community.

In 1911, J. E. Casely Hayford, a key figure in Fante cultural nationalism, published a book entitled *Ethiopia Unbound: Studies in Race Emancipation,* which he dedicated "To the sons of Ethiopia the world wide over." Inspired by Blyden, he writes, "Afro-Americans must bring themselves into touch with some of the general traditions and institutions of their ancestors, and, though sojourning in a strange land, endeavor to conserve the characteristics of the race" (1969 [1911], 165), arguing that Africa provided cultural grounding for African Americans and using more generally the notion of Ethiopianism to call for the unification of black people throughout the world.

Several decades later, Kwame Nkrumah would shift the emphasis in black Atlantic discourse from culture to development. When he visited the United States after becoming president of the newly independent Ghana, he invited African Americans, but specifically black professionals such as teachers, doctors, and dentists, to move to Ghana and to help develop the nation (Gaines 2006, 90). Rather than stressing African Americans' connection to Ghana as a result of their African ancestry and forcible removal from the continent through the slave trade, Nkrumah focused on their potential future connections through a commitment to the goal of African development. The access that the African American professional class had had to American educational opportunities, in the same way that he himself had had such access in the United States, could, he argued, be put to use in the service of Ghanaian development. In this vein, in 1958, he also hosted in

Ghana the All African People's Conference. Many African Americans responded to this call, although Ghana never saw an organized back-to-Africa movement of African Americans like those to Liberia and Sierra Leone. Nevertheless, as a result of more individualized travel, since the late 1950s, Ghana has received the most African American expatriates of any African nation (Jenkins 1975, 151). Many prominent African Americans visited Ghana during this period as well, including Richard Wright, Malcolm X, Maya Angelou, and Martin Luther King Jr.[2] In addition, W. E. B. Du Bois moved to Ghana late in life and was buried there.

The development of an African American expatriate community in Ghana led to well-known conflicts and suspicions on the part of Ghanaians (see Jenkins 1975; Gaines 2006). Nkrumah's efforts notwithstanding, their belonging to the nation was not a foregone conclusion. Despite the participation of some African thinkers in the construction of ties between Africa and the African diaspora, within the popular imagination in Ghana, it has often been trumped by other discourses.

For African American expatriates, not only did this period immediately follow Ghanaian independence, it also corresponded with the era of the Civil Rights movement in the United States, which led to their deep political engagement. In the midst of turmoil and violence in the United States, Ghana represented to them a land where black people could live in true freedom. Many African Americans were actively looking for an alternative to the discrimination that they faced in American society as well as a way to express their commitment to the liberation of all black people. Living in the midst of the violence of the Civil Rights era in the United States, this newly independent African nation gave these African American expatriates hope for the possibility of a free black community. It offered an escape from U.S. racism and the opportunity to realize a black nation. It also may have satisfied an idealized desire for a return to their homeland (Jenkins 1975; Lake 1997; Gaines 2006; Angelou 1986). Contributing to Ghana's development, as I discuss further below, was therefore a commitment that many readily embraced.

Despite Nkrumah's focus on economic development, other African nations focused more heavily during this period on black Atlantic cultural connections. In 1966, Senegal held the first world festival of *arts nègre*. This festival was followed by the grander Second World Black and African Festival of Arts and Culture, or FESTAC, which was held in Nigeria in 1977. Locating these festivals in Senegal in 1966 and in Nigeria in 1977 positioned them as the self-designated homelands of the black diaspora, which makes sense in the context of shifting global economic and cultural influence among West African nations. In the 1960s, Léopold Senghor, the president of a newly independent Senegal, championed Negritude as a pan-African arts movement; thus, his hosting of a pan-African arts festival allowed him to celebrate the notion of a set of cultural orientations that he believed united African peoples throughout the world. FESTAC followed the oil boom in Nigeria, as result of which it became the richest African nation. Nigeria also became a key player in the Organization of African Unity, thereby cementing its position as the leading African nation (Apter 2005). In his monograph exploring the history of FESTAC and its connection to the oil economy in Nigeria, Andrew Apter describes the narratives of black unity that it produced in seeking to position Nigeria as the "exporting nation" of black culture. This notion worked through links supported by the historical record, like those to Cuba, as well as through contemporary processes of wealth. Nigeria continues to play an important role in diasporic conceptualizations of an African homeland. It is often considered to be the *locus classicus* of African diaspora studies, and many of the African-based religious beliefs and practices of African Americans are derived from Nigerian religions (Matory 1999, 2005). But despite its dominance in the realms of scholarship and religion, Nigeria's political instability has discouraged diasporic travel to this popular religious homeland. If the oil boom positioned Nigeria at the center of the black Atlantic world, Apter argues, its bust left it clinging to the margins.

In 1977, the television miniseries *Roots* aired in the United States. As its title suggests, *Roots* stresses the African ancestry of African Americans and positions life in Africa as the prelude to the horrors of slavery. In large part as a result of this record-breaking series, the slave trade became the primary basis through which many African Americans started to view their connection to the African continent. The slave trade began then to do the work that had been done in the past by theories of cultural retentions and African development agendas. African Americans embraced their African ancestry and the history of their enslavement furthermore because, as Clarke notes, "*Roots* contributed to a narrative shift from what was popularly represented in schools as black Americans being victims of slavery who were *saved* by Abraham Lincoln, to blacks as noble survivors and agents of their own freedom" (2004, 140–41). While providing a more empowering image of slavery, like the narratives that described a savior Lincoln, it too was romantic in that it did not challenge the contemporary American power structure. African Americans may be agents in this story of the slave trade, but it is nonetheless a triumphant tale that does not attend to continuing forms of oppression.

As a result of the scripting of this empowering yet nonthreatening view of slavery, after the airing of *Roots*, countless novels were written, films produced, and historic plantation sites marketed in which the history of slavery was explored (see Berlin 2004). Some of these, like Toni Morrison's *Beloved*, provided alternative narratives of slavery. Through her vivid illustration of the "double-sidedness" of modernity (Bauman 1989) in which the terror of slavery is always a haunting presence, Morrison constructs a tragic story that challenges teleological narratives of black triumph and provides instead "an expression of the temporal experiences of African Americans, who are often denied a future and are therefore haunted by or retreat to the past" (Davis 1998, 256–57). Indeed, this description is strikingly similar to Scott's description of tragedy in which he discusses the "contingencies of the past" and "the uncanny ways in which its remains come back to usurp our hopes and subvert our ambitions" (2004, 220). At the same time, *Beloved* is also widely interpreted as a protest narrative[3] similar to the protest narrative that Rodney's discussion of the slave trade provides. There are clearly then multiple narratives of the slave trade in the American public sphere that have made this history of interest to a diverse body of African Americans. The greater affordability of air travel as well as the expansion of the black middle class in the United States allowed more and more African Americans to travel to Ghana to explore this history once the market responded to their burgeoning interest with the development of what has come to be known as diaspora tourism.

Castle Histories

The popularity of slavery narratives among African Americans was a major factor in the Ghanaian tourism industry's decision to focus on the slave trade, and there were few sites more fitting for this endeavor than Ghana's Cape Coast and Elmina castles. The sheer size and structural integrity of Cape Coast and Elmina castles provided the main arguments for their centrality to such narratives. They are massive structures, occupying nearly 100,000 square feet each, that sit on the shoreline of each town. They are made up of former storerooms, soldier's quarters, apartments for the governors, churches, courtyards, watchtowers, and ramparts that are still lined with canons trained at the sea. The *Maison des esclaves* on Gorée Island in Senegal as well as *La route de l'esclave* in Benin are other sites of such com-

7 Cape Coast Castle

memorative work. However, because these are French-speaking nations, undoubtedly many American tourists choose Ghana over Senegal and Benin to experience this history. The grand scale of Ghana's castles coupled with the nation's status as an English-speaking, politically stable West African nation has led to its emergence as a primary imagined homeland among African Americans, despite the fact that it accounted for only 13 percent of the British slave trade (Richardson 1989, 13). Since the growing instability in Nigeria, Ghana has been called "a model democracy—an oasis of peace and stability in turbulent West Africa." (*NPR Morning Edition*, May 26, 2005). Its remarkable stability and freedom from state violence, while surrounded on either side by the same in Cote d'Ivoire and Togo, have led many to consider it the leading nation of West Africa, if not of the continent as a whole, despite evidence of its economic troubles provided by examples like its joining the Highly Indebted Poor Nations Initiative.

Although they dominate the landscape of Cape Coast and Elmina, prior to the 1980s, the castles had not received a great deal of attention as important historical monuments. Before their conservation, they served primarily mundane functions including housing the post office and law court. An article in the *Ghana Teacher's Journal* in April 1958 suggests that students visit the castles as "places of historical interest," although no further information is given as to their specific significance. In 1970, the offices of the

8 Elmina Castle

Ghana Museums and Monuments Board (GMMB) moved to Cape Coast Castle. In an effort to expand the castle's significance as a tourist site, the GMMB proposed the establishment of a museum of West African history within the castle. The idea for the museum had taken shape by 1970. Planners intended it to represent West African history as a whole, but at least one of the planners argued that the museum should focus on the slave trade. Dr. R. Hurl of the Institute of African Studies at the University of Ghana, Legon, wrote in a memorandum about the museum, "Although the final aim of the Project is to arrive at a comprehensive museum of West African History with a strong cultural base, it might be useful to articulate the phases of implementation so as to emphasize what may be the most unique and significant aspect of Cape Coast and the other castles built along the coast: The Slave Trade" (quoted in Simmonds 1972, 7).

In the end, the museum represented the long history of Cape Coast and not just the period of the slave trade. Several international organizations made donations to the museum project including the British Museum and the City Museum in Liverpool and the Department of Geography at the University of Copenhagen (Duah 2000). The museum, which was named the West African Historical Museum, opened in 1972 with an exhibit that contained three main themes. The first display panel traced events in West Africa, North America, and Europe starting from 500 B.C. Next, several ancient African empires were addressed, along with Arab expansion in West Africa and the periods of Portuguese, Dutch, Danish, and French influence. Finally, the early history of West Africa including some aspects of the slave trade and other forms of trade, fishing, technology, the forts and castles, and warfare were addressed (Duah 2000, 119).

In his account of the creation of the museum, Francis Duah (2000) asserts that local people were receptive to its development and were involved in the process. He notes that one fisherman became a part-time model maker of fishing canoes at the museum and that several retired civil servants donated their own research materials or family documents on local history. Thus, although the museum was small in scale and consisted primarily of display cases placed against the walls of a long, narrow room, because of its at least partial focus on local history and culture, rather than focusing exclusively on the stigmatizing history of the slave trade, it appears to have been well received. In the same year, the dungeons at Cape Coast Castle were excavated. The dungeons had not been cleaned out since the last group of captives left; rather, the rubbish left by them was covered with a layer of sand and lime (Simmonds 1973, 268). During the excavation, eighteen inches of dirt and waste were removed from the floors.

Six thousand visitors were reported at Cape Coast Castle in 1972, including 1,487 school students from thirty-eight schools. The castle caretaker also served as a guide who would show visitors around, though there was no official interpretation of the site. Among international visitors, Richard Wright was one of the most famous. In his book *Black Power* he discusses his trip to Ghana, including his visit to Cape Coast and Elmina castles, which he suggests are vehicles for reconstructing the painful history of the slave trade (see chapter 7). In addition, a 1972 report of Cape Coast Castle notes that it received several international visitors including a parliamentary delegation from Barbados and forty-four members of the Morehouse College Glee Club, suggesting that even then, the castles were sites of sparse yet visible diaspora tourism (Simmonds 1972, 9–10).

Except for schoolchildren, local residents rarely took tours of the castles or viewed the structures as historic sites. Older Cape Coast residents with whom I spoke noted that during the 1950s, 1960s, and 1970s, anyone could go into the castle and look around and usually did not do so with the guide. They would simply walk around while going to the post office or other offices within the castle. In addition, the castle courtyard was often used for concerts and other events, functioning in many ways as the town civic center.

While their role in the slave trade did not lead to the treatment of the castles as special sites, they did have other important resonances. The site of Cape Coast Castle was once considered to be sacred space in the local cosmography. The rocks on which the castle was built form the shrine of Nana Tabir, one of the local deities of Cape Coast. Cape Coast has seventy-seven state gods (as opposed to household deities), and Nana Tabir is one of the most important of these. The god inhabits the rocks, and offerings are made there to him. In particular, Nana Tabir is responsible for the well-being of fishermen and traders (Graham 1994, 114). When the British built the castle on this site, local residents were forced to move the shrine to a different location. Thus, the building of the castle represented an act of immeasurable harm to local believers.

In 1977, the shrine was brought back to the castle, and the Traditional Council of Cape Coast hired a permanent priest to care for it. The shrine is located within the male slave dungeon, in front of one of its walls. The British built this wall once the slave trade was abolished to block off a tunnel leading from the dungeon to the point of departure where slaves were transported to the slave ship. The shrine is of particular importance during *Fetu Afahye*, the annual Cape Coast festival. *Fetu Afahye* takes place in September and celebrates the beginning of the fishing season as well as the yam harvest. During the festival, a bull is sacrificed at the Nana Tabir shrine. But because Cape Coast is heavily Christian, and many residents in fact eschew "traditional" religious practices, few people worship at the shrine during other times of the year. All the same, the castle simultaneously served as administrative space, tourist space, and sacred space during this period.

In 1979, the United Nations Educational, Scientific, and Cultural Organization (UNESCO) named both castles World Heritage Sites as a result of their nomination by Kwesi Myles, a Ghanaian museum professional and the secretary general of the Organization for Museums, Monuments and Sites of Africa. The UNESCO list, which had begun one year previously, sought to encourage preservation of historic sites as well as to give them recognition and bolster tourism. Such a designation was considered to be quite fitting, not only because of the significance of the castles to the slave trade, but also even in terms of their impressive size for such ancient structures. In the end, however, neither the establishment of the West African Historical Museum nor UNESCO's recognition of the castles led to the emergence of the slave trade within public history in Cape Coast and Elmina.

Indeed, up until quite recently, many local residents appear to have known little about the history of castles. They were not mentioned in any of the conventionalized narratives I describe in part 1 as places in which slaves were kept. Before the development of diaspora tourism, many men and women without formal education were in fact unaware of their significance to the slave trade. Indeed, even in 2001, when I asked an elderly woman with no formal education what one castle had been used for in the past, she stated it was the place where the post office was located. I then asked her what it had been used for before then, to which she replied that she had no idea. Ato, a young man and one of the tour guides at Elmina Castle who grew up in Elmina, confirmed that when he was growing up in the 1980s, before organized tours began, people often went to the castle to look around, but they knew nothing about its history. In most cases, the castles are viewed as profane spaces recognized primarily for their sheer size and beauty. Ato said of the level of interest of local people in the castle, "The only thing they want to see is the fact that it is so huge. That's it." He also said, "With the exception of the few who come to the castle to know what happened here, they will usually say, 'It's beautiful, I don't know how they built such a house in those days.'" Indeed, many people recited similar views of the castles. Yaw is a young entrepreneur in Elmina. I asked him if he ever wondered about the castles when he was young, to which he responded, "If there was anything to have actually made me to wonder it was the question how did they come by these huge buildings, structures here and there. They might have used a lot, you know, strength, energy, a whole lot, materials. How did they come by all these things at that time, about five hundred years ago and more." As these comments indicate, because of the reticence of previous generations to discuss the slave trade, the castles long remained profane structures within the landscapes of Cape Coast and Elmina, appreciated primarily for their size and beauty. As a result, while residents regularly entered the castles, they did not view them as important historical monuments, and if they were uneducated, did not associate them with the slave trade.

Conserving and Commemorating the Slave Trade

The significance of the castles and of the slave trade in general began to change in 1989 when the then regional minister Ato Austin traveled to the United States under the sponsorship of the Ministry for the Central Region to explore the options for the development of Cape Coast and Elmina castles as tourist sites. During this visit, he and his delegation met with various organizations and were eventually awarded $5.6 million from USAID for the implementation of the Natural Resource Conservation and Historic Preservation Project for the conservation of the castles. The Midwestern Universities Consortium for International Activities managed the grant, and several nongovernmental agencies served as subcontractors, including the Smithsonian Institution, Conservation International, the United States Committee for the International Council of Monuments and Sites, and the Debt for Development Foundation. This grant led to the castles becoming major tourist sites, with serious attention being paid to the history of the slave trade. As such, they became extremely popular destinations for diaspora tourists, and African Americans in particular.

Initially, however, neither a desire to commemorate the slave trade nor connections to the African diaspora were the driving forces behind the castles' conservation. A report on the conservation project describes the logic of their conservation as follows:

> Cape Coast Castle is a Ghanaian landmark, huge and picturesque. One mighty wall overlooks the shore, where clumps of sea-washed rocks are interspersed by soft, brown sand. Fishing craft are drawn up on the beaches as they have been for hundreds of years. Another wall oversees the busy life of the town, hazed by the smoking of the day's catch. The interior of the fortress has plenty of room for a major display of the nation's life. And Elmina, a relic of the earliest Portuguese landings along this coast, has a history that certainly would be a draw. Columbus, as a young man, is said to have learned navigation here. Later as "Admiral of the Ocean Sea," he supposedly stopped here to take on provisions for his great voyage of discovery. (Hyatt 1997, 5)

This construction of the significance of the castles makes no mention of the slave trade and therefore does not appear to challenge the dominant historical discourses discussed in part 1. On the contrary, the mention of Columbus invokes the age of exploration, a key romantic narrative of the modern age and an invocation as well of forms of connection between Africa and Europe.

Other projects during this period, however, explicitly invoked black Atlantic connections, particularly PANAFEST, a pan-African arts and culture festival that was the brainchild of Ghanaian playwright Efua Sutherland. In January 1991, an experimental national phase of PANAFEST was held in Cape Coast. Following its success, in 1992, the first official PANAFEST was held in Cape Coast and Elmina. Since then, it has become a biannual festival that draws tourists and performers from throughout the African diaspora. Like earlier pan-African festivals, it was based on an idea of cultural connection among Africans throughout the world. Its highlights include a grand *durbar,* or procession of chiefs and people in Cape Coast. Hundreds of tourists gather to see the parade of chiefs in full regalia, to watch indigenous dances and musical performances, and to hear welcoming speeches by tourism and government officials. Entertainment events include a beach party and a concert of international performers that have included the Boys Choir of Harlem and the Uthingo Dance Company of South Africa. Finally, a major component of PANAFEST is a visual arts exhibition once held at the Center for National Culture in Cape Coast, where vendors rent booths to sell their goods. Tourists can buy all of their Ghanaian souvenirs, from African clothing to wooden sculptures, here in a one-stop shopping experience, which thus underscores the touristic nature of the event.

PANAFEST then represented a shift in the nature of pan-Africanism in Ghana. While in the 1960s and 1970s, pan-Africanism involved the permanent resettlement of Africans in the diaspora in Ghana, since the 1990s Ghana has witnessed the expression of pan-Africanism through their temporary travel. In addition, while in an earlier period African Americans linked colonialism in Ghana to their struggle for civil rights, today the slave trade is central to many African Americans' constructions of their connection of Ghana.

Both projects however have been heavily concerned with development, although as I discuss more fully in chapter 7, they have defined it in very different ways. PANAFEST has addressed development concerns through the convening of conferences that address the theme of the event. The themes in 1999 and 2001 were "Uniting the African Family: Youth—The Agenda for the New Millennium" and "Bridging the Technology Divide," respectively. Finally, the organizers of PANAFEST demonstrated a burgeoning interest in commemorating the slave trade by including tours of the castles. These three agendas are clearly articulated in the PANAFEST Foundation's statement of its goals as the desire to "[e]stablish the truth about African history and our experience, using the vehicle of African arts and culture; provide a forum for the promotion of unity between continental Africans and those in the Diaspora; and develop a framework for the identification of issues and needs central to Africa's development and the improvement of the quality of life" (Atafori 1999, 6).

PANAFEST served to increase African American interest in the castles and their conservation. Two African American performers, Isaac Hayes and Dionne Warwick, who were part of a tour of the castles sponsored by the Nation of Islam, became interested in the conservation project. In 1992, the newly formed African American Society to Preserve Cape Coast Castle, represented by Isaac Hayes, pledged to raise $10 million for the preservation of the castle, although this goal was never met (Kreamer 2006, 454–55). But more than tourists, the African American expatriate community had the largest impact on the conservation of the castles. Today, this community numbers approximately one thousand individuals (Zachary 2001), most of whom reside in Accra, with a handful in and around Cape Coast. Certainly at this post-*Roots* moment, these individuals view the castles as sacred sites. For this reason, they worried about the conservation plan's lack of emphasis on the slave trade. Many among them, furthermore, were generally distrustful of the United States (having chosen to expatriate for this reason). The involvement of U.S. institutions like the Smithsonian thus increased their suspicion.

Examples of the conflicts that resulted from this fear are numerous. When the castles' conservation began, in addition to stabilizing the castles and providing modern plumbing facilities, the preservation team applied a mixture of lime, sand, and cement to the castle walls to remove the black mold stains that result from exposure to the coastal salt air, a process known as whitewashing. Members of the African American community in Ghana immediately responded to this act, concerned that it was an attempt to beautify the castles and thereby erase all evidence of the slave trade. Some charged that the whitewashing of castle walls and other improvement efforts were an attempt to whitewash history and, essentially, to erase the history of the slave trade. In particular, plans to clean up the dungeons met with fierce opposition. Apart from their excavation in the 1970s, the dungeons in both castles had lain unused for centuries and were still filled with layers of earth, human waste, and remains from the captives who were kept there centuries ago. In addition to their excavation, which served to make the dungeons accessible to visitors, the conservation team placed lighting in the dungeons to allow visitors to see their way into them. Fear that the dungeons would be completely sanitized angered many members of the African American community in Ghana.

Imahküs Vienna Robinson, an African American resident of Cape Coast, published an article in the journal, *Uhuru*, entitled "Is the Black Man's History Being 'White Washed': The Castles/Dungeons of the African Holocaust" (1994) in which she asked,

Are flowers being planted in the ovens at Auschwitz where millions of Jews perished? Have the Death Chambers of horror been brightly painted to somehow camouflage or silence the cries and screams of people who were brutally tortured and murdered? Think about that and then think about the Cape Coast and Elmina Castle/Dungeons on the Gold Coast of West Africa, where you can still hear and feel the presence of our African Ancestors when you enter the dark Dungeons and tunnels. But will this still be true when they finish renovating the Castles and painting the insides of the Dungeons? (1994, 48)

False reports that the dungeons were to be painted a "festive yellow" sparked much of the anger on the part of the African American community (Kreamer 2006, 453). In her article on Cape Coast Castle, Christine Mullen Kreamer argues that concerns that the castles, and particularly the dungeons, be left in their original condition "had less to do with historical accuracy and more to do with a feeling of something old, dark, tragic, and, to some degree, terrifying" (2006, 452). Indeed, not only the dark, dank conditions of the dungeons but also the black stained exterior walls of the castles created a menacing image that many deemed appropriate for a site of mourning.

More serious concerns arose over the inappropriate usages of the castles, including the use of one of the dungeons in Elmina Castle as a gift shop. Planners argued that the room had essentially been used as a warehouse to store goods, but historical evidence showed that it had indeed at one point been used as a dungeon, which was enough for opponents to protest the placement of a gift shop there. Under intense pressure, the gift shop was finally moved to one of the upstairs rooms in the castle.[4] Another controversy involved the placement of a restaurant over the male dungeon in Cape Coast Castle. Planners argued that as a tourist site, the castle should provide visitors with a place to buy refreshments. But opponents noted that the dungeons are equivalent to a cemetery, not an average tourist site, and argued that no one would ever dream of placing a restaurant in the middle of a cemetery.[5] In a story featured in *U.S. News and World Report* about the debate entitled "Africa's Cleaned-up Slave Castle," Nana Okofo Iture Kweku I, a member of the African American community in Ghana, is quoted as saying, "You're going to beautify it and tell my son there was no slavery" (Ransdell 1995, 33).

The debate surrounding this and other issues reached such monumental proportions that in 1994, a conference on the preservation of the castles as well as of a military fort in Elmina was held. Dr. Robert E. Lee, another quite prominent member of the African American community in Ghana, delivered a paper entitled "On the Meaning of the Slave Forts and Castles of Ghana." In it, he argued that Africans in the diaspora, as the descendants of slaves, some of whom passed through the castles, are the most important stakeholders in the matter of the castles' conservation and interpretation:

> These are the people who have a serious interest in the dungeons of the Slave Forts of Ghana. These slave forts are the clear outposts and last place seen before leaving—forever. To these descendants, coming back to Africa through the Slave forts is a necessary act of self realization; a recapturing of the "Lost Soul of Black Folk." It is like lying on the psychiatrist's couch and getting rid of a great burden which has been borne for centuries . . . Even today, the spirits of the diaspora are somehow tied to these historic structures and coming to stand under these forts and experience the feelings of walking in the damp, murky dungeons is a reminder of their ancestors' anguish and despair. (1994, 2–3)

Lee eloquently expressed a view of the castles as sacred space and insisted that they be treated as such, and that they should not, as he feared tourist officials intended, become "disco houses or hotels for fun lovers." He ended by strongly reiterating his view that the castles should be seen as the proper heritage of Africans in the diaspora: "the one deserving the most important consideration at this time is the slave himself; therefore, his/her descendants are the ones that this conference must address and keep in mind as we meet and decide on policy" (1994, 4).

In southern Ghana, where the slave trade invokes forms of discrimination against certain family members and particular regions, and where discussions of race have historically involved the condemnation of "Africans" as an undifferentiated category for their participation in the slave trade, the notion of commemorating the slave trade struck many to be a dangerous proposition. For this reason, several Ghanaian officials sought to reduce the amount of focus on the slave trade in the interpretation of the castles. In one report, they stressed the importance of representing the castles' "total history" and not just the history of the slave trade, noting that the castles "started as trading posts, changed into slave castles and then into administration centers."

An alternative interpretation of the castles as sacred space was addressed during the conference. In the report of the committee on philosophical and historical considerations, committee members listed the following as one of its philosophical considerations: "The Committee views the monuments as places that are 'sacred' places of pilgrimage and high cultural and spiritual importance for Ghanaians, West Africans, and the African diaspora. The centres are not secular and mundane places and should thus be regarded as 'special places' when it comes to the matter of usage" (1994, 1). The committee also recognized the African American diaspora (a telling reduction of the African diaspora to African America), along with the local Ghanaian population, companies, and traditional authorities as important stakeholders in the conservation of the castles. The influence of African Americans in the interpretation of the castles as sacred space proved to be profound.

The committee concluded that the castles should be developed as tourist sites; they should be "an organic museum and not a cemetery." But while they decided that tourism should be encouraged, they agreed that a certain degree of sensitivity must be employed at the castles and that inappropriate activities and usages should be stopped, including the holding of "musical extravaganzas" and the existence of a restaurant above the male dungeon in Cape Coast Castle. They also agreed that the dungeons should be left intact. The committee compromised on the significance of the slave trade at the castles. Some members argued that the castles should be marketed for the slave dungeons. Of particular interest, some committee members noted that highlighting the history of the slave trade could remove the aura of fear that surrounds it in Ghana. The report includes a reference to this fear that states, "There was [*sic*] general concerns that among local Ghanaians and the African diaspora for a long time, the old people have tried to discourage the children from enquiring into the historic past of the slave trade. There was concern that the bitter truth about the past be ascertained, documented, and disseminated" (1994, 4). The effects of this project in the face of opposition will be the topic of the final chapter. Making the castles into sites of pilgrimage in a narrative of slavery, sites to construct the horrors of the slave trade and to envoke the suffering of black people, was conceived of by many African Americans as a prelude to the redemption figured in stories like *Roots*.

While the report expresses hope for what remembering the slave trade might mean for Ghana, the example of the United States should serve to temper it. Today, even more so than in the decades following the airing of *Roots*, slavery is well represented within mainstream films and museums in the United States. Indeed, Ira Berlin argues that "[s]lavery has a greater presence in American life now than at any time since the civil war" (2004, 1251). Many of these representations, however, paint slavery as a closed chapter in

American history. The 2004 film *Amistad* provides a key example. In telling the story of a shipboard slave revolt, it ultimately celebrates the American legal system. Clearly, interest in slavery does not mark a readiness to address the structural nature of racism. Within these arenas, rather, "the renaissance in interest in slavery . . . has become an emblem, sign, and metaphor for the failure to deal directly with the question of race and the long legacy of chattel bondage" (Berlin 2004, 1259). Similarly, in his discussion of the discomfort caused by the Disney Corporation's plans to open an exhibit on slavery, Michel-Rolph Trouillot writes, "To condemn slavery alone is the easy way out . . . What needs to be denounced here to restore authenticity is much less slavery than the racist present within which representations of slavery are produced" (1995, 148). As I argued in part 1, public representations of the slave trade in many ways do not serve the interests of Ghanaians. But neither, of course, do they always serve the interest of African Americans. Commemorating the slave trade is not a sign that a given society has overcome slavery's horrors. Romantic or otherwise Disney-esque representations do not even always participate in the process of such a healing. At the same time, they hold a revolutionary yet rarely realized potential to critique the very foundations of contemporary forms of oppression. For this reason, the commemoration of the slave trade in Ghana has inspired both skepticism and hope. While diaspora tourism, as I discuss in the final section of this chapter, has opened a space for the construction of a protest narrative, many of the narratives told at the castles today are rather romantic narratives of black triumph. A prime example, to which I turn next, is the celebration of Emancipation Day. The highlight of the 1998 celebration was the reinterment of the remains of two slaves named Crystal and Samuel Carson from the United States and Jamaica. What better way to ensure that these conceptualizations take root, planners decided, than through the interment of diasporic bodies.

Little is known of Crystal, an unidentified slave from Jamaica who was given her name because of a crystal found on her body. In contrast, Sonny Carson, a black nationalist figure and community activist in New York, petitioned the U.S. government for permission to move the remains of his great-great-uncle Samuel Carson, who, according to him, became an officer in the United States Navy after he escaped his plantation in South Carolina after the Denmark Vesey rebellion. Sonny led a delegation of thirty individuals to Ghana to accompany the bodies.

The reinterment inscribed new meanings onto various sites in Ghana including Accra, Cape Coast, and Assin Manso, the three sites of the celebration, creating a sacred landscape that was recognized primarily by visitors from the diaspora. The program began in Accra, where the caskets were escorted by ten riders on horseback followed by members of the Ghana actors' guild enacting the march of slaves in chains. The caskets were then laid in state in front of the Nkrumah mausoleum where a vigil was held with performances by bands and traditional musical groups. Holding this event in Accra, and in particular at the Nkrumah Mausoleum, was an attempt to link the celebration of emancipation to the anticolonial struggle and to Ghana's proud status as the first sub-Saharan African nation to achieve independence. In addition, as "Rawlings's holiday," the opening of Emancipation Day at the mausoleum was an attempt to link Rawlings to the tradition of Nkrumah as a hero of Pan-Africanism. But without a clear political agenda, it remained an unconvincing link to many observers.

The next day, the remains were transported from Accra to Cape Coast Castle by sea. They were taken to shore on canoes and then carried through the Door of No Return, a reversal of their imagined departure. For many Africans in the diaspora, this reinterment represented the reestablishment of links between Africa and the diaspora. The physical transplantation of human remains from American soil to African soil was not only symbolic of this reconnection, it represented the achievement of the imagined dream of so many African slaves, to return to their own soil.

The spiritual nature of this reinterment was everywhere evident. One witness reported that as the caskets were being readied to be carried into the castle, they became so heavy that eight men could not lift them. He explains this strange occurrence as follows: "The ancestors resisted mightily . . . until we assured them that they were being returned through the dungeons this time, not taken away" (Kemp 2000, 21). After a ceremony at Cape Coast Castle, the remains were then transported to Assin Manso, the site of the Slave River, where they were finally buried. This river, located several kilometers inland from the coast, is reported to be the last place where slaves in transit to the castles had an opportunity to bathe. As such, it has become an important site in the reconstruction of the slave route in Ghana and is imagined as the last point in which enslaved individuals still held on to some measure of humanity by having the right to bathe before entering the wretchedness that characterized life at the castles and during the Middle Passage.

Now at the annual Emancipation Day celebration, a procession of chiefs walks to the river to perform burial rites, and children perform dancing and drumming while tourists approach the river in turn. At the riverbank, many tourists collect water or sand to carry home with them.

9 Tourists at Emancipation Day event, Assin Manso

This activity underscores the solemnity of the occasion in which the "celebration" of Emancipation takes on a tone more of reflection than of merriment. But the need to entertain tourists has led to certain incongruities from the perspective of tourists, including the Miss Emancipation Day beauty pageant held during the Emancipation Day program of 1999.

During this celebration, a Monument of Return was commissioned at the Assin Manso, and in 2001, a ceremony was held at the newly completed memorial, which consists of paved graves for the two "returnees" as well as an archway announcing the entrance to the path leading to the Slave River. The focus on return is designed to position Emancipation Day as the redemption of all African slaves, to recast the history of the slave trade from one of black wretchedness to one of black triumph. This notion of triumph is particularly evident during the candlelight vigil held at Cape Coast Castle every August 1, when names of important black ancestors on both sides of the Atlantic are read out to the assembled crowd, who sit packed together in the eerie atmosphere of the castle at night, each holding a candle against the encroaching dark. When midnight strikes, an announcer declares emancipation to raucous cheers, thereby celebrating the end of oppression by commemorating the 1834 emancipation of slaves and their own early-twenty-first-century catharsis.

This moment allows diaspora tourists to cast their own bodies in a ro-

10 Entrance to the Slave River, Assin Manso

mantic narrative of black triumph. That August 1, 1834, particularly for African Americans, may not be the date of their specific ancestors' emancipation is of little concern. What matters is that emancipation is part of their history whenever and wherever it occurred. For Ghanaians, however, the emancipation of slaves in the diaspora means little. While the focus on the Slave River turns attention to the suffering of Atlantic slaves prior to their export, the ultimate focus of Emancipation Day is their redemption, which occurred off of the continent. In this way, Emancipation Day marginalizes African experiences and positions Ghana as merely the site of diaspora's birth and baptism into slavery.

In addition to this reduction, within the construction of black diasporic struggle by the tourism industry, southern Ghanaians have at times been placed in a position of blame. During the first PANAFEST, several Ghanaian chiefs gathered in Accra to perform a ceremonial washing of stools and skins, the symbols of chieftaincy in Ghana, and to ask forgiveness for the complicity of their predecessors.

As I discuss in chapter 4, there are certainly many local understandings of slave dealing as wrongdoing and indigenous means of addressing it in West Africa. Most commonly, however, the proper vehicle of expression for this transcript is ritual, a closed, private sphere, not the open, public sphere of discourse. Indeed, the most significant difference between these other examples of ritual acknowledgment of the slave trade and the ceremony that took place during Emancipation Day is that while the meanings of the former may form part of an elite knowledge to which not everyone in the community has access (indeed those in charge of the knowledge may actively block its dissemination outside of the realm of ritual), in the case of the latter, the ceremony was accompanied by public discourses designed to ensure that the public had a clear understanding of its purpose.

In an article in the *Daily Graphic,* the major daily newspaper in Ghana, a tourism official described the purposes of the reinterment, as follows: "The current Ghanaian leadership believes that the pooling of the strength of the over one billion Africans scattered all over the globe is necessary for any meaningful development . . . We can only encourage further these Africans in the Diaspora to join forces with us if we can show remorse for our actions in the guilt of enslaving them. The repatriation and re-interment of these remains would signify our willingness to accept them" (Nunoo 1998, 5). Describing the passing through the Door of No Return, he stated, "This act, as is believed, would reverse all curses pronounced on us Africans by those enslaved African ancestors. But naturally and more physically, it will mean the living African's willingness for the return of all his brothers in the Diaspora. It would symbolize an acceptance of them as brothers and our preparedness to allow them to take part in the future development of this continent" (Nunoo 1998, 5). Not only did the celebration of Emancipation Day create new ritual acknowledgments of African responsibility for the slave trade, but it also placed this blame in the most public of forums, the press. The discourse of African culpability has gained even greater visibility since. There are more plans for chiefs to issues apologies for the slave trade during Emancipation Day in 2007 (see the conclusion). Diaspora tourism has thus opened Ghana up to the risk of the very censure that local demands for silence regarding the slave trade attempt to avoid.

In contrast to discussions of African culpability, during these same years, many African Americans were involved in attempts to hold Western nations accountable. In 1997, members of the United States Congress, led by Tony Hall, proposed the issuance of a formal statement of apology to African Americans on behalf of the U.S. government for slavery. Former president Clinton implied his support for the proposal but later decided to abandon it because of strong public and governmental opposition. But the following year, on his multination trip to Africa, Clinton, speaking in Uganda, stated, "Going back to the time before we were even a nation, European Americans received the fruits of the slave trade . . . and we were wrong in that" (*Washington Post*, March 25, 1998, p. A01). This apparent apology, made on the African continent no less, stirred up much debate back in the United States, upsetting many government officials who no doubt feared that Clinton's apology would lend credence to African American demands for reparations.

Such demands demonstrate the use of the slave trade as a means to talk about oppression in clear-cut racial terms and to argue that racial oppression continues today. The fervent attacks on proposals for reparations and an official apology for slavery demonstrate a reluctance to address this interpretation of the slave trade. Indeed, while George W. Bush condemned slavery as "one of the greatest crimes in history" during a visit to Gorée Island (Berlin 2004, 1254), he did not apologize for the role of the United States in it, again disconnecting present-day problems from this past atrocity and thereby ignoring contemporary white privilege. The threatening nature of the notion of American and European culpability for the slave trade became painfully clear during the United Nations Summit on Racism, Xenophobia, Racial Discrimination, and Related Intolerance, which was held in Durban, South Africa, in 2001. While Germany's foreign minister offered an apology for the slave trade on behalf of the Federal Republic of Germany, other Western nations including the United States refused to follow suit (Constable 2001). The call from both diasporic and continental quarters for reparations during the summit strengthened the narrative of the slave trade as a story of black struggle against white oppression. The reparations discourse represents an example of a discourse about the slave trade that critiques continued Western domination and racial inequalities.

While arguments for reparations have been criticized by some as an unfeasible solution, they usefully provide a narrative of the slave trade as the creation of a system of oppression that has yet to be overcome. These arguments furthermore demonstrate that protest narratives that use the history of the slave trade are not solely the province of black literary figures like Morrison. On the contrary, such narratives have been embraced by a much larger swath of the African American public. During the Emancipation Day celebrations in 2001, which took place during the run-up to the Durban conference, there were many lively discussions in Ghana regarding the idea of reparations for the African continent for the slave trade, and these discussions regularly resurface each year. As a result, they provide an alternative narrative about the slave trade in Ghana that is focused on European culpability for African underdevelopment, recalling Rodney's text. However, as I discuss in the next chapter, such arguments must jockey for position among more dominant narratives that position diasporic triumph at the center of discussion.

Exhibiting the Slave Trade

In contrast to the major focus within the celebration of Emancipation Day on diasporic redemption, other arenas of diaspora tourism have paid greater attention to Ghanaian history. In an attempt to make it more relevant to local residents, the Cape Coast Castle Museum parallels this story with the story of other historical struggles in Ghana. The development of this museum was part of the conservation project at the castles. The Smithsonian Institution in conjunction with the GMMB was charged with transforming the small West African Historical Museum at Cape Coast Castle into a major museum of national and international significance. The Smithsonian team was led by Vera Hyatt and also included Christine Mullen Kreamer, an art historian, and Fath Davis Ruffins from the Smithsonian's National Museum of American History. Despite the leadership of American museum professionals in the project, Hyatt sought to involve Ghanaians heavily in the process. But because Ghana lacked a class of museum professionals, she first had to train them. In 1992, the Smithsonian sponsored five Ghanaians to travel to the United States to train at the Smithsonian in various museum-related fields including architecture, graphic design, and carpentry (Hyatt 1997). James Anquandah, a professor of archaeology at the University of Ghana, Legon, led the content committee.

The committee decided that the main theme of the exhibit would be trade and entitled it "Crossroads of People, Crossroads of Trade," an attempt no doubt to reflect the "long history" of the region that local residents had so feared would be reduced to simply the stigmatizing history of the slave trade. Nonetheless, the final exhibit, which opened in December 1994, revealed the dominance of a narrative about the slave trade, and more specifically, a notably romantic one.

The exhibit has four sections, which cover the early history of Ghana and the coming of the Europeans, the transatlantic slave trade, the African diaspora, and the Central Region today.[6] The first section includes archaeological evidence of Ghana's early history. The early European trade is represented with brass weights used to measure gold and European household items found on the coast. The exhibit then turns to the forts and castles and includes a model of Elmina Castle. In the next section, the slave trade is represented through large murals replicating European observers' depictions of the slave trade. After passing these murals, the visitor enters a small room constructed to resemble the hold of a slave ship, with rough wooden planks on the floor, walls, and ceiling and minimal lighting. An illustration of the packed condition of slaves fills one of the walls. Leaving this room, the visitor steps up onto a raised platform surrounded by ropes. This room is a recreation of a slave auction block. Murals on the walls recreate eighteenth-century town life in the United States, complete with signs announcing the sale of slaves.

Continuing into the next room, the exhibit addresses the African diaspora. Plantation life is represented through photomurals interspersed with pictures of famous African American freedom fighters including Sojourner Truth, Toussaint Louverture, Harriet Tubman, and Frederick Douglass to represent resistance during the slave era. Later freedom struggles are represented by pictures of Marcus Garvey, Malcolm X, Martin Luther King, Jr., and W. E. B. Du Bois. Here, the African diaspora is reduced primarily to the United States. Exhibit text explains this reduction: "The full story of the African Diaspora in North and South America and the Caribbean is too complex to detail in this brief presentation. Consequently, the exhibition focuses on British North America," again reducing the diaspora to African Americans.

Throughout the bulk of the exhibit, the historical narrative is painted as a romantic one of suffering and triumph.[7] Within this story, Africa is merely the source of slaves who suffer through the Middle Passage and plantation life to emerge as the proud community of diaspora blacks, represented almost exclusively by African Americans. However, separately and seemingly incongruently, in one corner of this room, the Ghanaian freedom struggle is represented by pictures of Kwame Nkrumah and the five other men, Danquah, Ofori Atta, Akufo Addo, Obetsebi-Lamptey, and Ako Adjei, known collectively as the Big Six, who are popularly recognized as the primary agitators for independence. Kreamer explains that originally exhibit planners intended to juxtapose the stories of the struggle for freedom in the Americas and Ghana, with greater emphasis placed on Ghana's independence struggle, but they were pressured from a group of African Americans to increase the emphasis on the African diaspora, which now composes 90 percent of this section of the exhibit (Kreamer 2006, 442). The juxtaposition of these histories points again to the idea that the slave trade is not the history of Ghana and that therefore other histories must be told to fill its place.

Following the display of the freedom struggle of African Americans and

Ghanaians is a showcase of the wealth and beauty of the Central Region, focusing heavily upon what are commonly considered to be traditional aspects of culture while minimizing the significance of European influences. It includes a full-size brightly painted fishing boat, a model of an *asafo* shrine, and replications of royal regalia to represent the importance of chieftaincy in this region. For this section, local chiefs, fishermen, *asafo* company members, and shrine priests were consulted in order to ensure that their perspectives were represented in the exhibit. This focus was undoubtedly an attempt to include a section that would resonate with Ghanaians in general and local residents in particular.

As a result, this representation of the Central Region is completely disconnected from the slave trade as it provides no discussion of how it affected the region. Given the dearth of discourses that explore the slave trade in southern Ghana apart from discourses about African responsibility, it seems that there were few stories to be told about the trade that would not further stigmatize the region. Instead, the legacy of the slave trade, as it is in other arenas, is ignored. In its place is a picture of the color, wealth, and pageantry of the Central Region, thereby drawing a romantic conclusion to the story of Ghanaian independence.

Perhaps if the exhibit had focused on the North, it might have addressed the slave trade as part of Ghanaian history. Indeed, in 2001, a temporary exhibit was shown in Cape Coast Castle that highlighted the resistance of the Sankana and Gwelu, two groups in the Upper West region, to the slave trade.[8] It represented this history as the foundation of their pride in their communities. But here too, the romantic tone of the exhibit overlooked the widespread poverty of the North, which along with the history of the slave trade forms an argument not for romance but rather for protest.

In addition to the Cape Coast Castle Museum, a second museum was established in Elmina Castle as part of the conservation and interpretation project. Unlike the Cape Coast Castle Museum, this museum focuses much more on local history and culture. The exhibit, entitled "Images of Elmina across the Centuries," which opened in August 31, 1996, is located in the old Portuguese church, which had at one point been used as a slave auction hall. The exhibit consists of panels that describe different aspects of Elmina including the environment, people, neighbors, culture, trade with Europeans, the impact of European contacts, architectural history, and the Asante at Elmina, who became a sizeable population during the era of Atlantic trade.

This exhibit heavily stresses the effects of the European presence on local culture. Text in the people, neighbors, and culture section states, "Since the late fifteenth century, the Edinas have come under the influence of Europeans who have taught them skills of masonry, carpentry, metalworking, among others. This is reflected in modern technology, which to a large extent follows European models. However, traditional methods that evolved in pre-European times are still practiced among the Edinas and seen in potting, building technology, woodcarving, metal technology, and others." In the impact of European contacts section, the influences considered include formal Western education and the adoption of loan words from European languages such as *brodo* from the Dutch word for bread, *brood*. This section also mentions the introduction of European religions, crops, and judicial systems. Finally, it addresses the development of a multiracial community that continues to have a presence in Elmina today. The exhibit mentions the existence of European surnames such as Viala, Plange, and Duncan in Elmina today as evidence of its multiracial past and features a picture of a contemporary family in Elmina of what would be considered to be light-skinned individuals, apparently as evidence of their mixed-race heritage. The section on architectural history stresses the castles as well as the Dutch merchant homes in Elmina. The slave trade is addressed in the section on trade and includes a display of shackles, but overall, the exhibit stresses European influences on local cultural practices, institutions, and technological skills. In doing so, it portrays the European presence as part of the cosmopolitan identity of Elmina. In this way, the Elmina Castle Museum reflects local constructions of history in which the slave trade is not central. In its celebration of European influences on local culture, it mirrors popular regional histories.

In addition to the Cape Coast Castle Museum and the Elmina Castle Museum, a third museum was developed in 1997 also within Cape Coast Castle. The Building History Museum developed out of a master's thesis on the architectural history of the castle by Seidu Yakubu Goodman, a student in architectural conservation studies at the University of York in England. The development of this museum demonstrates the desire among some members of the GMMB to stress the castle's significance as an architectural marvel. This interpretation appeals to many Ghanaian visitors who visit the castles precisely because of their grandeur and are curious about how they were built. Many European tourists are similarly intrigued by the physical splendor of the castle and the European origins of its design. They approach their visits as they might approach a visit to a historic castle in Europe and appreciate the romantic associations that the notion of a castle conjures, similar to the function of the Save Elmina publications. In this way, they tie the castle to their own heritage as a source of pride and ignore its ignominious history.

Touring the Slave Trade

Tours of the castles are the final and most important arena in which the tourism industry constructs the history of the slave trade. As a result of conservation efforts at the castles, today, both Elmina and Cape Coast castles receive numerous visitors. At Cape Coast Castle, visitation rose from nine thousand visitors in 1992 to almost 30,000 visitors in 1995. These visitors include both domestic and international tourists. In 2000, Cape Coast Castle received 34,871 visitors. Out of these, 10,219 were international visitors and 24,652 were Ghanaian visitors (Visitor Record, Cape Coast Castle). Elmina castle has visitation numbers as high as 100,000 (recorded for 2000), although visitation rates tend to be closer to those of Cape Coast Castle. It also has a similar demographic breakdown. Generally speaking then, domestic tourists represent approximately 70 percent of all visitors to the castles, and international tourists make up the remaining 30 percent.

GHANAIAN VISITORS

Ghanaian visitors consist largely of school groups. For instance, out of the 24,652 Ghanaian visitors to Cape Coast Castle in 2000, 14,758 were children, SSS students, and university students, which amounts to approximately 60 percent of domestic tourists (Visitor Record, Cape Coast Castle). In Cape Coast and Elmina, virtually all students visit the slave castles, and most do so numerous times over the course of their educational career. Many teachers in other regions also take their classes on field trips to the castles, often traveling long distances to visit these sites. Other Ghanaian visitors to the Central Region, often on day trips from Accra and other nearby cities, take advantage of the opportunity to do some sightseeing, and at the top of their lists are the castles. Because one of the major reasons for travel in Ghana is to attend funerals, large groups of mourners can frequently be seen in the castles, often still in their funeral clothes. Local residents, other than students, rarely visit the castles unless they are accompanying out-of-town

11 School girls on tour at Cape Coast Castle

friends or relatives. The continued lack of local interest despite the fact that the castles have become major tourist sites is fairly typical of tourist sites throughout the world. In Washington, D.C., for instance, residents rarely visit the Capitol and the National Monument, and New York residents rarely visit the Statue of Liberty.

The majority of domestic tourists view the castles as ordinary tourist sites. Indeed, a typical day trip to the Central Region includes visits to one or both castles as well as a visit to Kakum National Park to walk over the rope bridges that hang suspended high above the forest floor. Most of these tourists equate visiting the castles to visiting the park, as recreational activities and regional attractions. Thus, upon entering the castles, Ghanaian visitors appear to have little sense that they may be embarking upon an emotionally trying experience. On the contrary, as stated above, many visitors stated that their interest in the castles stemmed from their massive size and beauty. They are often interested in the castles as architectural marvels worthy of admiration and not as sites of historical trauma. Ghanaian tourists therefore frequently approach the castles in a festive mood. As I discuss below, this attitude is quickly challenged by some of the tour guides who are pointedly concerned with transforming Ghanaian attitudes toward the slave trade and creating an awareness of its gravity.

DIASPORA TOURISTS

According to estimates, 10,000 African Americans visit Ghana each year (Zachary 2001), which if accurate suggests that they constitute approximately 12 percent of all recreational tourists, a significant percentage of the tourism market. The importance of this segment of the tourist market is noted in the *Tourism Development Plan for the Central Region,* which states, "A special interest market for the Central Region are African-Americans whose ancestors originated in West Africa and were sent overseas from the slave-trading castles and forts along the Ghana coast. Sometimes called Roots Tourism, this specialized tourist market has already commenced to develop in Ghana and the Central Region" (Ministry of Tourism 1996, 41).

For these tourists, the castles are sacred space, and their visits to them are often imagined as a pilgrimage. In writing about an African American heritage tour to Gorée Island, a similar departure point for slaves in Senegal, Ebron similarly describes tourists as pilgrims. She notes that the site "resonated with an already strong African American 'structure of feeling'" (1999, 923). She describes the group's approach to the slave fort: "The walk from the ferry provided several apprehensive moments and perhaps even a sense of awe brought about by the meeting of the myths of our American home with the material site, the slave fort, the place where it all began" (1999, 921).

For many diaspora tourists, Cape Coast and Elmina castles are similar sites of memory and mourning, places in which they recall the horrors of the slave trade. They are Pierre Nora's (1994) quintessential *lieux de mémoire,* or sites of memory. Nora argues that *lieux de mémoire* exist "[w]here memory crystallizes and secretes itself at a particular historical moment, a turning point where consciousness of a break with the past is bound up with the sense that memory has been torn—but torn in such a way as to pose the problem of the embodiment of memory in certain sites where a sense of historical continuity persists" (1994, 284). The forced migration of their ancestors represents a great tear in the fabric of memory for Africans in the diaspora, and returning to the site of their departure is an attempt to find a site for the embodiment of memory (see also Davis 1997).

Through their visits to the castles, these tourists seek to construct the atrocities of the slave trade. Such an objective, while hardly conforming to common notions of tourism as a quest for pleasure, is similar to the aim of Jewish Holocaust tourism (see Kugelmass 1994). Tourism that involves exploring historical atrocities has gained popularity because of its role in constructions of diasporic identity.

On Tour at Cape Coast Castle

In his article, "Tourism in Ghana: The Representation of Slavery and the Return of the Black Diaspora," Edward Bruner (1996) explores the differences between African American and Ghanaian interpretations of Elmina Castle's significance. He argues that while African Americans view the castle as part of the legacy of slavery that must be preserved, most Ghanaians "are not particularly concerned with slavery" (1996, 292). Furthermore, he argues that Ghanaians disagree with African Americans' emotionalism, stating that "[f]rom a Ghanaian perspective, they become almost 'too emotional,' suggesting that Ghanaians do not understand the feelings of diaspora blacks" (1996, 293). In this way, he presents a radical dichotomy between the views of African Americans and Ghanaians. While colonialism did not lead Ghanaians to resent whites, he argues, the experience of slavery and racism in the United States has led African Americans to harbor a great deal of resentment toward them. While Bruner provides a useful opening to the study of visitor reactions to the castles I have argued that Ghanaians attempt to marginalize the slave trade not because they are untroubled by this history. On the contrary, I argue that they are greatly preoccupied with it, preoccupied more specifically with its stigmatizing effects. As a result, their responses to castles vary, depending upon the narrative structure of the story of the slave trade with which they are presented.

I gleaned these responses through my participation in over fifty tours at both Elmina and Cape Coast castles. On these tours, I not only observed the tour guides' presentations but also paid close attention to the responses of the visitors. I also often interviewed visitors after the tours in order to learn more about their reactions. The structure of each tour varied depending on the tour guide and the audience. Tour guides altered their presentations significantly according to whether the audience was composed of whites, Ghanaians, or blacks from the diaspora. On tours, particular areas within the castles were, as I discuss below, crucial sites in which differences between African American and Ghanaian perceptions of history became apparent.[9]

Upon entering Cape Coast Castle, visitors buy their tickets, and then, if the tour is not yet ready to begin, they are directed to one or both of the museums. Once the tour begins, visitors gather around the entrance of the

12 Entrance to the male slave dungeon, Cape Coast Castle

male slave dungeon, where the tour guide proceeds to explain the origins of the castle and its use during the slave trade.

SORROWFUL SPACE

At the entrance of the male slave dungeon, a plaque reads,

> IN EVERLASTING MEMORY
> Of the anguish of our ancestors.
> May those who died rest in peace.
> May those who return find their roots.
> May humanity never again perpetuate
> Such injustice against humanity.
> We, the living, vow to uphold this.

Before visitors enter the dungeon, they are reminded that they are about to enter a site of sorrow. The plaque suggests that they approach the dungeon as they would a cemetery. It also stresses the importance of this site to Africans in the diaspora as "those who return." Visitors enter the male slave dungeon by walking down a steep tunnel into a dark underground chamber. Small windows located high above the dungeon floor provide the faintest

13 Inside male slave dungeon, Cape Coast Castle

light. While electric lighting has been added in order to allow visitors to see, when the tour guide flips the switch to turn them off, tourists are engulfed in darkness just as the captives once were.

A distinctively unpleasant smell fills this dark space that tour guides often remark is the smell of the blood, sweat, feces, and corpses that rotted for centuries in this place, which is also, they explain, the substance on which we are standing. Up to 1,000 men were kept in this space, the guides explain, often stressing the horror of their living in their own waste.

Both Ghanaian and African American tourists exhibit shock, horror, and sadness at the site of the dungeons. Indeed, I witnessed many visitors crying on tours of the castles. But along with sadness, many African American tourists experience intense anger. Tour guides at both castles often tell tales of African Americans becoming enraged on tours and occasionally attempting to attack white tourists. Bruner similarly describes such attacks and the desire, as one woman stated after visiting the castle, "to go out and strangle a white person" (1996, 296). In contrast, a great number of Ghanaian visitors exhibit little or no anger in response to the dungeons. These visitors are able to maintain a critical distance from this history, suggesting that, as

I discuss further in the next chapter, even when confronted with the horrors of the slave trade, they do not identify with its victims, viewing it instead as the history of others.

SACRED SPACE

As stated above, most African American tourists approach the castles as sacred space. Before ever setting foot within the castles, they have reflected upon their special nature and have prepared themselves mentally and emotionally to enter them. Renée Kemp, an African American television news reporter, wrote an article about her experience visiting the castles while on assignment in Ghana. She recounts a comment made by another African American whom she told she was going to the castle. He warned her, "Get ready . . . Sometimes the spirits there are very active" (2000, 21). Many visitors collect dirt from the dungeon floor, as they do at Assin Manso, in order to possess a remnant of the past. Their desire to possess a piece of the dungeons is a testament to the role of monuments in both containing memories of the past and providing a route to those memories. The possession of soil from the dungeons is also a statement of their having borne witness to this past and their insistence on never forgetting it. To this end, the soil is sometimes used in their own spiritual ceremonies.[10]

The sacred aspect of the castles is highlighted on the tour at the Nana Tabir shrine, which occupied the third room of the dungeons. A sign announces that the shrine is there in honor of the "ancestors" who passed through the dungeons. The fact that the shrine preceded the slave trade is not stressed; rather, tourists are told that the shrine's priest who is almost always standing by, will pour libations in honor of those slaves who died. Most African American tourists agree to the brief ceremony and appear to appreciate the spiritual component of the tour. The few words spoken by the priest, in Fante, but translated loosely by the tour guide, and the simple pouring of libations reinforces their construction of the visit to the castle as a pilgrimage. It imparts a spiritual component, which is deemed necessary to any true pilgrimage. But while African American tourists appreciate the spiritual nature of this ceremony, they experience it at a distance. First, because it takes place in Fante, the notion of the ceremony as something foreign is underscored. In addition, tourists are asked to donate money afterwards, which most do gladly, suggesting that they retain a sense of themselves as tourists, or spectators of a religious spectacle, rather than as participants in a religious practice. Thus, African American visitors accept the shrine as

14 Nana Tabir shrine inside male slave dungeon, Cape Coast Castle

clearly something that lies outside of their own spiritual frameworks but that they can accept as part of a Ghanaian spiritual framework, with which they hope to establish a relationship neither as voyeurs nor as adherents.

In contrast, Ghanaian visitors have dramatically different responses to the shrine. While African Americans simply embrace the shrine as part of a religious tradition other than their own, many Ghanaians, particularly Pentecostal Christians, are highly disturbed by it. Pentecostal churches, which are quite popular in southern Ghana, not only demand that their followers reject indigenous religions, they also describe in great detail the evils that these religions represent. Indeed, traditional priests are widely viewed to be powerful and dangerous figures. Meyer (1998) notes that, for this reason, Pentecostal Christianity in Ghana demands "a complete break with the past." Thus, when unsuspecting Pentecostal Ghanaian visitors encounter the priest at the castle, they are disturbed and often frightened. On one tour with a small group of sss girls, when the girls reached the doorway and spotted the shrine, they stopped cold and stood frozen in place with fear, refusing to enter the room. On another tour, a teacher accompanying a group of jss students from Kumasi also seemed to be quite frightened of the priest and asked the tour guide, "Is he very powerful?"

Needless to say, the priest did not pour libations for these visitors. Oftentimes, tour guides do not bother to ask Ghanaian visitors if they want the priest to do so for them, anticipating their response in the negative. Tour guides assume their discomfort with the shrine and explain its presence by stating that it is there to welcome back Africans in the diaspora. On one tour of JSS students from the Western Region, one of the teachers accompanying them asked, "Why do you choose this traditional method to welcome them home?" The tour guide responded that this was the way they were worshipping before they were taken away. The teacher then asked, "What if someone returns who is a Christian?" thereby stressing the shrine's incompatibility with Christianity. The tour guide conceded that a Christian from the diaspora probably would not like seeing the shrine, but he attempted to assuage the group's discomfort with the shrine by suggesting that it was there for African Americans alone and not for Ghanaians, the implication being that naturally it does not fit within their perception of a Ghanaian (read: Christian) religious framework.

The irony here is astounding. The shrine's meaning has undergone numerous reinscriptions. Not only is it a traditional shrine that was only replaced within the castle in 1979, but it has become part of the tourism industry's representation of Ghanaian culture to Africans in the diaspora. But the shrine's meaning is reinscribed a third time by Ghanaians who reject the incorporation of the shrine as part of their religious tradition, which leads tour guides to suggest that its significance derives from the meanings that African Americans, not Ghanaians, attach to it. Thus, during castle tours and outside of its official clan usages, the shrine is a site of the contestation of different identities. Africans Americans embrace the shrine and through it imagine a connection to "traditional African religion," while Ghanaians assert the strength of their Christian faith by rejecting the same.

NATIONAL SPACE

After viewing the shrine, visitors travel back up out of the dungeon and into the bright light of the courtyard. They are shown the three marked graves in the courtyard, those of colonial Governor George Maclean, Letitia Landon, his wife, and the African minister, Philip Quaque. The graves are another site of contestation. For Ghanaians, particularly schoolchildren, the graves recall popular historic figures. George Maclean and Philip Quaque are names that they have heard repeatedly in their classrooms. But not only are these individuals familiar, they are also celebrated national heroes. Tour guides discuss George Maclean in particular in highly favorable terms. They stress that he was fair and honest and that local people truly admired him, recalling the manner in which school textbooks describe him. Thus, for Ghanaian visitors, the graves, unlike much of the rest of the tour, introduce an aspect of their history with which they are quite familiar. Situated on the tour in between the male dungeons and the female dungeons, both places that introduce a history that they find for the most part new and shocking, the familiarity and positive nature of the history that the graves represent is a pleasant divergence, again pointing to the idea what while the slave trade is the property of the African diaspora, Ghana has other histories.

Many African Americans, on the contrary, have radically different reactions to the graves. Most know nothing of any of the figures buried there before entering the castle but upon learning that two of the graves belong to Europeans, become automatically disturbed to see the preservation and representation of the history of the Europeans who lived in the castles. On one tour that I observed with two African American women, at Maclean's grave one of the women asked, "What was so special about him?" Her anger was barely contained at having to stand at the gravesite of the European governor. The tour guide, aware of her resentment from having just emerged from the male slave dungeon, tried to explain that Maclean was governor after the slave trade had ended and that he ordered the tunnel in the male slave dungeon to be sealed and furthermore tried to convince the local people to stop trading in slaves. He added that Maclean brought the British legal system to Ghana and arbitrated cases with respect for traditional legal practices, and as a result, he was beloved by the local people and his name became a household word. Both women became very quiet after the tour guide's explanation, but they clearly were angered by the representation of European benevolence within a site that they construct as one of the greatest examples of European brutality. By the end of the tour, both women were in tears.

For many African American tourists, the placement of the graves on the tour after the male dungeons increases their indignation with any discussion of Europeans, but particularly with one that presents them in a favorable light. The contrast between the mounds of dirt and filth within the dungeons that represent the only graves of the slaves who died in the castle with these neat, well-marked graves serves to heighten their anger and disgust. Also, the ropes surrounding the graves and the tour guides' attention to the personalities buried there suggest to them a level of respect that many find difficult to accept. Naana Ocran, the museum educator, explained to me that African Americans "do not like to hear that whites were friendly with some of the Africans" but said that she feels it is important to "tell them the truth." Some African Americans feign stomping and spitting on the graves, although out a sense of respect for rules of proper deportment, most refrain from actually doing so. Nonetheless, through their performance of disrespectful acts, African American visitors seek to signify their disgust for Europeans who lived at the castle. This performance stands in complete opposition to their performance of solemnity in the dungeons, and the contrast between the two serves to heighten the significance of each.

After stopping at the graves, visitors pass over the rampart, which is lined with cannons facing the sea, ready to attack interlopers. The rampart passes over the tunnel from the male slave dungeon.[11] At the end of the rampart, visitors are shown the doorway from which male slaves emerged, near the entrance to the female slave dungeons. There are two separate rooms in which female captives were kept. They are not underground but are equally dank and disturbing. There is also a small room next to one of the dungeons that we are told held women who were disobedient, who possibly refused rape, and who were kept in solitary confinement as punishment. The female slave dungeons evoke similar emotions as the male slave dungeons, with the added horror of the discussion of rape, which I discuss further later in this chapter.

DIASPORIC SPACE

Immediately outside of the female slave dungeons is a set a huge wooden double doors with a sign above them that proclaims that it is the "Door of No Return." Here is where, visitors are told, slaves departed the castle to board slave ships, leaving Africa for the last time, never to return. The tour guide opens the doors, and visitors are invited to walk outside, where they find a small beach and a bustle of activity, men mending fishing nets, children swimming in the ocean, and women relaxing and fanning infants. Here tour guides explain that during the first Emancipation Day celebrations, the remains of two diaspora slaves were brought back to Ghana and were taken through this door, in a reversal of their original journey out of Africa, to Assin Manso, the site along the slave route where captives had their last bath. Here the remains of the two slaves were reburied. Now, above the entryway back into the castle, the words "Door of Return" are painted in bright colors. Both African American and Ghanaian visitors are told that today, when we exit the Door of No Return, we can return again and that

15 Door of Return, Cape Coast Castle

the Door of Return is meant "to welcome our brothers and sisters in the diaspora home" and to let them know that they should see Ghana "as a gateway to the rest of Africa."

African American visitors often applaud at this point in the tour. It represents the climax of the tour; after the demoralizing experience of the dungeons, the Door of Return brings a redemptive quality to the story of enslavement. Their "return" to the castle itself becomes a triumph over the ghastly history of slavery that they have just imagined. The Door of Return, similar to the shrine, is represented to Ghanaian tourists as mostly of interest to African Americans. During one tour, the tour guide told a group of JSS students that if they know any African Americans, they should tell them to come back home.

For diaspora tourists, the tour often ends soon after the Door of No Return. Back inside the castle, visitors pass storerooms that were used to store nonhuman commodities. They then come to the condemned cell, where pirates and unruly slaves who had been condemned to death were kept. The room is small and cramped, and when the door is shut, there is no light. The guides explain that prisoners were simply kept in this room with no food or water until they perished. Many prisoners could be kept in the room at the same time, and the guards waited until all of them had died to open the door and remove the bodies; thus, living prisoners were kept with rotting corpses.

The condemned cell invokes some of the strongest emotional responses from visitors. The images of dying prisoners and the barbarity of their deaths invoke shock and grief in most visitors, and therefore the condemned cell is included on all tours. Other parts of the castle are, however, frequently omitted from the tour for diaspora tourists. Tour guides explained to me that African Americans are not interested in seeing the governor's quarters and often become angry if this part of the castle is included on tours. The upper floors of the castles are often omitted from Ghanaians' tours as well, although if tour guides feel that they are interested in seeing the rest of the castle, they will take them through the upper levels. These floors, however, are always included on tours for white Americans and Europeans. Tour guides take them through the governor's large apartment, which now stands empty, but which they can imagine once held fine furnishings. There are also wonderful views of the town and the ocean from up here, and tourists often pause to take in the view and snap pictures.

For African American tourists, however, their tours focus heavily on the slave dungeons and the story of the slaves that were kept there, their departure from the castle, and the tourists' own return, cast as a redemption of those enslaved individuals themselves, creating a romantic narrative that again positions their own bodies as markers of a black triumph. Tours are thus structured to position the history of the slave trade within a narrative of diasporic overcoming. Once again, Ghanaians are largely omitted from the story.

On Tour at Elmina Castle

Despite the institutionalization of a romantic narrative at the castles, tour guides themselves may challenge it and provide alternative accounts of the slave trade. In addition to the senior tour guides, many of the guides are sss graduates fulfilling their national service requirements. Because they are largely young people who often through individual research have become experts in the history of the slave trade, they are a unique group. Rather than being limited to the scant information provided about the trade in school textbooks, many of them have read widely from an international body of scholarship on the slave trade. Of special significance to the story, many have read Rodney's *How Europe Underdeveloped Africa,* which is now on sale at the castle. Additionally, they regularly gain knowledge from conversations with diaspora visitors who often bring with them a great depth of knowledge about the slave trade. In this way, they are part of an "Afro-Atlantic dialogue" of which diaspora tourism is the catalyst but which it does not necessarily control. In what follows, I present one specific tour that I observed at Elmina Castle in order to discuss how the tour guide refashioned the narrative of the slave trade from the diasporic romance story that has become conventionalized within diaspora tourism to one of protest.

Felix was one of my favorite tour guides at Elmina castle. Not only is he well versed in the history of the slave trade, having read extensively on the subject, but he also regularly engages international and, in particular, African diasporic dialogues about the trade. He closely followed, for instance, the media coverage of the United Nations summit discussion of the slave trade and reparations. As a result of his expansive knowledge, he was particularly interested in conveying the ways in which Ghanaians were and continue to be affected by the slave trade. Therefore, he takes his role as an educator quite seriously. I often observed Felix's tours, which always provided a cutting critique of Europeans and stressed the inhumanity of the slave trade.

One day, Felix gave a tour to a group of Ghanaian university students. The tour, as always, began in the central courtyard, just beyond the entrance to the castle. The students gathered around Felix as he opened the tour. He began with a discussion of early European perceptions of Africa, European expansion into the New World, and the resultant need for slave labor. He explained that the first Europeans came to Africa as missionaries and traders in commodities and used the castle rooms as storehouses, but with the development of the slave trade, those same rooms were converted into dungeons.

Unlike at Cape Coast Castle, the tour at Elmina Castle proceeds first to the female slave dungeons. In the dungeons, an unpleasant stench is still present. Felix explained that two hundred people were kept in each small cramped room, which drew a response of exclamations of disbelief from the students, their shock and horror at the treatment of these slaves was quite apparent. The entire area around the female slave dungeons provides a unique opportunity for a discussion of the particular treatment of enslaved women. The female slave dungeons surround a small courtyard paved in stone. Two circular indentations are noticeable on the stone floor of the courtyard. Felix explained that these indentations were made from cannon balls to which "unruly women" were chained. As their punishment, they were forced to stand all day chained in the courtyard, unable to move, under the intense glare of the sun.

What Felix described next, however, was the most significant part of his discussion of female slaves. He pointed out the balcony that overlooks the courtyard and explained that it was the governor's balcony. Every so often, all of the women in the dungeons were assembled in the courtyard as the governor stood above them. He would then choose one woman from among them, and that woman was taken by the guards, bathed with water from a cistern in the courtyard, and taken up a staircase that leads from the court-yard, through a trap door, and into the governor's quarters.

As Felix described the governor's selection of women, a female student remarked, "First Lady!" which drew a round of laughter from the group. This laughter indexes the marginal nature of the slave trade within the Gha-naian historical consciousness. The rape of black women is a common trope of oppression among African Americans and draws the strongest emotional reactions perhaps of any of the horrifying facts of slavery because it power-fully exemplifies not only the complete dehumanization of enslaved people who did not have power over their own bodies but also the special vulner-ability of black women. It is not, however, recognized as such in Ghana. On the contrary, the students believed that the governor's selection of a woman was not for the purpose of rape but rather in order to establish a relationship with her and perhaps even to marry her. Their laughter illustrated a percep-tion not of women's greater vulnerability but rather of their greater access to power through their potential sexual relationships with European men. In this way, their reaction reflects the fact that during the Atlantic trade, many local women gained wealth and status through their relationships with Eu-ropean men (see chapter 1). But also, the laughter of the students attests to the lack of solemnity that the slave trade evokes. Because it has so small a role in Ghanaian public discourse, there is no sense of what would consti-tute an appropriate or inappropriate response to its discussion. Whereas the deportment of African American tourists within the castles attests to the demands of their historical consciousness for a posture of solemnity to address the topic of the slave trade, Ghanaian historical consciousness re-quires no such comportment.

Felix addressed this remark by elaborating on these relationships and ex-plaining that although some African women married European merchants and became prominent figures, this was not the case for the women in the castle.[12] He also noted that this was rape and not love and pointed out that these actions violated the very Christian ethics that most Europeans traders on the coast espoused. Finally, he added that the Europeans brought many diseases to Africa through these encounters. He concluded that there are two sides of the coin and said, "I leave you to make your judgment." He framed all of these points as different scholarly opinions, thus allowing him to take an impartial stance while simultaneously giving the condemnation of these rapes scholarly backing. The students responded to his presentation by immediately adopting a more solemn air.

We then went through the male slave dungeon to the Door of No Return. There, Felix quoted a description by a European observer of the conditions of the slaves in an attempt to bring to life the experiences of the enslaved. This description succeeded in invoking a response of horror and disgust from the students. Felix also returned to historiography to cite the theory that slavery is a global phenomenon that has included the Hebrews and ancient Greece and Rome as well as Africa. He then explained that slavery within Africa took a very different form from slavery in the Americas because in the case of the former, slaves could become incorporated into the families of their owners. He also told the students that in the beginning of transatlantic slave trade, Europeans raided African villages, but they soon began soliciting the aid of African chiefs by forming alliances with them. Some chiefs, he noted, even gave the Europeans their own children, supposedly to be educated in Europe. He discussed the role of guns and alcohol in the slave trade and then stated that Africans often traded "old cups, old knives, chamber pots, matches" for people, in order to emphasize the denigration of human life involved—that people could be equated with these inconsequential things. He also explained that the British and Dutch often incited internal rivalries in order to spark wars for which they supplied arms so that they could then take the prisoners from each side as slaves. Felix in this way argued that they were responsible for establishing the order in which Africans were ensnared. He carefully made the history of the slave trade relevant to Africans by constructing it as a story of their entrapment within a global system reaching far beyond the realm in which they might have agency.

We then passed the Portuguese church. Because of Felix's efforts to communicate the evil of the slave trade, the placement of a church within the castle struck the students as ironic. One asked, "What could they be preach-

16 Door of No Return, Elmina Castle

ing in there?" which this time drew not laughter but rather sighs and expressions of indignation from the group. The mood had clearly shifted from the lighthearted one of a few moments earlier to a gloomy pensiveness.

After having referenced it indirectly several times, at the end of the tour, Felix cited Rodney's thesis in his book, *How Europe Underdeveloped Africa* (1982), explicitly. He explained that when Europeans arrived in Africa, Africans were forced into a colonial trade with them, providing people and other primary products (raw goods) in exchange for secondary products (manufactured goods). He then asked, "And what do we trade today? Primary products." As I discuss in chapter 5, Rodney is largely responsible for the reformulation of the slave trade as part of a protest narrative whose effects continue to be felt today rather than as the basis of portrayals of "savage Africa." Felix's use of Rodney is fitting given his desire to tie the history of the slave trade to contemporary problems *in Africa* rather than presenting it as being simply about the creation of the African diaspora.

Felix then began to explain, "So, in the past it was primary products, in the present it is primary products," at which point someone interjected, "In future it will be primary products!" The mood had shifted again, this time to a strange mix of jocularity and pessimism, a puzzling combination, although one that I often encountered in Ghana. It derives from the same set of emotions that compels nervous laughter. It is a response to the recognition of the tragic nature of existence.

Felix responded, "Well, the future depends on the present. When we hear about Africa today, what do we hear about? Poverty, ignorance, war . . ." in this way, acknowledging the cause of the students' melancholy. He encouraged them, however, not to accept this state of affairs but rather to work to change it, in this way transforming pessimism into inspiration, seeing tragedy as the basis for protest. He then concluded by stating simply that we must learn from the past, which raised a round of applause from the group.

During his hour-long tour, Felix succeeded in altering the ways in which these students thought about the slave trade. While they began the tour with little understanding of the horrific nature of the trade, they ended the tour not only understanding its horror but also gaining a perspective on the importance of this history to an understanding of contemporary global inequalities. For them, as for many Ghanaian visitors, the tour represented a process of transformation of their historical consciousnesses toward, as I discuss more fully in the following chapter, the formulation of a protest narrative.

7 » *Navigating New Histories*

In 1996, the Ghanaian poet Kwadwo Opoku-Agyemang published a collection of poems devoted to Cape Coast Castle. In doing so, he sought to subvert common practices of sequestering the slave trade in Ghana. In one of these poems, he notes the silence that surrounds the slave trade in Ghana. He writes,

> Too many sad stories are lost to stain
> In the castle's cracks and leaning turrets
> Too long have I stood silent in the shadows
> Where people got carried away by the bargain
> I am waiting, will till freed
> And our memory cleared of weed. (1996, 14)

History in Ghana is indeed thick with weeds. The men and women whom I have described in the preceding pages must sojourn through a tangle of discourses about the slave trade in an attempt to construct family, regional, and national histories. They are constantly wary of the sharp thorns that tear at their identities from multiple directions. They have learned to stay on clearly marked paths in order to avoid emerging with the burrs of perversion, savagery, and depravity attached to them. This is certainly no stroll down memory lane.

Diaspora tourism, however, charts a different course that charges through largely unknown territory. So what happens when Ghanaians encounter this new path? Do they steer well clear of it, or do they soldier through? And if they take this path, are they pricked by history, or do they manage to clear their memory of its weeds?

In truth, the path has not been made clear. Many of the Ghanaians who have participated in diaspora tourism continue to view the commemoration of the slave trade as a dangerous road to go down. They often contest both the centering of the slave trade and the imagined geography of diaspora and homeland that it produces. They keep on following the signposts that direct them away from the slave trade, and in this way they actively disengage with this history. For others, however, particularly educated youth, the slave trade has become fodder for their formulation of protest narratives. They have begun to embrace this history in ways that challenge conventional narratives of family, region, and nation, and in doing so, they embrace a black Atlantic identity. They do so not by adopting diaspora tourism's romantic narratives wholesale, but rather by refashioning them in order to create a new route that can connect their past to the future. I argue then, with apologies to Robert Frost, that for educated youth in Ghana today, two roads diverge in the construction of history. Embracing the slave trade remains, however, the one less traveled. In what follows, I discuss the reactions of Ghanaians who have been exposed to diaspora tourism to both the slave trade and to the notion of a transnational black community. My starting point, however, is on the other side of this road. I begin with the African diaspora.

Well-Seasoned Travelers

As I discussed in chapter 6, for diaspora tourists, the castles are sites of pilgrimage that evoke the horrors of the slave trade and the suffering and struggle of black people. While the tourism industry encourages them to view these pilgrimages as a prelude to the redemption figured in stories like *Roots*, for most diaspora tourists, they seem to function instead as a key element in the construction of a protest narrative, an African diasporic tradition that includes Morrison's *Beloved* and the reparations movement. Gilroy, who calls this tradition a counterculture of modernity, finds further examples of its articulation within black music. He argues that black love songs in particular "preserve and cultivate both the distinctive rapport with the presence of death which derives from slavery and a related ontological state that I want to call the condition of being in pain" (1993, 203). As a result of their emplacement within this tradition, diaspora tourists are primed for what they encounter in the slave dungeons. When they enter the dungeons, it is almost as if it is not their first time. They have been down this road before and are well-seasoned travelers.

Diaspora tourists respond to the dungeons with oftentimes intense emotional reactions, suggesting that they are recalling crucial yet exceedingly painful collective memories that are already deeply engrained in their historical imaginations. This connection is expressed through bodily practices during commemorative ceremonies and in the castles, including weeping, standing silently and solemnly, and sometimes flaring into anger. They are also quite adept at narrating the experience of their encounter with these memories, often with great feeling and eloquence. This encounter resonates not only, as Ebron notes (1999, 2002), with a "structure of feeling" but also with an existing structure of discourse. Indeed, many African Americans and other members of the African diaspora have documented the experience of visiting the castles in newspaper editorials, journal articles, films, and books (see especially Gerima 1993; Hartman 2007; Phillips 2000; Richards 2005). The emplacement of the castles in a tradition of such narrations dates back at least to Richard Wright's visit in the 1950s. In his book *Black Power,* he describes the "awe-inspiring battlements of the castle with its somber but resplendent majesty" and reflects on the images that the dungeons conjure, writing,

> A tiny pear-shaped tear that formed on the cheek of some black woman torn away from her children, a tear that gleams here still, caught in the feeble rays of the dungeon's light—a shy tear that vanishes at the sound of approaching footsteps, but reappears when all is quiet, a tear that was hastily brushed off when her arm was grabbed and she was led toward those narrow, dank steps that guided her to the tunnel that directed her feet to the waiting ship that would bear her across the heaving, mist-shrouded Atlantic. (1954, 341–42, quoted in Bruner 1996, 292)

Many tourists with whom I spoke provided similar descriptions of the castles. The castles are sites in which they imagine the slave trade in all of its gruesome detail. Violet is a seventy-two-year-old woman originally from Jamaica who now lives in Florida. Recounting the first time she entered the dungeons, she said,

> My very first step down, I felt a sort of queasiness, and my hair rose up on my head and a shiver went through my body. And I can't put the rest

into words, I just can't . . . I felt that I could hear the moaning. I could hear the moaning and I could see the filth and I could smell it. And it's not until now that I want to cry. I didn't want to cry then, but now I want to cry. How in the world could human beings survive something like that? I think that's when I really felt what they must have felt. (Holsey 2004, 172)

Visitors are often assaulted by the presence of spirits through sound, smell, or even sight. Indeed, the sensory experience of the dungeons, which dominates their descriptions, seems to bring an experiential knowledge of what transpired in these spaces.

In addition to sensing the spirits of the dungeons, many visitors also experience an intense sense of identification with the captives once held there, as if the visitors have slipped into their place (see also Richards 2005). Violet expressed this feeling, stating, "I could feel the flesh falling from my body." In this way, she suggests that her physical presence in the dungeons allowed her not just to imagine the past but to almost experience it herself, in the same way that the main character in the film *Sankofa* is transported back in time and space into slavery in the Americas as a result of venturing into the slave dungeons. She describes the necessity of her empathic experience: "Maybe because I wanted to feel a little more of what my ancestors suffered. It wasn't pleasant, it was horrible." Thus, for her, imagining the emotions of the dungeons' captives is a painful but important act of self-realization. Similarly, Ella, a middle-aged African American repeat visitor to Ghana, expressed her sense of pride that arose from the ability of her ancestors to survive their enslavement:

I was overwhelmed at first and very saddened by the fact, but I came away with strength! I came away with strength knowing that if my ancestors, if I survived all that through my ancestors, I'm a very strong person. I came from a very strong stock to have survived the capture and the entrapment and the dungeon and being taken through the middle passage and another four hundred some years through just abject poverty and beaten. I mean, I survived all that, and I can claim all that? I am so strong! Nobody in this world can claim [that they are] stronger that I am. And that's what I went away with, with a sense of strength. And my daughter said too, we analyzed, and my daughter said they're the strongest of the strong, they're the strongest of the strong. And if my ancestors can survive that, certainly I can survive what I'm going through no matter what it is. I have no excuse. None. (Holsey 2004, 172–73)

I discuss the content of Ella and Violet's statements elsewhere (Holsey 2004) and note in particular that the purpose of their collapsing of the experience is clear: in claiming the strength of those who survived slavery as their own, they arm themselves to battle their own personal experiences of racism. It leads them to believe that they too can survive. Such is particularly true for middle-class, educated individuals, many of whom not only see members of their own families continuing to suffer but who have also been exposed to representations of African Americans such as those found within "culture of poverty" theories. While these racist views serve to destroy any sense of pride in their communities, diaspora tourism helps them to reconstruct or re-member their communities as ones comprised of strong and proud survivors.

In addition to my desire to share the passionate ideas that they articulated, I quote these women again here to point out the eloquence with which they expressed them, which at times rivals Wright's. The poetic flow of their language suggests that they had already begun a process of reflection and narration of their experiences in order to share them with others back home. Indeed, after her first trip to Ghana, Ella wrote an account of her experience that she shared with family and friends. The narration of their experiences, as I mention above, has become a key cultural practice among diaspora tourists with both personal and political significance. Clearly, many visitors to the castle become more than tourists, more than even pilgrims: they become witnesses. The gravity with which they take their role as witnesses to the history of the slave trade is plain. African American journalist Renée Kemp explicitly expressed her vow to pass on her experience. She writes, "If I don't see these shores again, I tell myself, this handful of home will remind me of the ancestors' requirement of me: 'Tell them that you know of us,' they say. I give them my word" (2000, 29). To this end, Kemp describes experiencing the female slave dungeon in Cape Coast Castle. She writes,

> I say nothing. But of course I know that they are there. The presence of spirits is even stronger here than in the men's dungeon. I want to feel the stone floor beneath my feet; to feel what those women felt standing in this place. I step out of my sandals and feel the surface of the floor against the soles of my feet, then kneel and touch it with the palms of my hands. A child was delivered on this spot. A young girl died over there. A woman braided another's hair in this corner to pass the time. Over there a teenager wept for her mother. "We are in every crevice of this place," they seem to be saying. "Please don't recoil from us now." (2000, 28–29)

Just as Richard Wright imagined the experience of slaves in the dungeons almost fifty years ago, Kemp's physical contact with the castle floor allows her to imagine birth, death, weeping, and the both mundane and sacred act of a woman braiding another's hair.

Kemp expresses a sense of pride quite similar to that expressed by Ella, stating, "I am filled with a profound feeling of pride and gratitude to be the descendant of ancestors who were able to survive entombment in these dungeons, the hell of the ocean's 'middle passage,' and the indignities of that 'peculiar institution' called slavery" (2000, 29). Her pride is in fact what leads her to feel that she has a responsibility to share her experience with others so that it gains a purpose greater than an individual, fleeting occurrence. While popular historical narratives in the United States stress freedom as the essence of American-ness, structural racism, the progeny of slavery, continues to dismember African American subjectivity. For many African Americans then, remembering their enslaved ancestors is an act of protest. The castles inspire this protest, and diaspora tourists are thereby strengthened by these visits. They come away armed to do battle with inequality.

First Encounters

In contrast to the powerful and moving stories related by African American tourists, the responses of Ghanaian visitors are usually much less coherent. Because the operation of the slave trade on the coast in general, much less in the castles, is not part of a public discourse, visiting the castles often serves as their first encounter with this history. They cannot therefore *re*-member it; they must absorb this history for the first time. For many, the only information they have about horrors of the slave trade is the little they learn about them in JSS. For this reason, Ghanaian visitors to the castles are often shocked by what they learn. Indeed, when I spoke to Ghanaian visitors, I found that many of them expressed disbelief at what they were told. One student told me, "When my friends came here, they told me what they saw over here, but what they said, I didn't believe it. I didn't believe them until I came to see it myself . . . Even these places, at school, we learned it in the books that this and this is what happened, but we didn't believe it. We thought it was just something they made up—or let's say a story, a funny story." The limited amount of information presented in schools often leads students to simply dismiss the slave trade. Theresa, a student from the Brong Ahafo Region, who felt a similar disbelief, said, "When we were children in school, we read about the castle, but we didn't believe it, so we've come today to see whether or not what we read is true or not, that's why we came. That's also part of the purpose of coming here. When we were children, we didn't believe that it was true, that that's what happened, so we've come to see it for ourselves." When I asked her if she thinks other people similarly do not believe what they have heard about the slave trade, she responded, "Oh yes, a lot of people wouldn't believe it. That's why we have taken pictures, so that when we go we can show it to them so that they will also know that the thing is true, it really happened." Her companion added, "Some people, when you tell them, they will think that it is just an exaggeration. How we have seen it is how we describe it to them, but they think we are exaggerating."

To stress this point, Theresa offered an example: "Someone like my grandmother or my mother, if I tell her that this, this and that happened, I don't think she will believe it. Older people are illiterate so they can't read. Even we who can read, unless we come here, we will not be believing it. So if I go there and tell my mother that this, this, and this is true, I don't think she will believe it unless she sees it." Certainly, for uneducated Ghanaians, the castles may serve as their first encounter with this aspect of the history of the slave trade, with the story of what happened in the dungeons, whether through their own visits or through the stories and pictures of others. Even for those who have learned about the slave trade in school, as these comments demonstrate, this history remains abstract and even spurious.

Most Ghanaian visitors then approach the castles with little sense of solemnity, but many leave with a different posture toward this history. This transformation usually begins with bewilderment. Indeed, given the nonchalant attitude with which most Ghanaian visitors approach the castles, the response to actually viewing what lies within is often one of incomprehension. Such was the case for one visitor from the Brong Ahafo Region who said,

> I am very surprised because how can about a hundred people or whatever it is be kept in such a room or treated in that way? Okay, the purpose of the slave trade was to take the blacks to go to those areas to go and work for them [whites]. Why should they maltreat them in this way so that most of them were dying? I think they couldn't get the number that they were after because they came here to take people to go and work for them, maybe a hundred people might go and work for you. But you maltreat them and about sixty of them were dead and forty were taken. I don't understand why they did that. Why should they do that? Was that reasonable?!

This comment is telling because it expresses the common belief that the transatlantic slave trade was similar to domestic slavery: the enslaved people were essentially servants, occupying the lowest ranks of society, but still clearly maintaining their human worth. This misunderstanding of the slave trade is what leads many Ghanaians to disregard its significance. Thus, the realization that transatlantic slaves were treated as chattel and that their humanity was not recognized is often shocking and incomprehensible to them.

While the students on Felix's tour may have come away with an understanding of the significance of the slave trade to their own history, many visitors to the castles leave without any clear sense of the significance of the experience, despite the fact that they are horrified by what they learn. Some in fact maintain an emotionally detached stance even after their tours. In this way, they do not re-member the slave trade or, in other words, embrace it as a relevant history; on the contrary, they seem to reject this history, or to "dismember" it, and continue to distance themselves from associations with the slave trade. A woman from Saltpond, a nearby coastal town, who was at the castle accompanying a visitor from Japan, explained her detached attitude to me saying, "I have been here before, but I don't like to worry myself with these things, the dungeons and sad things like that." She also expressed the notion that the slave trade resulted in a positive outcome: "The White man is very wicked, do you know that? But now you are there [in the United States] so it is bad, but there is some good from it too, don't you think so?" (Holsey 2004, 178). Her comments demonstrate her rejection of the importance of the slave trade to the contemporary conditions of her community; she views it instead as only relevant to blacks in the diaspora and, furthermore, as having been to our benefit.

For many, however, their newfound sense of the horror of the slave trade, at least for the African diaspora, remains paramount. Once they accept the atrocities with which they are presented, many Ghanaian visitors express great sadness. A teacher from the Eastern Region commented on the emotional impact that the dungeons have: "It reminds me of the way they suffered here. Some of the students, they didn't even want to get in. They still feel the pains . . . The first time I entered the castle, I wept." A second teacher with the group described his first visit to the castle, suggesting the impact of the presence of African Americans on his own emotional response:

The first time that I came here was in '92 during the PANAFEST. I was here with a lot of African Americans. And some of them, they fainted, weeping when they had to enter the male slave dungeon. In fact, they wouldn't enter at first. I felt very, very, very sad. It was at that time that I began to see how wicked man had been to man, that people take advantage because of wealth, instead of seeing to their own welfare. And you see a lot of injustice that has been done, by both Africans and Europeans.

As his last comment suggests, with regard to the relationship of the slave trade to their own histories, many continue to view it as a story of African collusion, particularly teachers and students, who, as I discuss in chapter 5, have been trained to view the slave trade in this way. In this context, it remains a difficult history to embrace.

Charting a New Course

The tourism industry has recognized the continuing tendency to sequester the slave trade. Seth Nii Akele Nunoo of the Ministry of Tourism stated, "Unfortunately, because of the nature of our development, there will be some who will sneer at the stigma of slavery, and wonder why anyone should commemorate that shameful period in the history of man; others will try to damn this part of their rich heritage, but in so doing, they will deprive themselves of a share of the glory that belongs to those who fought against oppression" (1998, 1). His reference to the stigma of slavery points to constructions of perverse families, the savage bush, and the cursed continent that plague discussion of the slave trade. In this context, his suggestion that Ghanaians might instead fashion the slave trade as a story of their struggle against oppression is a radical departure from these conventionalized narratives. While the narratives presented in castle museums, on tours, and during celebrations of PANAFEST and Emancipation Day certainly demonstrate that the African diaspora has fought against oppression, they do not often suggest that Ghanaians have "shared" in this struggle. Diaspora tourism has, however, been accompanied by an educational campaign that has attempted to refocus attention onto the slave trade. These attempts, however, have not met with much success. While they attempt to chart a new course, they often revert to familiar paths.

The most significant move toward developing a new narrative about the slave trade outside of the realm of tourism has been the revision of school textbooks. In September 2001, the Ministry of Education released a new syllabus for social studies in JSSS. The ministry's focus on JSSS most likely arises from the fact that not only do a larger percentage of students attend JSS than attend SSS, but that in JSS, social studies is a required course. One of the major changes in this syllabus was an expanded emphasis on the slave trade. This change is a result of a number of different factors, not the least of which is the impact of recent international attention to the slave trade. UNESCO, which operates an Office of Education at the Ministry of Education in Accra, oversees the Associated Schools Project Network, which links schools in nations around the world—including Ghana—through various educational goals. One of its programs is the Transatlantic Slave Trade Education Project, which was designed to expand and improve education about the slave trade. This program involves primary schools and JSSS in Accra, Cape Coast, and Elmina. The project hosted international teacher training workshops, including a 2000 conference at Tulane University in New Orleans, Louisiana, entitled "Breaking the Silence—Teaching about the Transatlantic Slave Trade." The UNESCO Office for Education in Ghana has also held national teacher training workshops for JSS teachers. The creation of a new history syllabus was a logical next step.

With the Ministry of Education's release of the new JSS social studies syllabus, emphasis on the slave trade has reached a new height. In JSS 1, under a unit on the arrival of Europeans in the Gold Coast, after addressing the role of Europeans in education, trade, and missionary activities, teachers are instructed to address the "Transatlantic Slave Trade and its Effects." The syllabus states in its objectives that students will be able to "give reasons why the Transatlantic Slave Trade was started by Europeans, describe the operation of the transatlantic slave trade, give reasons why the slave trade continued for more than 400 years (1450–1850), state the major reasons for the abolition of the slave trade, and describe the effects of the slave trade on Africa and the African in general" (Ministry of Education 2001, 5–7).

Despite the comprehensiveness suggested by these goals, the new syllabus continues to stress familiar themes. African collusion in the slave trade is heavily stressed. In the new syllabus, teachers are directed to "highlight the role of some of our chiefs in capturing and selling their own people to white people" (Ministry of Education 2001, 5). In stating that "our chiefs" sold "their own people," the syllabus, like many of its forebears, posits a corporate African identity. In this context, it appears that *all* chiefs sold slaves and that therefore every community participated in the trade. The syllabus furthermore explains that chiefs sold slaves out of greed. Finally, the syllabus states that one of the results of the slave trade was the demoralization of Africans who "suffered loss of image and self respect" and "suffered loss of confidence in their ability to rely on their own minds and efforts to develop" (Ministry of Education 2001, 7). Taken together, these points paint a picture of Africans participating in their own destruction out of their own stupid greed. This analysis ignores the geopolitics of the slave trade in which certain groups enslaved members of other groups. School textbooks seem to be wary of pointing to this fact, perhaps out of fear that to do so would be to condemn particular groups in the nation. As I argue in chapter 5, a more nuanced appraisal of African participation in the trade that points to the constraints within which African rulers and merchants operated rather than its attribution to simple greed might decrease this fear; however, the syllabus chooses to simply spread the blame evenly across the entire society.

The syllabus continues the historiographic tradition of using the history of the slave trade to condemn Africans. This argument, like the one in Boahen's text, sets the stage to argue that through their participation in the slave trade, Africans caused deleterious effects on the entire country and indeed continent. As discussed earlier, this argument dates back to the abolitionist movement and supported the institution of colonial rule. It is now being revisited in order to provide a rationale for African underdevelopment. But the same fears that Sarbah had of the former, namely, that it provided an argument for the disenfranchisement of Africans, who have destroyed themselves out of greed, suggest that this interpretation of the trade is unlikely to be any more popular than the old one.

Finally, in its description of abolition, the syllabus states the major reasons behind it as

i. Humanitarian reasons given by Granville Sharp and William Wilberforce
ii. Revolt of slaves in America, Brazil, and the West Indies
iii. Unprofitability of the slave trade by the early 1800s due to the Industrial Revolution in Europe which made it cheaper to use machines instead of intensive human labour. (Ministry of Education 2001, 6)

In addition to British humanitarianism, this construction of abolition assigns agency to slaves in the New World and stresses economic motives for abolition. In the latter, it illustrates the influence of Eric Williams's work. But nowhere in this discussion do Africans on the continent figure. The story of resistance to the slave trade remains the story of Europeans and blacks in the diaspora, while African agency is only evident in their participation in the trade. Thus, the construction of the history of the slave trade in the new syllabus suggests that despite a much more in-depth analysis of the slave trade, many of the same issues persist.

In addition to changes to this syllabus, several television programs have been devoted to the slave trade. *Krokrokroo* is a popular Saturday morning children's program. It addresses various issues regarding national history, politics, and culture. In September 2001, one of its programs addressed the slave trade. It focused heavily on abolition, showing a scene in which Ghanaian children dressed in black robes and white wigs reenacted a debate between members of the British parliament regarding whether or not the slave trade should be abolished. Just as in schools, *Krokrokroo* represents the slave trade as a tale of Africa's salvation by Europeans. This program thus defined abolition as a story of the British, with no significant African actors. It did, however, insist on the presence of African resistance in other contexts by juxtaposing British efforts to abolish the slave trade with Yaa Asantewaa's struggle against the imposition of colonial rule.

The same episode of *Krokrokroo* included the performance of a skit about Yaa Asantewaa. Yaa Asantewaa, the queen mother of the Ejisu, led the Asante in an attack against the British in 1901. The inclusion of this story within the same episode appeared to be an attempt to recover a notion of African resistance given that no such resistance appeared in its representation of the slave trade. In the skit, a young girl playing Yaa Asantewaa gave an impassioned speech about her refusal to submit to European rule. Yaa Asantewaa has become a symbol of African resistance in Ghana, and as such, her story forms an important part of the history taught to children. In JSSS, although the social studies textbook includes only one paragraph about her, it includes a large picture of her and suggests at the end of the chapter that students enact a play about how Yaa Asantewaa became the leader of the Asante army. In addition to Nkrumah, Yaa Asantewaa is another central icon within children's perceptions of history and provides an ideal image of African agency, which, remarkably, is gendered female. Just as in school textbooks, by juxtaposing her story with the history of the slave trade, the program attested to the ill fit of the latter within the romantic register of children's history lessons, with their major focus being on African resistance.

The slave trade has also featured in local performances in Cape Coast and Elmina. I attended one play put on by the Center for National Culture (CNC) in Cape Coast about the slave trade. It was attended my many local residents including several groups of schoolchildren. This play showed Europeans capturing Africans, thereby reversing conventional historical constructions of the acquisition of slaves as a wholly African affair. Because it contradicts the information found in textbooks, however, many of those in the audience simply rejected it. For instance, as I discuss in chapter 5, Miss Mensah took her students to see the play. When its representation of slave capture came up in class discussion, however, she told the students, "I think it was a big lie. I didn't like it." Thus, this representation met with no more success than the other attempts I have mentioned.

Moving Ahead

Within SSSS, while the syllabus has remained the same, diaspora tourism has influenced both the presentation of the history of the slave trade by teachers as well as its reception by students. Miss Mensah not only took her students to the CNC play, she also took them to Elmina Castle. Many of the students had also attended the previous PANAFEST and Emancipation Day celebrations. And they had likely read and seen some of the numerous newspaper articles and television programs that have been written and have aired since diaspora tourism has taken off. It is for this reason that Miss Mensah felt it necessary to take the slave trade seriously. She recognizes that she is not the only source of information that her students have, but she seeks to be the dominant one. Recall her directive with regard to the slave trade discussed in chapter 5: "We should put it behind us and not dwell on it. Now we have Emancipation Day, we were emancipated a long time ago. We should move ahead." In order to move ahead, she insists, they must turn away from the slave trade.

For her students, their tour of the castle did not appear to radically alter their views of the slave trade. Discourses they heard during PANAFEST and Emancipation Day, however, did have a significant impact. These events provided an arena for discussions of the need for reparations to the African continent that gained in popularity as a consequence of the United Nations Durban summit. As a result of these events, some students were quite savvy in drawing connections between the slave trade and Ghana's current place in the global economy. Some in fact brought up the issue of reparations in class. In response, Miss Mensah reiterated her point that they should not look for compensation but rather should move ahead.

Miss Mensah's lecture succeeded in convincing many of her students to follow her directive. Comfort was one of these students. I talked to her and several of the other students after their last lecture on the slave trade to see what their reactions were to the material they had just covered. She was particularly struck by the emphasis on African collusion in the slave trade, which was an element of the trade that she had just learned of for the first time. She said, "I learned a lot here, and it's very detailed. And I got to know that one of the main things which helped encourage the slave trade was our own people were involved in it, getting of the slaves and everything. So I think that if we weren't involved in it, it wouldn't have started, in the first place or [at least] it wouldn't have continued."

For this reason, Comfort does not see the slave trade as a story of European oppression and certainly does not believe that contemporary Europeans should be held accountable. She continued,

Personally, I don't feel any negative, I don't have any negative attitudes toward Europeans because—they did some wrong things to Africans in the first place, but maybe it's because I didn't go through it, the slave trade or something, that's why I'm saying this—because it's like the slave trade, it's both the Africans and the Europeans who contributed to it, so I don't really see why I should have any ill feelings toward the Europeans. I feel quite okay around them.

In noting that both Africans and Europeans participated in it, Comfort takes a detached stance toward the slave trade, devoid of any emotional content. She suggests that her lack of ill feelings results from the fact that she is so removed from this long-ago historical episode and did not herself "go through it." She argues that, as a result, she does not harbor any resentment toward contemporary Europeans. Her passionless response echoes Miss Mensah's classroom manner.

Because it had been a hot topic in class, I asked her if she thinks that Europe should pay reparations to Africa, to which she replied, "No, I don't think so because I don't see what they owe us. Europeans gained from the trade and Africans gained in some way. We gained education, we gained some sort of civilization through the slave trade, so I don't see why they have to pay again for nothing they've done." Comfort is a model student, having absorbed all of the arguments that Miss Mensah made about the slave trade. For her, the slave trade was a sad chapter in human history for which no one group can be blamed. Therefore, it is a story with no redeeming quality, no struggle between good and evil, no victory for righteousness. It also resulted, according to her, in some positive outcomes, including even providing "civilization," which undermines the idea that it is responsible for Africa's underdevelopment. In this context, there is no strong motivation for remembering the slave trade. It is a story that is best forgotten.

Ruth is one of Comfort's classmates. For her, Miss Mensah's take on the slave trade was also well received. The message of African collusion was foremost in her thoughts. When I asked her when she had first learned about the slave trade, she replied,

> When I came here and I started learning about it, I realized that we all had a part to play in the slave trade. The locals, the indigenous people sold the black people themselves and it wasn't the whites who were forcing them, but they were being sold. And here, it's made me be a bit levelheaded about the whole thing. When I came here, I realized that they were to blame, but we were also partly to blame, the blame is to be shared equally between the blacks and the whites because they all contributed or helped in some way.

African collusion was the most significant aspect of the lesson for many students. Ruth equates understanding the role of Africans in the slave trade to being "levelheaded," thereby implying that any rational person who was presented with the facts regarding African involvement in the slave trade could not blame Europeans.

We also discussed the effects that the slave trade has had on Africa. While she discussed its negative effects, Ruth, like Miss Mensah, was quick to also stress the benefits of the European presence in Africa. She argued,

> I think the effect has been both positive and negative, but to the larger extent, I think the effects have been very negative because some of the people who were sold, in fact, all of the people who were sold were in their prime, in their youth, and they could have contributed in a very good way to the development of Africa, and they could have helped make Africa what we probably can never be . . . But there are positive effects too . . . We've also become a bit developed. Some of the things we now have, education, Christianity, some crops were not locally grown in Ghana and other parts of Africa, but now we have them.

In recognizing that the slave trade did have negative effects, even, as she argues, if the European presence ultimately had several advantages, Ruth still struggled somewhat with a notion of the specter of white oppression that the history of the slave trade raises. Attempting to play down these feelings, she said, "Well, what they did was unpardonable, it was very bad, but I don't have any ill feelings toward them because it wasn't—the blame cannot be put on the whites or the Europeans because we also had a part to play in the slave trade. So I have no ill feeling toward them, just that, well . . . sometimes I do have a little, just a little . . . but then I don't really have any bad feelings." She attempts, nonetheless, to remain levelheaded and concentrate instead on the idea that the slave trade, as the motivation for the early European presence, had positive effects. For her too then, the slave trade cannot be used to explain contemporary economic woes or to comment on the racialized nature of European oppression. It is not a very good story at all.

Although Ruth suggests that her views are largely shaped by what she has learned in school, her family background plays an important role in her reactions to the slave trade as well. When I asked how she thinks her parents feel about the slave trade, she replied, "My daddy works in Australia, so I think my daddy is a bit levelheaded, he's come to appreciate what the whites are doing and I think he's forgiven them and has no ill feeling toward the whites because he works for a white company." She suggests here that constructing the slave trade as a story of white oppression would render interactions with whites difficult. For Ruth, levelheadedness is then a matter of practicality. For those who aspire to work in high-level positions, as do most of these students, the likelihood of working with Europeans is quite high. Ruth constructs her father as a model of how to remain levelheaded in interactions with whites, which includes not attributing oppression to Europe or Europeans, in order to succeed.

As a result of Miss Mensah's presentation of the slave trade, Comfort and Ruth learn to forget this chapter of history. They succeed in becoming levelheaded young ladies, not only in their own estimation, but certainly in Miss Mensah's as well, by adopting a detached, rational, and practical perspective that the slave trade is best left in the past. The elite status of the girls in this school plays a role in the decision of some of them to eschew more radical critiques; they are, after all, there to become proper young ladies, not revolutionaries. In particular, Ruth's father's employment overseas and his ability to be successful in the international economy leads her to accept views that support a global order founded on the dominance of Western nations. This acceptance points to a conservative definition of progress. It views fostering good relationships with Europe and the United States as the best route to greater access to flows of wealth that they control. For this reason, it discourages a critique of the historical foundations of their wealth in the slave trade.

Escape Routes

This construction of progress is common in Cape Coast and Elmina. Men and women in these towns tend to see forging connections with people from other nations as crucial to advancement of any sort. Constructions of a cosmopolitan past form one strategy for forging such a connection. They are attempts to gain symbolic capital that coastal residents hope to transform into international interest in their towns and thereby into real capital. While older individuals may stress the need for investments in development, youth almost always tie progress to the ability to travel. While travel is one of the most commonly expressed desires of Ghanaian youth, the extreme difficulty of obtaining visas often keeps them imprisoned within their national borders. In this context, they constantly seek ways to escape.

In this context, the presence of international tourists takes on special significance and helps to explain why many local residents do not wish to construct their past international relationships in terms of exploitation. It offers an explanation as to why, in other words, when discussing the slave trade, many stress an equal responsibility of Europeans and Africans. After all, many youth seek to benefit from the international tourists of all types that have become a focal point of life for residents of Cape Coast and Elmina.

Yaw is a young man who grew up in Elmina. Describing playing near the castle as a child, the most likely place to meet tourists, he said, "We would go and swim around the castle. They used to organize these beach activities, so we would go there to swim, we would go there to play games. All of us at a point in time, we have followed these whites. Almost everybody in Elmina, whether big, average, small, whatever, has had that kind of life at a point in time."

The idea that all children at one time or another have followed "these whites" captures the nature of their dependency. Older children may follow tourists in hopes of engaging them in conversation, selling them trinkets, or, best of all, obtaining their addresses. Some individuals do benefit from their relationships with tourists. For some, the acquisition of a foreigner's address may lead to a pen pal relationship, financial support, or even a possible invitation to the United States or Europe, all part of their cosmopolitan dreams, which sometimes, as Yaw notes below, come to fruition. It is this tenuous hope, Yaw suggests, that causes residents to remain silent with regard to the atrocities involved in Europe's historical relationship to Ghana. Indeed, Yaw was adamant that there are no negative views of foreigners in Elmina. He insisted,

Instead of becoming angry and then living in hatred, we've rather developed a kind of love, friendliness, hospitality, that sort of thing. So this idea of a young kid seeing a white woman or a man, and yelling *buronyi, buronyi, buronyi* [foreigner]! you know that kind of excitement, that kind of happiness you know, trying to follow the person up to a particular distance you know for as long as that foreigner can have these kids around him or her . . . so it was that friendly atmosphere.

And some of those whites too, they were nice, some of them were kind. I remember up to my secondary level, I had this white friend in America. He used to send me anything that I needed, as far [as he was able], he did his best, okay. So some of us saw it as a privilege because maybe there were certain things our parents couldn't offer and some of these friends who were kind and nice enough would do that, you know they would pay your school fees, they would occasionally send you a few things, and until today it's even becoming more lucrative or maybe more deeper with the kids of today . . . and it's like we are finding it very difficult to check it, and it is because the atmosphere is friendly and it is peaceful, and there's love. So I think it's still the same, just that more kids are getting into it these days. Most of them are not going to school because they think that they are making enough money from these their friends.

Despite his attention to the ways in which some visitors have helped local people including himself, implicit in Yaw's comment is a critique of the relationships between tourists and locals. His comment that many youth are dropping out of school to panhandle from tourists points to the dangerous problem that the tourist presence has created. Despite the development of tourism, Elmina and Cape Coast remain the same marginalized towns that they have been since the departure of the Dutch and British. The small amounts of money that children who drop out of school may earn from their interactions with tourists do not make up for their lack of basic education. While many youth like Comfort and Ruth might therefore express their appreciation for the contributions that have been made by Europeans in the past and, in this way, situate their desires to benefit from them in the present, many simultaneously recognize the fact that they are disempowered by the unequal nature of these relationships. This recognition has not dismantled the public discourse that describes the "friendly atmosphere" of the coast. In this way, it is similar to narratives of the cosmopolitan coast discussed in chapter 5 that coexist with statements like "you know these whites."

In addition to approaching white tourists, Christian faith has become another site of both a literal and figurative interaction with foreigners. The recent explosion of charismatic churches in Ghana attests to the reformulation of the Christian community as a global construct with back-and-forth communication between Africans and Europeans, not to mention people from all other corners of the world. Unlike the missionary churches of the past, which represented major faiths such as Methodism, Anglicanism, and Catholicism, the fastest-growing churches in Ghana today are these charismatic churches. Many of these churches, having originated in Ghana, have set up branches in other countries and attest to their international-izing aims through names such as International Central Gospel Church and Harvest Ministries International (van Dijk 1997). Conversely, some of these churches are established churches in the United States and Europe that have set up branches in Ghana. While their congregations are largely Ghanaian, through their connections with churches abroad, they imagine themselves as part of an international community. Thus, millennial mission work forges an international community based on faith.

In addition to the notion of an international Christian community as an ideological construction, these churches also often lead to actual international travel by many Ghanaian church members. Church leaders, through their ties to churches in the West, often procure opportunities for Ghanaians to travel abroad to attend church conferences or for more permanent reasons and to be received by those churches into an already existing network, leading Rijk van Dijk to argue that Ghanaian Pentecostal leaders often serve as brokers who "link information and interaction flows between different cultural contexts" (1997, 149). Within this construction, international church conferences replace PANAFEST and Emancipation Day as relevant community-building events. The remembrance of the slave trade is equally irrelevant in the context of an ideology in which the only histories worthy of deep reflection are those found in the Bible. The success of internationally oriented charismatic churches in Ghana demonstrates the desperation felt by many Ghanaians.

Indeed, the embrace of international tourists and the success of charismatic Christianity are due to their imagined abilities to respond to the fantasies of travel that many Ghanaians harbor, who otherwise see few opportunities for travel or advancement. In the discussion of this bleak situation, the slave trade often arises in a cynical comparison. I often heard people say that if a slave ship were to dock off the coast of Ghana today, bound for America, and Ghanaians were told that they could get on but that they would have to endure the same conditions that the slaves did, the boat would still be full of volunteers. Such comments index the marginalized position in which Ghanaians find themselves with regard to the global economy, their sense indeed of abjection. While these statements are no doubt made for their shock value, they nonetheless illustrate a view of entrenchment in place that is itself a form of enslavement in the new millennium from which many Ghanaians seek escape by any means (Holsey 2004, 179).

The Long Road Home

Along with expressing their sense of abjection, the slave ship comment also points to a view of African Americans as the lucky ones. Ironically then, in contrast to the focus of many Ghanaians on finding routes out of their country, many diaspora tourists are searching for ways to establish roots in it. The comment also makes a mockery of diaspora tourists' romantic visions of Ghana. Stories about these romantic visions are widespread. One story that I was told in Ghana (see Holsey 2004, 166) focuses on an African American man who had some evidence that his family descended from Ghana. He knew the name of this family, so he employed a company to help him to track down the Ghanaian descendants. The company located the family, and the man promptly traveled to Ghana to meet them. When he arrived, he was taken to their village where he was met by a man who was to take him to the family's house. When the man saw him, he simply stared in disbelief. The American asked him what it was, but the other man simply replied, "Wait and you will know." As they walked through the village, other people stopped and stared. Again the man became curious, but his companion repeated, "Wait and you will know." When they finally reached the house of the family that he believed to be his relatives, a group of people emerged from the house, and the man discovered that he looked remarkably similar to all of the members of the family. They welcomed him having no doubt that he was indeed their kin.

This fantasy trope of transatlantic reconnection uses phenotype as the proof of a connection not only to Africa as a vague continental homeland but to a particular family in a particular village. The specificity of this connection is the object of a great deal of diasporic longing. In the absence of phenotypic certainty, many diaspora blacks articulate an almost mystical sense of belonging. As one African American visitor stated, "I understand, with my first whiff of Ghanaian air, that absent any proof to the contrary, this is where my family's history begins" (Kemp 2000, 17). This construction provides an alternative sense of belonging to counterbalance the alienation that many feel in the United States. Such stories, however, suggest a happy ending in the diaspora's return to Ghana and do not cite the contemporary struggles in which Ghanaians are engaged. Their connection to Ghana is then based not on a shared struggle but rather solely on an ancestral link.

While the examples discussed above illustrate diaspora tourists' embrace of Ghana as an ancestral homeland, some diaspora blacks have made Ghana their contemporary home. Their expatriation from the United States forms a strong critique of American racial exclusion by highlighting the fact that it has forced some African Americans to give up on the United States altogether. This subversive act discloses the failure of American multiculturalism and, in doing so, puts the image of the United States at risk. The event that brought this fact to my attention was the publication of an article in the *Wall Street Journal* in 2001 about African Americans living in Ghana. The article painted a bleak picture of their lives, suggesting that they were not made welcome by Ghanaians and that life in Ghana for them was exceedingly difficult. This article was quickly disseminated, passed around over e-mail accounts to members of the African American community in Ghana, and it sparked a firestorm of responses. Many complained both orally and in print that the assumptions of the article were false and that the comments of the individuals who had been interviewed were taken out of context.

In other contexts, African American expatriates have noted that many aspects of their lives in Ghana are indeed difficult. David Jenkins conducted interviews with many of these individuals in 1973. He notes the inconveniences and culture shock that they face. One of his informants, a young African American woman, explained, "You're away from racism, and that's the plus side. But when you get here all your supports are removed too. Not just family and friends or anything, but all the other things, community, television, familiar food, a familiar street with lots of things you understand going on in it, all these things support you" (Jenkins 1975, 172). African American women who have married Ghanaian men, who make up a large percentage of the expatriate community, often discuss the difficulties they find in negotiating their relationships with their husbands and in-laws. Obiagele Lake notes that in describing her situation, one woman stated, "If your husband dies and you're from another country, you could find it's not unusual that the extended family will come in. They come in quite nicely at the beginning, being quite helpful during funeral time. And they could be quite hostile too. And it's quite possible that they want to take most of your things away. They don't even ask, they demand it!" (Lake 1997, 56).

Certainly, many African Americans do find life in Ghana less than perfect and, at times, downright trying. That they remain in Ghana suggests then that even with these difficulties, they prefer life there over life in the United States. In fact, their continued residence in Ghana itself serves as a critique of racism in the United States; it boldly reveals the hypocrisy of American society that makes life unlivable for its own citizens if they happen to be black. Given this commitment, they found the suggestion in the *Wall Street Journal* article that African Americans are actually better off in the United States and not in Ghana particularly galling.

The motivation behind this suggestion was not lost on members of the African American community. The article's appearance in the *Wall Street Journal* in particular, they suggested, was an attempt to dissuade well-to-do African Americans from moving to Ghana or otherwise investing their money in this or any other African nation. By suggesting that their presence is not welcome there, they believed that the article was attempting to tell African Americans not to bother with Ghana but rather to keep their money and, as an extension of that, themselves in the United States. This interpretation, which appears to be quite plausible, suggests a growing recognition in the United States of the wealth of middle-class African Americans, which, if combined with an ideological commitment to Ghana, would deprive the U.S. economy of the potential benefits of their wealth. Thus, the challenge that the notion of diaspora poses to U.S. narratives of freedom was made explicit in this episode.

The Ghanaian state, furthermore, has encouraged the subversion of these narratives. Former president Rawlings sought to grant African Americans dual citizenship to Ghana. The extension of this right, he argued, would certainly encourage African Americans to make long-term investments in Ghana. In 1999, during a visit by former U.S. president Bill Clinton, Rawlings stated that black Americans who so desired would be eligible for Ghanaian citizenship. This proclamation caused a great deal of excitement among African Americans both in the United States and in Ghana, many of whom struggle with visa issues once in Ghana, although the bill ultimately failed to win approval at that time. Ways to aid diasporic resettlement in Ghana are, however, currently being considered. Through both touristic travel and the hope of future dual citizenship, many middle-class African Americans embody a degree of what Aihwa Ong (1999) terms "flexible citizenship" that increases not only their sense of freedom but also significantly affects their status in American society.

While diasporic practices of embracing Ghana and remembering the slave trade form part of a powerful oppositional stance with regard to U.S. narratives of freedom, they often simultaneously rely on romantic narratives of Ghana. In particular, by stressing citizenship as the solution their problems, African Americans imply not only their affection for Ghana, the land of their ancestors, but also their allegiance to Ghana, the contemporary nation-state. After all, while they cannot rely on the United States, they suggest a belief that they can rely on Ghana to protect their freedom.

Deterring the Diaspora

African American discourses about the slave trade and African belonging have become the object of a great deal of debate among coastal residents in Ghana. In this way, African Americans have contributed significantly to the public discourse about the slave trade in Ghana not only through their role in shaping diaspora tourism but also as tourists and expatriates. In response to their claims of belonging, many Ghanaians challenge the diaspora/homeland construction on several grounds. Some do so because they believe that diaspora blacks were well incorporated into their new societies. For this reason, even evidence of the diaspora's dreadful separation from the African continent does not necessarily lead to calls for reunion. This view also explains comments about the "positive" outcomes of slavery like the one made by a woman who told me, "but now you are there [in the United States] so it is bad, but there is some good from it too, don't you think so?" Many in fact believe that slaves were simply low-status individuals in the New World, particularly in the United States (which tends to occupy the Ghanaian imagination as the principal destination of slaves), and that their descendants ultimately benefited from their ability to be absorbed into a first world nation. The popular images of blacks that they receive, which frequently represent their affluence and success, have led many to believe that all blacks in the diaspora are wealthy (Holsey 2004, 178).

In addition, many reject constructions of Ghana as homeland in order to protect the distinctiveness of their regional identity. The notion of homeland holds great significance in Ghana, where it is rendered more specifically as "hometown." One's hometown is the place from whence the original ancestor of the lineage came. Thus, people identify very strongly with particular places, and one of the first questions asked of strangers is "what is your hometown?" Individuals take great pride in their ability to trace their lineages back to a specific place and continually maintain their ties to these places. They may live quite a distance from their hometown but will regularly return for local festivals and to visit family members. Thus, despite being displaced from one's hometown, an individual maintains spiritual and emotional ties to that place. Indeed, people are ideally buried in their hometown. For these reasons, there is quite an emphasis on knowing unequivocally the location of one's hometown.

Hometowns are also significant because of the particular histories that are attached to them. As I discuss in chapter 4, residents of Cape Coast and Elmina have developed elaborate histories of their towns' past cosmopolitan status as central nodes in the Atlantic economy. These histories, furthermore, take shape in direct opposition to descriptions of the North as the site of enslavement. Within this imagined geography, the African diaspora's ties are, if with anywhere, with northern Ghana. In this context, many coastal residents view constructions of Ghana as a whole as the homeland of the black diaspora as the extension of the history of the North to the entire country. They reject the homeland/diaspora construction then as part of a rejection of a national identity fashioned in this way.

At times, they also contest the mapping of the slave trade onto their nation by pointing not to the regional specificity of the origins of slaves but rather to the fact that slaves were taken from countries other than Ghana. When I asked one young man if he thought African Americans should be granted dual citizenship, he responded,

> Not all black Americans because we are not the only blacks on this continent. There are other countries. I wouldn't say that Ghana is the only black country where they were taken as slaves. The slave trade didn't happen only in Ghana, but because of history and the familiarity, if I should say, the famous being of our destination, it has been the center of the history of the slave trade. So they always say Ghana, Ghana. Most of the people believe that all those in the Americas, black Americans are from Ghana, but I don't think so.

In this way, he attempted to lessen this history's stigmatizing effects by emphasizing that it is not his nation's special property.

Cape Coast and Elmina are particularly important sites in the discussion of Ghanaian views of diaspora blacks because residents of these towns have frequent interactions with them. On one hand, some local residents reference the fact that they are "the ones who were taken away," which reflects their understanding of the historical links between Ghana and the African diaspora (see Hartman 2006; Hasty 2002). At the same time, small children often follow behind African American tourists calling "*oburoni!*" or "foreigner." *Oburoni* (or *buronyi* in Fante) is an Akan word that has become a bone of contention between Ghanaians and blacks in the diaspora, who, having been told that *oburoni* means "white man," find themselves to their dismay called by this term. In actuality *oburoni* means "those who come from over the horizon." This is not a racial label then but rather a demonstration of the ways in which Ghanaians often identify people by the places from which they come, in quite literal terms. Indeed, the Americanness of African Americans is quite significant from the point of view of Ghanaians. For them, African American and white tourists sometimes occupy the same mental space; they are all privileged foreigners.

Despite the hopes attached to all types of tourists, and sometimes especially to black tourists, rarely does their presence lead to substantial new opportunities for local residents. In many ways, the nature of tourism in fact discourages the creation of meaningful bonds between tourists and residents. Many tourists, particularly those on package tours, arrive on large tour buses, visit the castles, and then return to their buses, without ever having any contact with local residents outside of the ones that are directly involved in the tourism industry such as tour guides. When they do happen to spot them on the street, children often approach these tourists with a chant that enacts an imagined conversation with them: "*Oburoni*, how are you? I'm fine. Me too." As I note elsewhere, the fact that local children have developed this chant demonstrates that tourists are a welcome and amusing presence. At the same time, however, the chant demonstrates the one-sided nature of the relationship between residents and tourists: the child must carry on both sides of the conversation because the foreigner rarely answers back (Holsey 2004, 178).

The image of diaspora tourists, in particular, moving through these towns without answering back, thereby leaving local residents stuck in place, demonstrates that the intellectual construction of homeland and diaspora relies not only on practices of travel but also, as Clifford (1997) has noted, on practices of dwelling. While diasporic subjects may travel back to the homeland, those in the homeland must remain stationary. They must after all be there to greet the diaspora upon its return. Many local adolescents have begun to do just that. Standing outside the castles, they cheerfully shout out to diaspora tourists, "Welcome to your homeland!" But besides these savvy youth who employ the language of homeland strategically in their panhandling endeavors, to most residents, the imagined geography that positions their country as a homeland, a space upon which so many longings and so much sadness are placed, is often difficult for them to comprehend (see Holsey 2004, 178).

Black Atlantic Identities

Despite popular perceptions of diaspora tourists' sole interest in romantic narratives of transatlantic connection, many, as we have seen, are engaged in the production of powerful protest narratives. Mobilizing the slave trade within protest narratives is not, however, the sole province of the diaspora. While many Ghanaians quite adamantly minimize the significance of the slave trade, as more and more are exposed to alternative discourses about this history, some of them, particularly the educated youth who make up the largest percentage of castle visitors, are beginning to construct their own critiques. Indeed, as I discuss in this final section, just as some tour guides at the castles challenge the dominant narratives within diaspora tourism, some of their Ghanaian audience members have taken these challenges outside of the arena of the castles. In this way, diaspora tourism has served as a catalyst for the production of protest narratives. These narratives do not derive directly from diaspora tourism's dominant discourses but rather from the refashioning of them, in which both tour guides and visitors participate. Indeed, local residents' critical approach to these dominant discourses bears primary responsibility for the emergence of the slave trade as part of public youth discourse in Cape Coast and Elmina today.

To make this case, I return to Miss Mensah's classroom. I have noted that many of the students were successfully immunized from the influences of diaspora tourism by their teacher's directive to forget about the slave trade. During my observation of class discussions and student comments and reactions, I noticed a group of girls who did not fit this pattern and indeed seemed to be quite resistant to Miss Mensah's presentation. They were the ones who somewhat unsuccessfully attempted to start a conversation about reparations. After class, I sat them down to ask them about their reactions. They spoke quite passionately about racism, African underdevelopment, and the need for an apology from Europe for the slave trade. It is difficult to trace precisely the origins of the counter-discourse that they created. They had heard the same lectures and been on the same castle tour as the other girls in their class. Their radically different perspective suggests not that they necessarily had a greater level of exposure to alternative discourses about the slave trade, but rather that they were more attuned to them. They likely already had critiques of racism and underdevelopment well formed in their minds. Learning about the slave trade and, particularly, it seemed, about reparations through PANAFEST and Emancipation Day simply gave them a new language with which to discuss it. As a result, their experiences in the castle and the classroom articulated with a blossoming political consciousness.

The teenage years are a crucial time in the development of a political consciousness. They are a time in which boys and girls are ripe for the embrace of critical evaluations of conventional discourses and, oftentimes, of their own parents' outlooks. Schools, furthermore, are important participants in this process, and history courses in particular are especially important. As Lesley Sharp notes, "[I]t is in the schoolroom that historical, and ultimately, political, consciousness are forged. Thus, students' shared critical vision (that is, what Freire 1985 refers to as *conscientização*) of their personal trials, of the colonial past, and of the current nation are rooted in a dialectic of state ideology and pedagogical praxis. In the end, students' narratives expose the provocative and potent nature of collective memory in forging political consciousness and action in youth" (2002, 5). Indeed, history classrooms often provide arenas in which radical visions are both formed and expressed. Despite the usual attention paid to male radicalization, in Cape Coast and Elmina, because of the nearly equal access that girls have to schooling, their radicalization must also be reckoned with. For all of these reasons, Miss Mensah's class provides a perfect arena in which to examine the alternative visions of history that youth embrace. Indeed, while some students came away with the message that they should indeed forget about the slave trade, others rejected their teacher's directive. The combination of the classroom setting and the background of diaspora tourism led them to refashion the history of slave trade.

In contrast to the tourism industry's romantic narratives, for them, the significance of the slave trade lies in its unveiling of the deep roots of global racism, a system with which Ghanaians continuously struggle. It points, in other words, to the tragedy of the Atlantic era. In this way, they find another way to combat the stigmatizing effects of the European constructions of this history that have led many Ghanaians to sequester it: they use it to create a protest narrative.

As I demonstrate below, this protest narrative contains several key elements. First, Europeans bear unequivocal responsibility for the slave trade. They make this interpretation not by discussing individual actors, but rather by focusing on the slave trade as a system of oppression that Europeans began and largely controlled. They also stress the negative effects that the trade had on the African continent and insist that any positive effects of the European presence do not lessen or excuse this impact. In this way, they also tie the slave trade to contemporary forms of racism from which, they argue, Africans continue to suffer.

Finally, they recognize that because antiblack racism is a global phenomenon, black people all over the world share in this suffering. For this reason in particular, this construction of the slave trade has also led to the embrace of a notion of black Atlantic community. While many Ghanaians contest contemporary discourses of diasporic belonging, there have been various discourses about black community in Ghana for at least a century that were likewise produced as a result of African American influences. Auntie Amma's proclamation, "I'm black and proud" demonstrates this fact (see chapter 4). For the younger generation in Cape Coast and Elmina and likely elsewhere in Ghana, however, their exposure to diaspora tourism's narratives about the slave trade are as much responsible for their articulations of notions of black Atlantic connections as are musical anthems and political movements. The focus on the slave trade as the basis of these connections, furthermore, contests conventional histories of families, the coastal region, and nation that sequester the slave trade from discourse, suggesting that these youth may begin to rethink these narratives. Their construction of a black Atlantic community also refashions diaspora tourism's formulation of community. In contrast to its positioning of Ghana as the homeland of the black diaspora, in their construction of the black Atlantic, Ghana and the diaspora are both places in which black people continuously struggle against oppression, thus making them natural allies.

One of the girls who embraced this construction of the slave trade was Anne. We sat and talked after one of Miss Mensah's lectures. Anne has very strong views about the slave trade and insists on its continued significance today:

The other time our teacher was saying that you should forget about the slave trade and all that and it's passed and all that and we should think about ourselves and all that, but I think it will never be forgotten because as of now there are so many people who would like to trace their roots to know where they come from, but who is going to help them? And all this is a result of the slave trade and the damage that it has caused. That's why I keep on saying that there's nothing that you can do about it. So I don't think it is something that we can ever, ever forget about because the effects are still with us. Maybe Europeans did a couple of good things, but then as a human being, if somebody does good things and bad things, the bad ones will definitely override the good ones.

Anne accepts the notion that the European presence benefited Africans but argues that the horrors of the slave trade override these benefits. These horrors include the diaspora's loss of the knowledge of its specific origins, a fact with which she deeply sympathizes. Because of these horrors, she cannot forget.

She was most struck by the discussion of the organization of the slave trade. For her, Miss Mensah's explanation of the treatment of slaves undermined her position that the slave trade is not a story of European oppression. Anne repeated Miss Mensah's description of the treatment of slaves, the images appearing to have been seared into her memory:

> Just two days ago our teacher was telling us how it was organized. I never knew the whites were so inhuman when they came here. How can you be so callous and insensitive? I mean, they packed the human beings like goods and commodities that were going to be sold. I mean they stripped them naked, both men and women and children, and they packed them, and they were lying in their own excreta and urine, and if you happen to die along the way, they just threw you overboard. How can you treat human beings like this? I mean, I don't know but I think it's time that the whites grew to realize what they did. I mean, it's like they should put themselves in our shoes, and try and imagine what we went through. I mean it's something that we cannot just go away like that with, so they better start treating us and behaving like what's expected of them. The earlier the better!

By stressing the atrocities committed specifically by European actors, Anne dismantles the conventional privileging of African participation. In arguing that Europeans should put themselves in "our shoes," furthermore, she suggests that Africans on the continent are rather the victims of their crimes, suggesting a shared oppression among those Africans and members of the African diaspora. While, as I mention above, many men and women reject the history of the slave trade by retreating to regional identification, others embrace it by reaching toward a pan-African politics.

Anne was obviously greatly pained by what she had learned, and this pain was transformed into anger directed toward whites. Her bitterness over past wrongs is also related to anger over contemporary racism. She commented on the racism that she sees today:

> Up till now, they still look down on us and I think its very, very bad because I can really say that if it hadn't been for us, I mean Africans, Europe wouldn't be what it is now. So at least, even they should give us the sort of respect. Up till now, when you go to Europe, they look down on Africans. If you go there, no matter how long you stay there, you are regarded as a third class citizen, and that is really bad because we've helped a lot and it's like right now, we can't go there and take the things that they have, you understand? So I really feel very, very bad about the Europeans.

In stating, "If it hadn't been for us, I mean Africans, Europe wouldn't be what it is now," Anne used Walter Rodney's argument. This perspective, furthermore, serves to counter her teacher's assertion that that the slave trade is not a story to dwell on. Anne stresses racism as the most important legacy of slavery, in contrast to local histories that tend to emphasize instead internal divisions between slave and free, North and South. In contrast to other Ghanaians who do not express anger toward whites, it is clear that this conciliatory posture is not adopted by all. Anne, as a radicalized youth, is emboldened by the classroom presentation of the slave trade, both in her strong opposition to the teacher's dismissal of the history of the slave trade and in her newfound understanding of its horrors.

Mary, another student in Miss Mensah's class, also expressed to me her objection to the idea that they should forget about the slave trade. Our conversation took place in October 2001. Because of its timing, she brought up the events of September 11 in the United States in her discussion: "Looking at what just happened in America, this bin Laden issue, America is demanding that bin Laden come forward and say that he's sorry. The same way we are demanding that they come forward and say they are sorry for all that they did. Do you think that America will ever forget about what happened on the eleventh of September 2001? There's no way. And that's the same reason why we will never forget about what they did to us in the past during the slave trade." She, like Anne, stressed that the slave trade is something that happened to "us." She furthermore suggests the need for an apology.

This suggestion shows the influence of the discussion of reparations that took place during Emancipation Day. Linking this discussion to September 11, Mary launches a critique of white terror.

Mary argued that white terror is not a thing of the past; on the contrary, today, the racism of the global economy continues to terrorize Ghana. She argued that the HIPC initiative, which Ghana had recently joined in order relieve some of its debt to foreign nations, represents a form of neoslavery: "I think this HIPC initiative is indirectly slavery, is indirectly servitude, because they tell us what to do in their own interest . . . So I think that we are still in servitude to them indirectly." This comparison points to slavery as a *system* of oppression created by Europeans in which the African continent was entrapped rather than as simply a series of depraved acts by both European and African individuals. For Mary, the classroom lesson on the slave trade allowed her to articulate a political consciousness of Ghana's status in the contemporary global economy. She continued,

> I think that we as blacks should emancipate ourselves of the fact that we are second-class citizens. It's time we start thinking of ourselves as people who can make it. There are blacks who made it. Nelson Mandela was a black and he was able to fight for South Africa. Nkrumah was a black and he was able to fight for Ghana. Kofi Annan is a black. Martin Luther King was a black whose ancestors were taken into slavery and was able to do it . . . So it is time you stop looking down on me. I have my pride and my dignity to keep, and until you stop trampling on my pride and dignity, there's no way I can go forward.

In this statement, Mary articulates explicitly the racial reasoning that she and some of her classmates employ. She groups Ghanaians, South Africans, and African Americans together under the category of black. The common experience of racism makes this category salient. Indeed, her awareness of the global scope of antiblack racism was particularly influential in her embrace of the history of the slave trade. This awareness derives in part, as her above comment demonstrates, from a familiarity with the Civil Rights movement in the United States and the antiapartheid movement in South Africa, both of which she compares with the independence struggle in Ghana. Cape Coast Castle Museum is certainly an important source for such information. But in contrast to its construction of parallel success stories in the diaspora and in Ghana, Mary suggests that only certain individuals have "made it" and that others should follow their example. She points, in other words, to an unfinished struggle of black people throughout the world.

This notion of a shared struggle is what allows her and other radicals in the class to claim the history of slavery as their own. In contrast to the coastal view of slavery in which individuals try to establish their identities as those who were not enslaved, Mary and girls like her identify with these struggles by embracing the history of the slave trade as the basis of a critical stance. This critical stance, embodied in Rodney's text and rehearsed on some castle tours, is adopted by many youth like Mary who view the significance of the slave trade in light of the contemporary oppression of black people both on the African continent and in the diaspora.

Yaa was the third radicalized youth with whom I spoke. She, like Anne and Mary, also spoke of the necessity of remembering the slave trade, stating, "The slave trade can never be forgotten . . . It's been how many centuries now, and people still cry over it, people still lament over it. It's a fact and it won't change, it's going to be there until we do something about it. It's not going to be forgotten." In speaking of what Europeans should do today with regard to Africa, Yaa said,

> They should stop looking down on us for one thing, and for another, they should stop discouraging us from getting to where we want to go. For instance, if I finish university and I want to get somewhere high, and maybe I go for a job interview or something at a very high institution, a black person goes, a white person goes, who do you think will be accepted? You understand. Meanwhile, I want to reach places, meanwhile, I'm better than the white person, but then the white person, just because of his skin color will get there and I will be in a bottomless pit!

Despite this description of a seemingly hopeless situation, Yaa expressed a dogged determination to fight against racism:

> The past is in the past, they [Africans in the past] were ignorant. Right now, this generation, there's nothing ignorant about us, and in the time to come, things are going to happen, and I mean things are going to happen because nobody is ignorant about the slave trade, okay? I mean, our generation, we all know about it, we know what it entails, we know, I mean we know what is going on right now, do you understand? And when we grow up and we take the position of those who are there right now,

we're not going to sit back and be puppets for those people to pull our strings to tell us what to do. I'm not going to sit down for someone to tell me what to do, you know what I mean? And I'm going to make sure that I get there, and no one is going to tell me what to do!

Yaa also connects the history of the slave trade to contemporary racism. She argues that her generation has been politicized by learning about the history of the slave trade, a key point that I am arguing here, and as a result, it will become the new vanguard that will combat postcolonial forms of oppression. Thus, Yaa places knowledge about the slave trade directly within her account of the development of a radical consciousness among today's youth.

For some students, like Ruth, their desires to benefit from Western capitalism lead them to eschew critiques of its historical foundations. For others, however, their same desires along with their recognition of the limited nature of their opportunities lead them instead to center such critiques. The diversity of the girls' responses demonstrates the current widening of historical consciousness, even for those on the same socioeconomic track. Indeed, for many of Ruth's classmates, the focus on forgetting the slave trade in school only serves to bolster their sense of outrage and their development of a political consciousness. For these students, learning about the trade helps them to articulate the link between past oppression and their present marginalization within the global economy.

While some of the girls in the class embrace the history of the slave trade as part of a protest narrative, they reject the narration of this history within a romantic register. For this reason, they were all skeptical of the celebration of Emancipation Day. While some view it to be simply irrelevant, arguing that it celebrates, after all, the emancipation of slaves in other parts of the world, others argue on the contrary that it is premature. During the year in which Emancipation Day was first launched, many people questioned its appropriateness by asking the question, "Are we emancipated?" This question reveals a sense of skepticism, a sense indeed of the tragic nature of history, by its assertion that given Ghana's position in the global economy, for them, emancipation is as yet unrealized. Neoliberal policies like the HIPC initiative certainly support this conclusion.

Anne suggested for this reason that Emancipation Day should be cancelled. She explained, "If you're not going to do anything to help the situation, why bring about this emancipation stuff and all that?" Another one of Miss Mensah's students, Georgina, also criticized Emancipation Day. She stated, "I think they should not celebrate it. But even when they want to celebrate it, they should put down some aims and objectives to help Africans come up in the economy. They shouldn't just come here and celebrate, celebrate, and not do anything about our plight. I think after they celebrate, they should try to do something for Africans."[1]

Many argued that not only are Ghanaians not emancipated but neither are blacks in the diaspora. Yaa, for example, critiqued racism in the United States when she expressed her skepticism with regard to the role of the celebration in bettering the lives of African Americans by stating, "I think Emancipation Day is in a way useful and in a way useless because, okay so you come back, you come back to your roots, you lament, you cry, you go back, you eventually go back to where you came from, and you are still looked down upon. So what is the use of coming here to remember your past?" Because it does not change the fact that African Americans are "looked down upon," Emancipation Day, she argues, is far from empowering. This position contrasts sharply to suggestions that African Americans are well positioned within American society, a belief that, as I discuss above, leads many to disregard the significance of the slave trade.

These comments suggest that even those who recognize the significant role that the slave trade played in the creation of contemporary global inequalities and, for this reason, believe in the importance of learning about it do not believe in the romantic remembering encouraged by the celebration of Emancipation Day. For them, the slave trade brings to mind contemporary forms of inequality, rather than a sense of relief over its abolition. For this reason, the most common objection to Emancipation Day that Ghanaians voice is that it is constructed primarily as a celebration, as a romantic conclusion to the historical episode of the Atlantic trade, and has not led to any serious economic developments. They suggest that if it is to continue, Emancipation Day should not be a celebration of a fait accompli but rather a program aimed toward the future goal of freedom broadly conceived for black people everywhere.

Through the launching of Emancipation Day, Rawlings sought to forge a connection between African Americans and Ghanaians. He imagined this connection as one in which African Americans would gain a personal experience of historical reclamation and a rebirth that the Ghanaian landscape could provide, while the Ghanaian economy would gain the influx of tourist dollars. Through these efforts, Rawlings sought to position himself as the inheritor of Nkrumah's legacy of pan-African leadership. Nkrumah had also stressed explicitly the importance of transatlantic ties to economic development, thereby providing an alternative geography to the metropole/colony geography of colonialism or the first world/third world geography of global capitalism, but he did so by positing the adoption of a socialist economic structure. Many of the African Americans who traveled to Ghana immediately following Ghana's independence imagined Ghana as an escape from the twin forces of racism and capitalism that ensured their marginalization in the United States, but the dream of an African socialist state quickly collapsed, and along with it, their dreams of realizing this alternative.

Indeed, instead of subverting global capitalism, most African Americans today travel to Ghana on trips sponsored by tourist agencies, themselves vehicles of global capitalism. In this vein, Ebron examines a "homeland tour" to Senegal and the Gambia that was sponsored by, of all things, McDonalds. She explains, however, that its sponsorship reveals the shift noted above in which "[o]ppositional identities no longer appear autonomous from global commerce, even to their most radically passionate adherents; instead, they are inescapably intertwined" (2002, 211). Rawlings' pan-Africanist agenda then, being based on tourism, was firmly ensconced within a capitalist framework by making the remembrance of the slave trade into a commodity that Ghana could sell to diaspora tourists. The launching of Emancipation Day might be viewed in fact as a triumph for capitalism; even memory could now be commodified. It is also a triumph of the notion of the nation-state as the guarantor of freedom.

This embrace of Western capitalism recalls Rodney's description of the slave trade in which he writes that African rulers "joined hands with Europeans" (see chapter 5). Similarly, Ghanaian novelist Ayi Kwei Armah has compared the postcolonial situation to the Atlantic era on these grounds. In his novel *Fragments*, he uses the image of Christianborg Castle to comment on contemporary political corruption. The castle, which is located in Accra, was the base of operations of the Danish trade in the Gold Coast. The Danish sold it to the British in 1850, who used it as their headquarters after they moved the seat of the colonial government to Accra (Lawrence 1964). Today, the castle is the seat of national government. Armah notes the irony of the use of a European trade fort that held slaves in the past by the Ghanaian government today. He writes that the old slave castle "had become the proud seat of the new rulers, the blind children of slavery themselves" (1970, 44). In this way, he argues that as the "children of slavery," postcolonial leaders reproduce its tyranny in a new form. This rare example of the appearance of the slave trade in Ghanaian literature anticipated the type of critiques that have become increasingly common today.

For many of the girls I discuss above, the history of the slave trade is only empowering to the extent that it is mobilized within explicit protest narratives. Their protest is aimed not only at a global system of antiblack racism but also at the Ghanaian state's failure to adequately address it. To do so, they reject the romantic narratives of nationalism provided within schools and elsewhere and the romantic narratives of diasporic reunion in an idealized Ghanaian homeland that are also nationalist. Because of the failure of both of these discourses to speak to contemporary conditions, they remain skeptical of them and seek instead to use the slave trade to critique the despair of the postcolonial moment. Appiah (1992) discusses similar forms of skepticism as part of what he calls a postnationalist consciousness. Postnationalism, as he describes it, results from the failure of nationalism to create an alternative sphere, such as Nkrumah's wished-for socialism. On the contrary, the nationalist era has seen few changes from the colonial era. Both are marked by "the incorporation of all areas of the world and all areas of even formerly 'private' life into the money economy" (Appiah 1992, 145). Thus, Appiah notes that those who express postnationalist sentiments reject the Western *imperium* as well as the nationalist project of the postcolonial bourgeoisie (1992, 152). Because postnationalism critiques the nationalist government's support of the global order that it claimed to challenge, it is also, Appiah argues, the postoptimistic era.

Ghanaians who critique romantic narratives of slavery and abolition demonstrate such postoptimism by critiquing the commodification of a potentially radical discourse and thus its domestication into a tool of the power structure. The postnationalist critiques that I have discussed argue for the replacement of a national orientation specifically with an emphasis on a broader black Atlantic community that continues to grapple with the effects of the slave trade. In this way, it is more similar to earlier formulations of pan-Africanism than to diaspora tourism's constructions of black community in that it depends on a recognition of antiblack racism in Ghana as well as in other parts of the world. Many of the above-mentioned youth demonstrated such an awareness. Their comments suggested that attending to the racist underpinnings of global capitalism is precisely what the current moment demands.

In making such observations, local educated youth suggest a different basis for a transatlantic connection. For instance, in response to the relocation of the two sets of remains to Ghana during Emancipation Day, one visitor to Cape Coast Castle, a young Ghanaian man, told me, "It's okay, but personally, I think that is not so important . . . Many of the Africans died [in the diaspora]. Their bodies have not been brought here. But the fact that *all Africans who are alive are coming together* is an indication that we don't want to forget our roots. We are one people. I think that is rather of more importance" (emphasis added; see also Holsey 2004, 176). Through these words, he critiques not only diaspora tourism but also many theories of the black Atlantic. He does so by summing up the emergent vision of a black Atlantic community in Ghana that is not based on romantic notions of shared African origins or even simply on similar historical experiences of oppression. He points rather to contemporary collaborations, on the actions of those *"who are alive."* Taken further, his comments point to the *strategic* decisions to remember their roots in the slave trade and thereby re-member themselves as "one people" joined in a struggle against the physical and ideological entrapments of the contemporary age.

CONCLUSION

When I returned to Ghana in 2005 to observe PANAFEST and Emancipation Day, I found that local residents had become increasingly critical of it. After I asked a friend his thoughts on PANAFEST, he replied, "PANAFEST? PANAFEST was a Pana-flop!" This term had become a popular joke about the struggling celebration that faced numerous problems. Local residents complained about its lack of organization, the high ticket prices, and sudden cancellations of performances. But a more fundamental problem remains in the structure of diaspora tourism in Ghana, namely, a problem with the stories it tells. Its stories, I have argued, are largely romantic. They celebrate the triumph of emancipation and the subsequent achievements of blacks in the diaspora. In addition, they encourage a reunion between the diaspora and Africa in which the diaspora can finally reclaim its roots. For many diaspora tourists these stories are empowering. They allow them to embrace an African homeland and thereby fill the gap left by their second-class citizenship in the United States. For many Ghanaians, however, the brand of pan-Africanism that diaspora tourism fashions is much more difficult to embrace. It is indeed a Pana-flop.

Nonetheless, diaspora tourism not only continues, it is in fact growing. To coincide with the two hundredth anniversary of the abolition of the slave trade in 2007, the Ministry of Tourism launched the Joseph Project. Using the Biblical story of Joseph's separation from his family as a parallel to the situation of many diaspora blacks, this project draws upon notions of their kinship to Ghanaians. The highlight of this project is a "healing ceremony" to take place in July 2007 that will bring together Africans on the continent and those in diaspora in order to address the legacy of the slave trade.

There have also been renewed calls to grant African-descended individuals dual citizenship to Ghana, thereby embracing them not only within a family idiom as kin but also within the framework of the nation-state as citizens. Along with this expanded vision of transatlantic connection, the landscape of diaspora tourism has also grown. At Assin Manso, the site of the graves of the two "returnees," there is now a prayer garden and a Wall of Remembrance where people from the diaspora can sign their names and thereby inscribe themselves into this site of remembrance. There are also plans to open a museum entitled the African Excellence Experience that will commemorate the lives of great figures in Africa and the diaspora.

These efforts suggest the elaboration of a romantic narrative of slavery that celebrates black triumph. This narrative, I have argued, while repeatedly enacted on Ghanaian soil, often excludes Ghanaians by positioning Ghana as merely the homeland of the diaspora. It also tends to overlook continuing forms of oppression, both on the continent and in the diaspora. In addition, it positions past Ghanaians as perpetrators of the slave trade and constructs a need for the "healing" of the supposed rift between Africans and blacks in the diaspora. Such celebratory narratives, of course, fit more easily within the structure of tourism. For this reason, these projects will no doubt encourage more diaspora tourists to travel to Ghana, and they may yet bring, as the tourism industry has long predicted, serious economic gains for the local economy.

If this does indeed happen, Ghanaians may become less vocal in their critiques. Their embrace of diasporic dollars will not, however, cancel their sequestering of the slave trade. After all, this sequestering is a response to the serious risks posed by their pathologization within discourses on human rights, development, and global capitalism, to name a few, and these processes show no signs of stopping.

For this reason, in part, this book has examined the ways in which men and women in Cape Coast and Elmina struggle against their marginalization in which the assignment of the slave trade as their special property is one enactment. I have argued that residents of Cape Coast and Elmina are in fact constantly engaged in negotiations of their position within a global economy of cultures and histories through the stances they take toward the slave trade. To this end, I have noted that refusing to speak about domestic slavery is an attempt to protect the coherence of families in Cape Coast and Elmina within which the descendants of both slaves and slave owners reside, as well as to present their families as proper "modern" families according to national and international definitions. In addition, I have argued that displacing slave raiding from coastal histories and onto the North is an attempt to avoid the stigmatization that this history attracts. Similarly, relegating slave commerce to nonexplicit narratives allows coastal residents to paint for themselves a cosmopolitan past and in this way to stake a claim to improved standing in the current global economy. Minimizing the slave trade within national history protects the narrative flow of colonial oppression and nationalist victory that allows Ghana to be viewed as member of a community of nations rather than as "a race of slaves." In these multiple contexts, I have argued that protecting one's identity from pathologization, whether it is the identity of the occupants of the same house, region, or nation, is an important and empowering act.

Despite the importance of these constructions of history, the identities that emerge from them possess their own inherent dangers that result from their erasure of various forms of oppression. After all, while family units are protected by narratives that sequester domestic slavery, discrimination against the descendants of slaves within families is silenced. Similarly, while coastal residents escape from stigmatization by their displacement of slave raiding from their community histories, northerners are heavily stigmatized. And while Ghana as a nation may celebrate its achievement of independence, this celebration ignores the harsh realities that many of its citizens face in the postcolonial era.

In addition, these identities require constant surveillance. While coastal residents have developed complex means of avoiding negative characterizations, none of them are permanent. They must constantly keep up their guard against the production of yet more instantiations of these very old stories. There is also the danger that these strategies may cease to work altogether. In particular, in the context of their increasing poverty, old constructions of history may no longer be tenable.

For this reason, I have also paid attention to the fact that some coastal residents have reversed direction and begun to mobilize the history of the slave trade in the same struggle in which attempts to sequester it from discourse are engaged. They do so by embracing a different conceptualization of this identity, a conceptualization that notes their struggle against the bonds of contemporary global structures of inequality. This reinterpretation, furthermore, has been heavily influenced by the diaspora. Diaspora tourism has in fact been the catalyst for such formulations. Local youth gain new perspectives on their history, not only from savvy tour guides, but also from the debates over diaspora tourism in which they engage. The question, "Are we emancipated?" as a common rejoinder to the announcement of the inauguration of the celebration of Emancipation Day in Ghana demonstrates a rejection of diaspora tourism's romantic narratives at the same time that it mobilizes a notion of enslavement in a radical critique of neoliberal policies. To this end, many Ghanaians also critique the apparent apoliticism of some African American tourists who appear to them to champion the remembrance of the slave trade while failing to mobilize its remembrance as part of a larger political agenda. Indeed, a growing number of women and men, and more especially girls and boys, have developed a critical stance toward contemporary problems that is nourished by an awareness of the slave trade.

To be sure, the formulation of these narratives by youth in Cape Coast and Elmina is unlikely to lead to a complete transformation of the ways in which history is imagined in these towns. Instead, coastal residents will no doubt continue to struggle with the emplacement of the slave trade onto their families and communities and nation. One arena of representation like the tourism industry is unlikely to completely change the shape of historical consciousness even in the best of circumstances. Public histories are varied and dynamic, but they are also sites of intense negotiation. These negotiations are not simply internal; they depend upon, as we have seen here, shifts in European historiography, the level of international interest that different regions can command in development projects, and the kinds of scrutiny applied to even the most intimate of spaces, like the family home.

Nonetheless, their refashioning of the slave trade demands our attention because it seeks not only to improve the position of Africans within the global economy but to challenge the roots of that economy itself. The history of the slave trade certainly has the potential to challenge Western capitalist exploitation as a modus operandi in global relations. In this way, Ghanaians' refashioned narratives have also led to the recognition of ties to the African diaspora based not on Ghana's position as its homeland but on a recognition of past and present shared experiences of oppression. While Ghana has long been the site of pan-African constructions of identity, the use of the history of the slave trade as the basis of these claims represents a shift of attention to the Atlantic era. This shift has occurred through a recognition of the fact that men and women on the African continent were caught up in a system of oppression in which they were alternately victims and pawns.

We have long understood that the African diaspora makes use of the figures of both Africa and the slave trade (see Scott 1991). In the process, however, it often reduces Africa to its womb. Rather than viewing the African continent as a dynamic place of ongoing struggles, it views it instead as its prehistory, as a remnant of a time that is now dead.[1] What Ghanaians' refashioning of historical discourse demonstrates is that it is not merely the homeland of the African diaspora; it is also a site of struggle against contemporary forms of racism in which it too can make use of the figures of both the slave trade and the diaspora. Africa is not dead, in spite of the corpses carried across the Atlantic for Emancipation Day.

The slave trade has never been solely the history of those who were captured from their homes, placed in chains, carried across the sea, and forced to toil on plantations. It is also the history of those in the bondage of the global system of oppression that emerged at the moment of this forced migration. This interpretation provides then a different vision of black Atlantic community that might be a stronger basis for connection than those based on overcoming the divide between those who were enslaved and those who remained. Rather than assert such a strictly delimited group experience, we might instead seek out the ways in which the repercussions of these experiences have been linked. The adoption of this black Atlantic identity furthermore is a challenge to white power, which was the basis of the slave trade and remains to a large extent the basis of contemporary global relations. If conceived of in this way, on this small stretch of the West African coastline and elsewhere in the Atlantic world, remembering the slave trade might steer the way toward a brighter horizon.

NOTES

INTRODUCTION

1   I am indebted to Matory's (2005) critique of collective memory studies for their suggestion of passivity. He suggests that scholars instead examine dialogues, which point both to an active process and to the involvement of multiple parties.

2   The exclusion of the slave trade from discourse extends to African literature as well, as Opoku-Agyemang notes. In speaking of the perception of the slave trade among the characters in Achebe's *Things Fall Apart*, he writes, "There is no residual hurt, no memory of anger or danger, no lingering knowledge of defeat or a heritage of resistance" (Opoku-Agyemang 1992, 69).

3   Very few scholars have addressed at length practices of sequestering the slave trade from discursive constructions of history in African communities. Bailey (2005) addresses oral histories of the slave trade among the Ewe in Ghana but in the spirit of attempting to prove their existence. While she outlines some possible reasons for the reticence of most people to discuss the slave trade in the introduction, she turns in the body of the book to histories retained by elders in the community. Larson (2000) examines the silences with regard to the slave trade within a collection of traditional texts in Madagascar and explores the politics of silence during the time period in which they were collected and recorded. Although this type of research moves us toward discursive constructions of history rather than symbolic ones, they are written histories and therefore do not necessarily reflect how contemporary people in Madagascar imagine their history within other arenas.

4   David Scott (1999) calls for this type of analysis with regard to colonialism. See chapter 5 for a fuller discussion.

CHAPTER 1

1 Most studies of the Gold Coast in the seventeenth and eighteenth centuries focus
on either the Fante states (McCarthy 1983; Shumway 2004) or on what became
the Gold Coast Protectorate, namely, the coastal areas of Ghana (Daaku 1970;
Kea 1982; Reynolds 1974). Exceptions include Feinberg's (1989) and DeCorse's
(2001) studies of Elmina and Graham's (1994) study of Cape Coast.

2 Akan is the language family dominant in southern Ghana and includes the Fante
dialect.

3 Lawrence (1964) and van Dantzig (1980) provide further details on the histories
of the forts and castles in Ghana.

4 The Danish traded from Christianborg Castle in Accra, but their trade remained
on a much smaller scale.

5 *Caboceer* is a corruption of the Portuguese term, *caboceiro* or "captain" (McCarthy
1983, 15, n.5).

6 References to the Fantes during this period refer to members of the Fante Confederation, not more broadly to Fante speakers. Historians therefore refer to conflicts between the Fante and Elminans.

7 The European companies on the coast held a large number of slaves who worked
for them at the castles. In 1816, the Royal African Company owned 454 slaves
(McCarthy 1983, 48), and the West India Company maintained approximately
six hundred slaves during the eighteenth century (DeCorse 2001, 35). Most of
the men worked as carpenters, bricklayers, and other skilled artisans, while the
women served as household servants and general laborers. Many of these slaves
were imported from other areas in West Africa. Some local people became castle
slaves after going to the castles to seek protection, particularly those who were
impoverished or who had been disowned by their families (McCarthy 1983, 48),
but the majority remained foreign-born slaves, which served to maintain distinctions between them and the townspeople (Reynolds 1974, 13).

   In addition to protection, castle slaves also received payment for their services to buy food. They lived in a separate area adjacent to the castles and formed
their own *asafo* company, which they named *Brofumba* or "white man's servants"
(van den Nieuwenhof 1995, 18). What defined their status as slaves rather than
as merely servants was that all of their actions were controlled by the companies,
and if they acted without the consent of their company, they could be sold overseas (McCarthy 1983, 48). In 1822, when the Crown took over control of Cape
Coast Castle, it freed the company slaves, but many of them continued to work
for the British as servants (Feinberg 1989).

8 In the Indonesian situation to which she refers, distinctions between Europeans and locals were more significant because of the presence of a large colonial bureaucracy, suggesting that the Dutch on the Gold Coast would have
been even more likely to embrace the idea of having relationships with local
women.

9 Dutch law also necessitated that fathers provide for their children born to African mothers out of wedlock (DeCorse 2001, 37).

10 I use this term following Gocking (1999), who elaborates on the significance of the Euro-African class in coastal Ghana.

11 This term often appears in the historical literature as *donko* or *donkor*.

12 This term, which refers both to northerners and slaves, is discussed in chapter 4.

13 Ferme (2001) similarly discusses the "retrenchment from modernity" of the Mende of Sierra Leone as a response to encounters with the slave trade.

14 Lovejoy and Richardson (2003, 105) make a similar argument with regard to the Efik traders at Old Calabar, namely, that the development of European tastes served as cultural markers that helped to distinguish them from those they dealt in as slaves.

15 Translation: 'People who wear native dress.'

16 The failure of the colonial system to reward coastal elites for their mimicking of the culture of the metropole is not only due to specific historical factors but also to the general design of colonialism in that it necessitates the continued subordination of its subjects. Bhabha's (1994) phrase "not quite/not white" captures the colonial power's requirement of the assimilation of its subjects, but also these subjects' ultimate failure, in order to maintain the legitimacy of its power. He states, "The success of colonial appropriation depends on a proliferation of inappropriate objects that ensure its strategic failure" (1994, 86). Thus, the colonial subject is perpetually striving toward an assimilation that she never achieves. This hypocrisy is, of course, at the heart of the colonial endeavor. As Comaroff and Comaroff describe it, "British colonialism, and colonial evangelism, was everywhere a double gesture. On one hand, it justified itself in terms of difference and inequality: the greater enlightenment of the colonizer legitimized his right to rule and civilize. On the other, that legitimacy was founded, ostensibly, on a commitment to the eventual erasure of difference in the name of a common humanity. Of course, had the difference actually been removed, the bases of overrule would themselves have disappeared. It was not; they did not" (1997, 396).

17 Sarbah along with many other prominent Fante nationalists like J. E. Casely Hayford (see 1969 [1911]) and Attoh Ahuma (see 1971) critiqued practices of European assimilation found in dress, speech, naming practices, and countless other arenas. But their attack on assimilation did not bear much fruit. Most of these individuals themselves failed to make such changes and ultimately embraced cultural nationalism as a literary project alone (Gocking 1984). Instead of a cultural renaissance, their critiques led only to greater awareness of Fante assimilation. Notions of Fante identity within the popular imagination of coastal residents at this time and, as I discuss in forthcoming chapters, in many ways since center around both their struggle for political autonomy from the British and their practices of assimilation. Their experiences of the slave trade, however, were not part of this equation.

18 Other scholars report his name as Caramansa. Although most scholars argue that Caramansa is a corruption of Kwamena Ansa, Claridge (1973) argues that the reverse is true.

19 The story of Kwamena Ansa was recorded by João de Barros, a Portuguese chronicler who was employed as a low-level officer at Elmina Castle in the 1520s. He wrote *Decades in Asia* in 1552 in which he describes the meeting between Ansa and D'Azambuja and the speeches given by each. P. E. H. Hair notes that it was not uncommon for historians of this era to invent the speeches of their subjects "expressing what might have been said, or at least silently thought, by the character on the occasion" (1994, 8). Sarbah relies on de Barros's account. For other discussions of this story, see Wartemburg (1950), Ellis (1964), Blake (1942), and Claridge (1915).

20 Christensen argues this point in his discussion of refusals of marriage proposals: "[T]he Fanti rarely use a direct negation on such an occasion, and resort to either a proverb or subterfuge to indicate refusal" (1954, 60).

21 Austen and Smith (1969) discuss the connection between arguments for abolition and the rise of colonial rule in West Africa imagined as the assumption of responsibility for those populations that had been demoralized by the slave trade.

CHAPTER 2

1 The names used in this text are pseudonyms, except for a few cases in which individuals requested that I use their real names. I use the terms "Auntie" and "Uncle" for many individuals because these are commonly used titles in Ghana for women and men who belong to the generation of one's parents and therefore titles that I frequently used when speaking to older individuals.

2 Cole (2001) similarly argues that memories of colonialism reemerge despite their submergence in Madagascar.

3 The ɔmanhene is chosen from a particular lineage. Within that lineage, only those who do not have slave ancestry are eligible.

4 See Antze and Lambek (1996) for a discussion of the connection between personal memory and social narrative.

5 Casely Hayford notes that in response to the question "'Who told you your family history?' the answer is often returned, 'My grandmother told me'" (1970, 79). Penningroth makes this point as well with regard to facts about ancestry (2003, 33).

6 Poku (1969) suggests that among the Asante, the taboos surrounding the discussion of slave ancestry have lessened since precolonial times. He describes the environment in which slave ancestry is discussed, "Only the simplest of precautions are taken before revealing secrets which 60 or 70 years ago might have proved fatal to the narrator—small children are chased away, and care is taken to see that no one of a discussed slave stock is likely to overhear" (1969, 36).

7 See Klein (1989). Also see Robertson (1983) for an example of a successful documentation of an oral history of slavery. In contrast, Poku (1969) notes that many individuals are willing to discuss their slave ancestry if approached privately.

8   See Massey (1994) on the significance of "a place to call home" in the postmodern age.

CHAPTER 3

1   I follow Shaw (2002) in her argument that memories of slavery, colonialism, and postcolonialism may become mapped on top of each other, with memories of each period contributing to an understanding of the others.

2   The first Methodist church in Ghana was established in Cape Coast in 1835. It was the second major European religion, after Anglicanism, to be introduced in Ghana by the British. Methodist missionaries built the Wesley Chapel in the center of town. In 1992, the Methodist Church in Cape Coast had 3,000 members (Arhin 1995, 41). For the history of Methodism in Ghana, see Bartels (1965), Debrunner (1967), and Southon (1934).

3   The story of the founding of the church in Obidan, which is recorded by several European writers, has long been part of the popular history of the Methodist Church on the coast, but in 1952, a church official declared that he wanted church members to celebrate the anniversary of the destruction of the shrine as the moment of the church's founding. He asked John Crayner, a former teacher and a member of the Methodist Church in Obidan, to research the story of Akweesi. Crayner discovered that his wife is the great granddaughter of Akweesi, and, therefore, he was able to access some of the details of the story that had previously remained hidden. During an anniversary celebration for Akweesi held in 1952, Crayner recited the story. He published the story in Fante in 1963 and in English in 1979 in a book entitled *Akweesi and the Fall of the Nananom Pɔw.*

4   Two contemporary accounts by McCaskie (1990) and Kea (2000) have analyzed this historical episode. In addition, Kea (1986) notes elsewhere that local priests became involved in practices of banditry. Thus, the disappearance of travelers near the shrine suggests their capture and enslavement by the priests, thereby challenging the popular notion of coastal immunity to enslavement, which I have argued is the hallmark of coastal identity. Whereas usually within public discourse danger and violence are displaced onto the North, memories of coastal cruelty emerge within stories of liminal spaces between coastal towns and the bush.

   The story of Akweesi and the *Nananom Mpow* has long been recognized as a sort of origin story of Methodism on the coast. The adage "the *Nananom* was made by man" is a popular saying in the region that summarizes the outcome of the story, namely, the exposure of the fraudulent nature of the shrine's claim of spiritual authority, which was in actuality the authority of the priests themselves, and its displacement by Christianity.

5   Brown similarly notes that many discourses in Britain erect a "moral cordon" around Liverpool such that it "becomes Britain's symbol, par excellence, of racial backwardness" thereby "absolving other places on the national map" (2005, 181).

6   Feature article of Sunday, February 20, 2005, on www.ghanaweb.com.

CHAPTER 4

1 The full text of this speech is available at http://www.koninklijkhuis.nl/content
.jsp?objectid=4172.
2 Takoradi and Tema later became Ghana's major ports.
3 Many scholars have made similar arguments regarding the selling of slaves
through their analyses of private and ritual discourses throughout West Africa.
For instance, Rattray (1932) notes the existence of a ritual practice among the Talensi in northern Ghana to purify the land when someone sells a member of his
or her own family into slavery. Scholars have noted similar practices throughout
West Africa. Robert Baum (1999) explains that within Diola villages in Senegal,
secret sacrifices must be performed by the descendants of those who sold their
children into the slave trade (see also Brown 2003). Thus, here not only is there
a notion of culpability that creates the risk of spiritual vengeance, but such culpability is passed down through families such that contemporary individuals must
still negotiate their relationship with the history of the slave trade. While these
examples focus on the selling of family members, the more general picture is
one in which the selling of slaves is tied to notions of immorality.
4 The belief in magically reproducing beads was reported as early as 1819 by Bowdich, a European observer who remarked, "The natives believe that by burying
the aggrey beads in the sand they not only grow but breed" (1873, 268).
5 Despite Ghana's relative political stability, and even the hopefulness inspired by
the swearing in of a new president during the year that I lived there, many of the
actions of government officials have led to the belief that the current government
is also a kleptocratic regime. During my time in the field, the affair that captured
everyone's attention was when the minister of sports was convicted of stealing
US $40,000 with which he had been entrusted to give to the members of the
national soccer team for their bonuses. (He claimed that the money had been in
a suitcase that he checked when boarding a flight and that when he arrived at his
destination and retrieved the suitcase, the money was gone). Theft, like enslavement, entails one person's gain at another person's loss.
6 In fact, when I asked a young man the literal meaning of the expression, he
struggled to translate it, thinking that the reference to the Dutch must be a reference to Dutch Komenda, a neighboring coastal town.
7 Feature article of December 21, 2004, on www.ghanaweb.com.
8 This nostalgia is distinct from the "imperialist nostalgia" that Rosaldo describes, which
is a nostalgia for the traditional culture that the imperialist has destroyed (1989).
9 Comaroff and Comaroff similarly note that "people who reject an ideological
message may yet be reformed by its medium" (1992, 259).

CHAPTER 5

1 See Kaba (2001) for an example of the negative response to the documentary.
2 Zachernuk (1998) provides an in-depth analysis of the notion of African

backwardness in school textbooks written by British historians during colonialism.

3　See www.edughana.net for more information on schooling statistics.

4　The book to which I am referring and which was in use in 2001 when I conducted this research is *Social Studies for Junior Secondary Schools, Pupil's Book Two.* It was published by the Curriculum Research and Development Division of the Ghana Education Service in 1988. Since then, as I discuss in chapter 7, the social studies syllabus has changed.

5　There is a large body of literature on this subject. See, for instance, Sharp (2001, 2002) and Wertsch (2002).

6　The title of this section is meant to invoke Frederick Cooper's article, "The Problem of Slavery in African Studies," which addresses domestic slavery in Africa. I explore here, in contrast, the problems associated with the study of the Atlantic slave trade in Africa.

7　In his discussion of West Africa historiography, Fage (1971) writes that 1948 marks the beginning of its modern period.

8　Fage expounds upon this argument in his 1969 article for which he is perhaps most well known outside of Ghana. The article set off a firestorm of responses, most notable of which are those of Rodney (1982) Inikori (1982), and Wrigley (1971).

9　Rodney would later fully expound on the negative effects of the slave trade in his book *How Europe Underdeveloped Africa*, which I discuss below.

10　See especially Inikori (1982), who argues with Rodney that Fage's argument cannot be supported.

11　Scott's description of tragedy points to this definition. He notes that "the colonial past may never let go" (2004, 220); at the same time, however, he writes, "The sense of the tragic for our postcolonial time is not the belief that we are likewise doomed, that change is futile, that in the end we are mere pawns of imperial tyranny" (2004, 221). He argues instead simply that our struggles must be tempered by knowledge of the contingencies of the past.

12　Similarly, in her discussion of the presentation of the history of the slave trade in Liverpool, England, Jacqueline Brown (2005) notes that some teachers fail to mention it at all and that even those who do may restrict their discussion to Liverpool, thereby limiting the scope of its significance and (inadvertently) providing a justification for its exclusion from the national consciousness.

CHAPTER 6

1　See Thomas (1999) for a discussion of the celebration of Emancipation Day in Jamaica.

2　See Gaines (1998, 2006), Jenkins (1975), Lake (1997), Meriwether (2002), and Walters (1993) for discussions of African Americans in Ghana during the independence era.

3　Davis writes that it constructs "an overt political agenda of social protest" (1998, 256–57).

4 Conversation with Albert Wuddah Martey, curator, Elmina Castle, May 2001.

5 See Bruner (1996), Singleton (1999), and Kreamer (2006) for other discussions of the debates surrounding the conservation of the castles.

6 There is also a film that is shown at the beginning of the exhibit that visitors can choose to watch. Here an image of contemporary Ghanaian culture is collapsed with its precontact culture, suggesting again that Ghana is merely the diaspora's past (see Richards 2005).

7 Richards argues that "administrators of these sites must devise a means of softening the horror by effecting a substitution in which a healthy actor or progress narrative stands in for the dehumanized body and tale of abjection" (2005, 632).

8 The exhibit, "Sighting Memories: An Exhibition of Poetry and Photographs Dedicated to All Those Who Resisted," was held at Cape Coast Castle from July 29 to August 3, 2001. The exhibit brochure states, "That our ancestors were enslaved does not make slavery our heritage. It is more reasonable and truer to the history to consider the ancestors' unbroken resistance to enslavement as our proper heritage."

9 I draw here on Tim Edensor's (1998) discussion of the Taj Mahal and of its interpretation by tourist officials and tourists in terms of specific symbolic realms, which he calls colonial space, sacred space, and national space. He thus applies Massey's (1994) formulation of the multiple and shifting meanings of place, by which she refers to larger locales such as towns and countries, to a particular structure, the Taj Mahal, a perspective that applies as well to the castles.

10 I brought soil back at my father's request, which he uses during Kwanzaa to pour libations in honor of our ancestors.

11 GMMB officials told me that they have plans to remove the wall blocking this tunnel so that visitors can walk through it and take the same path that male slaves took out of the castle, but for now, visitors must make do with walking over the top of the tunnel.

12 While some tour guides report that women who became pregnant in the castles were freed and occupied the large merchant houses in town, this was not likely the case. As I discuss in chapter 1, African women who married European men were more commonly from local, sometimes elite, families.

CHAPTER 7

1 I provide a further discussion of this comment and others responses to Emancipation and specifically, local critiques of its failure to bring economic development in Holsey (2004).

CONCLUSION

1 Early anthropologists created similar visions of Africa, as Johannes Fabian (1983) famously notes.

BIBLIOGRAPHY

Abu-Lughod, Lila. 1990. "The Romance of Resistance: Tracing Transformations of Power through Bedouin Women." *American Ethnologist* 17(1): 41–55.

Adams, John. 1966 [1823]. *Remarks on the Country Extending from Cape Palmas to the River Congo*. London: Frank Cass & Co. Ltd.

Aidoo, Ama Ata. 1970. *Anowa*. London: Longman Drumbeat.

Akantoe, Boniface. 1998. "The Impact of the Slave Trade on the Nankani." In *The Slave Trade and Reconciliation: A Northern Ghanaian Perspective*. Edited by Allison Howell. Navrongo, Upper East Region, Ghana: Bible Church of Africa.

Akyea, W. Nkunu. 2001. "A Touristic Dimension of the Historic and Political Role of Cape Coast in the Development of Ghana." In *Oguaaman: An Annal of History, Religion and Culture of Cape Coast*. Cape Coast: Africa Best Enterprise.

Akyeampong, Emmanuel. 2001. "History, Memory, Slave-Trade, and Slavery in Anlo (Ghana)." *Slavery and Abolition* 22(3): 1–24.

Allman, Jean. 1991. "'Hewers of Wood, Carriers of Water': Islam, Class, and Politics on the Eve of Ghana's Independence." *African Studies Review* 34(2): 1–26.

Allman, Jean, and John Parker. 2005. *Tongnaab: The History of a West African God*. Bloomington: Indiana University Press.

Alpern. 1995. "What Africans Got for Their Slaves: A Master List of European Trade Goods." *History in Africa* 22: 5–43.

Anderson, Benedict. 1991. *Imagined Communities: Reflections on the Origin and Spread of Nationalism*. Rev. ed. London: Verso.

Angelou, Maya. 1986. *All God's Children Need Traveling Shoes*. New York: Random House.

Antze, Paul, and Michael Lambek, eds. 1996. "Introduction: Forecasting Memory." In *Tense Past: Cultural Essays in Trauma and Memory*. New York: Routledge.

Appadurai, Arjun. 1996. *Modernity at Large: Cultural Dimensions of Globalization*. Minneapolis: University of Minnesota Press.

Appiah, Kwame Anthony. 1992. *In My Father's House: Africa in the Philosophy of Culture*. New York & Oxford: Oxford University Press.

Apter, Andrew. 2005. *The Pan-African Nation: Oil and the Spectacle of Culture in Nigeria*. Chicago: University of Chicago Press.

Arhin, Kwame. 1983. "Rank and Class among the Asante and Fante in the Nineteenth Century." *Africa* 53(1): 2–22.

———. 1995. "Cape Coast and Elmina in Historical Perspective." In *The Cape Coast and Elmina Handbook: Past, Present and Future*. Edited by Kwame Arhin. Legon: Institute of African Studies, University of Ghana.

Armah, Ayi Kwei. 1970. *Fragments*. Boston: Houghton Mifflin.

———. 1972. *Why Are We So Blest?* Garden City, N.Y.: Doubleday.

———. 1979. *Two Thousand Seasons*. London: Heinemann.

Atafori, A. Kapini. 1999. "Panafest'99: Festival with a Difference." *Business Watch* July: 3(6):5–9.

Attoh Ahumah, S. R. B. 1971 [1911]. *The Gold Coast Nation and National Consciousness*. London: Frank Cass & Co. Ltd.

Austen, Ralph A. 2001. "The Slave Trade as History and Memory: Confrontations of Slaving Voyage Documents and Communal Traditions." *William and Mary Quarterly* 58(1): 229–44.

Austen, Ralph A., and Jonathan Derrick. 1999. *Middlemen of the Cameroons River: The Duala and Their Hinterland, c. 1600–1960*. Cambridge: Cambridge University Press.

Austen, Ralph A., and Woodruff D. Smith. 1969. "Images of Africa and British Slave-Trade Abolition: The Transition to an Imperialist Ideology, 1787–1807." *African Historical Studies* 2(1): 69–83.

Bailey, Anne C. 2005. *African Voices of the Atlantic Slave Trade: Beyond the Silence and the Shame*. Boston: Beacon Press.

Baker, Lee D. 1998. *From Savage to Negro: Anthropology and the Construction of Race, 1896–1954*. Berkeley: University of California Press.

Bartels, F. L. 1965. *The Roots of Ghana Methodism*. Cambridge: Cambridge University Press.

Battaglia, Debbora. 1992. "The Body in the Gift: Memory and Forgetting in Sabarl Mortuary Exchange." *American Ethnologist* 19(1): 3–18.

Batten, T. R. 1953 [1938]. *Tropical Africa in World History*. Oxford: Oxford University Press.

Baucom, Ian. 2005. *Specters of the Atlantic: Finance Capital, Slavery, and the Philosophy of History*. Durham, N.C.: Duke University Press.

Baum, Robert M. 1999. *Shrines of the Slave Trade: Diola Religion and Society in Precolonial Senegambia*. Oxford and New York: Oxford University Press.

Bauman, Zygmunt. 1989. *Modernity and the Holocaust*. Ithaca, N.Y.: Cornell University Press.

Berlin, Ira. 1998. *Many Thousands Gone: The First Two Centuries of Slavery in North America*. Cambridge, Mass.: Harvard University Press.

————. 2004. "American Slavery in History and Memory and the Search for Social Justice." *Journal of American History* March: 1251–68.

Bhabha, Homi K. 1994. *The Location of Culture.* London: Routledge.

Blake, John. 1942. *Europeans in West Africa, 1450–1500.* London: Hakluyt Society.

Blier, Suzanne Preston. 1995. *African Vodun: Art, Psychology, and Power.* Chicago: University of Chicago Press.

Boahen, Adu. 1966. *Topics in West African History, Schools Edition.* London: Longman.

Bosman, William. 1967 [1704]. *A New and Accurate Description of the Coast of Guinea.* 4th ed. New York: Barnes and Noble.

Bowdich, T. E. 1873 [1819]. *Mission from Cape Coast Castle to Ashantee.* London: Griffith and Farran.

Brooks, George E. 1962. "The Letter Book of Captain Edward Harrington." *Transactions of the Historical Society of Ghana* 6: 71–77.

Brown, Carolyn. 2003. "Memory as Resistance: Identity and the Contested History of Slavery in Southeastern Nigeria, an Oral History Project." In *Fighting the Slave Trade: West African Strategies.* Edited by Sylviane A. Diouf. Athens, Ohio: Ohio University Press.

Brown, E. J. P. 1929. *Gold Coast and Asianti Reader.* London: Published on Behalf of the Government of the Gold Coast Colony by the Crown Agents of the Colony.

Brown, Jacqueline Nassy. 2000. "Enslaving History: Narratives on Local Whiteness in a Black Atlantic Port." *American Ethnologist* 27(2): 340–70.

————. 2005. *Dropping Anchor, Setting Sail: Geographies of Race in Black Liverpool.* Princeton: Princeton University Press.

Bruner, Edward. 1996. "Tourism in Ghana: The Representation of Slavery and the Return of the Black Diaspora." *American Anthropologist* 98(2): 290–304.

Campt, Tina M. 2004. *Other Germans: Black Germans and the Politics of Race, Gender, and Memory in the Third Reich.* Ann Arbor: University of Michigan Press.

Carsten, Janet. 1995. "The Politics of Forgetting: Migration, Kinship and Memory on the Periphery of the Southeast Asian State." *Journal of Royal Anthopology* 1: 317–35.

Casely Hayford, J. E. 1970 [1911]. *Ethiopia Unbound: Studies in Race Emancipation.* London: Frank Cass & Co.

————. 1970 [1903]. *Gold Coast Native Institutions.* London: Cass.

Chakrabarty, Dipesh. 1992. "Postcoloniality and the Artifice of History: Who Speaks for 'Indian' Pasts." *Representations* 37: 1–26.

Christensen, James Boyd. 1954. *Double Descent among the Fanti.* New Haven: Human Relations Area Files.

Claridge, W. Walton. 1964 [1915]. *A History of the Gold Coast and Ashanti from Earliest Times to the Commencement of the Twentieth Century.* Vol. 1. London: Frank Cass & Co.

Clarke, Kamari Maxine. 2004. *Mapping Yorùbá Networks: Power and Agency in the Making of Transnational Communities.* Durham, N.C.: Duke University Press.

Clifford, James. 1997. *Routes: Travel and Translation in the Late Twentieth Century*. Cambridge, Mass.: Harvard University Press.

Cole, Jennifer. 1998. "The Work of Memory in Madagascar." *American Ethnologist* 25(4): 610–33.

———. 2001. *Forget Colonialism?: Sacrifice and the Art of Memory in Madagascar*. Berkeley: University of California Press.

Comaroff, Jean, and John L. Comaroff. 1991. *Of Revelation and Revolution*. Vol. 1. *Christianity, Colonialism and Consciousness in South Africa*. Chicago: University of Chicago Press.

———. 1992. *Ethnography and the Historical Imagination*. Boulder: Westview Press.

———. 1993. "Introduction." In *Modernity and Its Malcontents: Ritual and Power in Postcolonial Africa*. Edited by Jean Comaroff and John Comaroff. Chicago: University of Chicago Press.

Comaroff, John L., and Jean Comaroff. 1997. *Of Revelation and Revolution*. Vol 2. *The Dialectics of Modernity on a South African Frontier*. Chicago: University of Chicago Press.

Connerton, Paul 1989. *How Societies Remember*. Cambridge: Cambridge University Press.

Constable, Pamela. 2001. "Consensus Lacking on How to Address Legacy of Slavery, Debate at World Racism Conference Focuses on Apologies vs. Reparations." *Washington Post*, September 2.

Cooper, Frederick. 1979. "The Problem of Slavery in African Studies." *Journal of African History* 20(1): 103–25.

Coupland, Reginald. 1933. *The British Anti-Slavery Movement*. London: Frank Cass.

Crayner, John Brandford. 1979. *Akweesi and the Fall of the Nananom Pɔw*. Cape Coast: Methodist Book Depot.

Cruickshank, Brodie. 1966 [1853]. *Eighteen Years on the Gold Coast of Africa*. Vols. 1 and 2. 2d ed. London: Frank Cass.

Curriculum Research and Development Division, Ghana Education Service. 1988. *Social Studies for Junior Secondary Schools, Pupil's Book Two*. Accra: Ministry of Education and Culture.

Curtin, P. D. 1975. *Economic Change in Precolonial Africa: Senegambia in the Era of the Slave Trade*. Madison: University of Wisconsin Press.

Daaku, Kwame Yeboa. 1970. *Trade and Politics on the Gold Coast: 1600–1720: A Study of the African Reaction to European Trade*. Oxford: Clarendon Press.

Davies, K. G. 1957. *The Royal African Company*. New York: Longmans.

Davis, Kimberly Chabot. 1998. "'Postmodern Blackness': Toni Morrison's *Beloved* and the End of History." *Twentieth Century Literature* 44(2): 242–60.

Davis, Olga Idriss. 1997. "The Door of No Return: Reclaiming the Past through the Rhetoric of Pilgrimage." *Western Journal of Black Studies* 21(3): 156–61.

Debrunner, Hans. 1959. *Witchcraft in Ghana: A Study on the Belief in Destructive Witches and Its Effect on the Akan Tribes*. Accra: Presbyterian Book Depot.

———. 1967. *A History of Christianity in Ghana.* Accra: Waterville Publishing House.

DeCorse, Christopher R. 2001. *An Archaeology of Elmina: Africans and Europeans on the Gold Coast: 1400–1900.* Washington, D.C.: Smithsonian Institution Press.

Der, Benedict G. 1998. *The Slave Trade in Northern Ghana.* Accra: Woeli Publishing Services.

Diouf, Sylviane A. 2003. "Introduction." In *Fighting the Slave Trade: West African Strategies.* Edited by Sylviane A. Diouf. Athens, Ohio: Ohio University Press.

Drucker-Brown, Susan. 1993. "Mamprusi Witchcraft, Subversion and Changing Gender Relations." *Africa* 63(4): 531–49.

Duah, Francis Boakye. 2000. "Ghana Museums and History: Cape Coast Castle Museum." In *Museums and History in West Africa.* Edited by Claude Daniel Ardouin and Emmanuel Arinze. Washington, D.C.: Smithsonian Institution Press.

Du Bois, W. E. B. 1989. *The Souls of Black Folk.* New York: Bantam.

Ebron, Paulla A. 1999. "Tourists as Pilgrims: Commercial Fashioning of Transatlantic Politics." *American Ethnologist* 26(4): 910–32.

———. 2002. *Performing Africa.* Princeton: Princeton University Press.

Edensor, Tim. 1998. *Tourists at the Taj: Performance and Meaning at a Symbolic Site.* London: Routledge.

Ellis, A. B. 1969 [1893]. *A History of the Gold Coast of West Africa.* New York: Negro Universities Press.

Elwert, Georg. 1989. *An Intricate Oral Culture: On History, Humour, and Social Control among the Ayizo (Bénin).* Berlin: Arabische Buch.

Everts, Natalie. 1996. "*Cherchez la Femme*: Gender-Related Issues in Eighteenth-Century Elmina." *Itinerario* 20(1): 45–57.

Fabian, Johannes. 1983. *Time and the Other: How Anthropology Makes Its Object.* New York: Columbia University Press.

Fage, J. D. 1955. *An Introduction to the History of West Africa.* Cambridge: Cambridge University Press.

———. 1969. "Slavery and the Slave Trade in the Context of West African History." *Journal of African History* 10: 393–404.

———. 1971. "Continuity and Change in the Writing of West African History." *African Affairs* 70(280): 236–51.

Fanon, Frantz. 1963. *The Wretched of the Earth.* New York: Grove Press.

———. 1967. *Black Skin, White Masks.* New York: Grove Press.

Feinberg, Harvey M. 1989. *Africans and Europeans in West Africa: Elminans and Dutchmen on the Gold Coast during the Eighteenth Century.* Philadelphia: American Philosophical Society.

Ferguson, James. 1999. *Expectations of Modernity: Myths and Meanings of Urban Life on the Zambian Copperbelt.* Berkeley: University of California Press.

———. 2002. "Of Mimicry and Membership: African and the 'New World Society.'" *Cultural Anthropology* 17(4): 551–69.

———. 2006. *Global Shadows: Africa in the Neoliberal World Order.* Durham, N.C.: Duke University Press.

Ferme, Mariane C. 2001. *The Underneath of Things: Violence, History, and the Everyday in Sierra Leone.* Berkeley: University of California Press.

Field, M. J. 1948. *Akim-Kotoku: An Oman of the Gold Coast.* London: Crown Agents for the Colonies.

Fortes, Meyer. 1969. *Kinship and Social Order: The Legacy of Henry Louis Morgan.* Chicago: Aldine.

Foster, Philip. 1963. "Secondary Schooling and Mobility in a West African Nation." *Sociology of Education* 37(2): 150–71.

———. 1965. *Education and Social Change in Ghana.* Chicago: University of Chicago Press.

Foucault, Michel. 1972. *The Archaeology of Knowledge.* New York: Pantheon Books.

———. 1982. "Afterward: The Subject and Power." In *Beyond Structuralism and Hermeneutics.* Edited by Hubert Dreyfus and Paul Rabinow. Chicago: University of Chicago Press.

Fynn, J. K., and R. Addo-Fenning. 1991. *History for Senior Secondary Schools.* Accra: Ministry of Education.

Gable, Eric. 1995. "The Decolonization of Consciousness: Local Skeptics and the 'Will to Be Modern' in a West African Village." *American Ethnologist* 22(2): 242–57.

———. 2006. "The Funeral and Modernity in Manjaco." *Cultural Anthropology* 21(3): 385–415.

Gaines, Kevin K. 1998. "The Cold War and African American Expatriate Community in Nkrumah's Ghana." In *Universities and Empires: Money and Politics in the Social Sciences during the Cold War.* Edited by Christopher Simpson. New York: New Press.

———. 2006. *American Africans in Ghana: Black Expatriates and the Civil Rights Era.* Chapel Hill: University of North Carolina Press.

Gates, Henry Louis, Jr. 2001a. "The Future of Slavery's Past." *New York Times,* July 29.

———. 2001b. "Preface." *William and Mary Quarterly* 58(1): 3–5.

Geertz, Clifford. 1973. "Deep Play: Notes on a Balinese Cockfight." In *The Interpretation of Cultures.* New York: Basic Books.

Gerima, Haile. 1993. *Sankofa* [film]. Washington, D.C.: Myphedus Films.

Getz, Trevor R. 2004. *Slavery and Reform in West Africa: Toward Emancipation in Nineteenth-Century Senegal and the Gold Coast.* Athens, Ohio: Ohio University Press.

Gillis, John R., ed. 1994. *Commemorations: The Politics of National Identity.* Princeton: Princeton University Press.

Gilroy, Paul. 1993. *The Black Atlantic: Modernity and Double Consciousness.* Cambridge, Mass.: Harvard University Press.

Gocking, Roger. 1984. "Creole Society and the Revival of Traditional Culture in Cape Coast during the Colonial Period." *International Journal of African Historical Studies* 17(4): 601–22.

———. 1999. *Facing Two Ways: Ghana's Coastal Communities under Colonial Rule.* Lanham, Md.: University Press of America.

Gomez, Michael A. 1998. *Exchanging Our Country Marks: The Transformation of African Identities in the Colonial and Antebellum South.* Chapel Hill, N.C.: University of North Carolina Press.

Goody, Jack. 1971. *Technology, Tradition, and the State in Africa.* London: Oxford University Press.

Graham, C. K. 1971. *The History of Education in Ghana: From the Earliest Times to the Declaration of Independence.* London: Frank Cass & Co., Ltd.

Graham, J. Erskine. 1994. *Cape Coast in History.* Cape Coast: Anglican Printing Press.

Greene, Sandra. 1997. "Crossing Boundaries/Changing Identities: Female Slaves, Male Strangers, and Their descendants in Nineteenth- and Twentieth-Century Anlo." In *Gendered Encounters: Challenging Cultural Boundaries and Social Hierarchies in Africa.* Edited by Maria Grosz-Ngaté and Omari H. Kokole. New York: Routledge.

———. 2003. "Whispers and Silences: Explorations in African Oral History." *Africa Today* 50(2): 40–53.

Hagan, George P. 1993. "Nkrumah's Cultural Policy." In *The Life and Work of Kwame Nkrumah.* Edited by Kwame Arhin. Trenton: Africa World Press.

Hair, P. E. H. 1994. *The Founding of the Castelo de São Jorge Da Mina: An Analysis of the Sources.* Madison: University of Wisconsin.

Halbwachs, Maurice. 1980. *The Collective Memory.* New York: Harper and Row.

Hancock, W. K. 1943. *Argument of Empire.* Harmondsworth: Penguin Books.

Handler, Richard, and Eric Gable. 1997. *The New History in an Old Museum: Creating the Past at Colonial Williamsburg.* Durham, N.C.: Duke University Press.

Hannerz, Ulf. 1992. *Cultural Complexity: Studies in the Social Organization of Meaning.* New York: Columbia University Press.

Hartman, Saidiya. 2002. "The Time of Slavery." *South Atlantic Quarterly* 101(4): 757–77.

———. 2007. *Lose Your Mother: A Journey along the Atlantic Slave Route.* New York: Farrar, Straus and Giroux.

Harvey, David. 1989. *Condition of Postmodernity: An Enquiry into the Origins of Cultural Change.* Cambridge, Mass.: Blackwell Publishers.

Hasty, Jennifer. 2002. "Rites of Passage, Routes of Redemption: Emancipation Tourism and the Wealth of Culture." *Africa Today* 49(3): 47–76.

Henige, David. 1973. "The Problem of Feedback in Oral Tradition: Four Examples for the Fante Coastlands." *Journal of African History* 14(2): 223–35.

Higginbotham, Evelyn Brooks. 1993. "The Politics of Respectability." In *Righteous Discontent: The Women's Movement in the Black Baptist Church, 1880–1920.* Cambridge, Mass.: Harvard University Press.

Holsey, Bayo. 2004. "Transatlantic Dreaming: Slavery, Tourism, and Diasporic Encounters." In *Homecomings: Unsettling Paths of Return.* Edited by Fran Markowitz and Anders H. Stefansson. Lanham, Md.: Lexington Books.

Hountondji, Paulin. 1983. *African Philosophy: Myth and Reality*. Translated by Henri Evans with the collaboration of Jonathan Rée. Introduction by Abiola Irele. Bloomington, Ind.: Indiana University Press.

Hyatt, Vera, ed. 1997. *Ghana: The Chronicle of a Museum Development Project in the Central Region*. Washington, D.C.: Smithsonian Institution.

Inikori, Joseph E. 1982. "Introduction." In *Forced Migration: The Impact of the Export Slave Trade on African Societies*. New York: Africana Publishing Company.

————. 2003. "The Struggle against the Transatlantic Slave Trade." In *Fighting the Slave Trade: West African Strategies*. Edited by Sylviane A. Diouf. Athens, Ohio: Ohio University Press.

Isichei, Elizabeth Allo. 2002. *Voices of the Poor in Africa*. Rochester, N.Y.: University of Rochester Press.

Jenkins, David. 1975. *Black Zion: Africa, Imagined and Real, As Seen by Today's Blacks*. New York: Harcourt Brace Jovanovich.

Jenkins, Ray. 1985. *Gold Coast Historians and Their Pursuit of the Gold Coast Pasts, 1882–1917*. Ph.D. diss., University of Birmingham, Alabama.

————. 1994. "William Ofori Atta, Nnambi Azikwe, J. B. Danquah and the 'Grilling' of W.E.F. Ward of Achimota in 1935." *History in Africa* 21: 171–89.

Jones, Adams. 1995. "Female Slave-Owners on the Gold Coast: Just a Matter of Money?" In *Slave Cultures and the Cultures of Slavery*. Edited by Stephan Palmié. Knoxville, Tenn.: University of Tennessee Press.

Kaba, Lansine. 2001. "The Atlantic Slave Trade Was Not a 'Black-on-Black Holocaust'." *African Studies Review* 44(1): 1–20.

Kea, Ray A. 1982. *Settlements, Trade, and Polities in the Seventeenth-Century Gold Coast*. Baltimore: Johns Hopkins University Press.

————. 1986. "'I Am Here to Plunder on the General Road': Bandits and Banditry in the Pre-Nineteenth-Century Gold Coast." In *Banditry, Rebellion and Social Protest in Africa*. Edited by Donald Crummey. Portsmouth, N.H.: Heinemann.

————. 2000. "'But I Know What I Shall Do': Agency, Belief and the Social Imaginary in Eighteenth Century Gold Coast Towns." In *Africa's Urban Past*. Edited by David M. Anderson and Richard Rathbone. Oxford: James Currey.

Kemp, Renée. 2000. "Appointment in Ghana: An African-American Woman Unravels the Mystery of Her Ancestors." *Modern Maturity* 43:17–29.

Kimble, David. 1963. *A Political History of Ghana: The Rise of Gold Coast Nationalism, 1850–1928*. Oxford: Clarendon Press.

Klein, A. Norman. 1981. "The Two Asantes: Competing Interpretations of 'Slavery' in Akan-Asante Culture and Society." In *The Ideology of Slavery in Africa*. Edited by Paul E. Lovejoy. Beverly Hills: Sage Publication.

Klein, Martin A. 1989. "Studying the History of Those Who Would Rather Forget: Oral History and the Experience of Slavery." *History in Africa* 16: 209–17.

Klein, Martin, and Paul Lovejoy. 1979. "Slavery in West Africa." In *The Uncommon Market: Essays in the Economic History of the Atlantic Slave Trade*. Edited by Henry A. Gemery and Jan S. Hogendorn. New York: Academic Press.

Korang, Kwaku Larbi. 2003. *Writing Ghana, Imagining Africa: Nation and African Modernity*. Rochester, N.Y.: University of Rochester Press.

Kramer, Fritz. 1993. *The Red Fez: Art and Spirit Possession in Africa*. London: Verso.

Kreamer, Christine Mullen. 2006. "Shared Heritage, Contested Terrain: Cultural Negotiation and Ghana's Cape Coast Castle Museum Exhibit 'Crossroads of People, Crossroads of Trade.'" In *Museum Frictions: Public Cultures/Global Transformations*. Edited by Ivan Karp, Corinne A. Kratz, Lynn Szwaja, and Tomás Ybarra-Frausto, with Gustavo Buntinx, Barbara Kirshenblatt-Gimblett, and Ciraj Rassool. Durham, N.C.: Duke University Press.

Kugelmass, Jack. 1994. "Why We Go to Poland: Holocaust Tourism as Secular Ritual." In *The Art of Memory: Holocaust Memorials in History*. Edited by James Edward Young. New York: Prestel.

Kumekpor, Maxine. 1971. "Some Sociological Aspects of Beads with Special Reference to Selected Beads Found in Eweland." *Ghana Journal of Sociology* 7(1): 100–108.

Lake, Obiagele. 1997. "Diaspora African Repatriation: The Place of Diaspora Women in the Pan-African Nexus." In *Gendered Encounters: Challenging Cultural Boundaries and Social Hierarchies in Africa*. Edited by Maria Grosz-Ngaté and Omari H. Kokole. New York: Routledge.

Lambek, Michael. 1996. "The Past Imperfect: Remembering as Moral Practice." In *Tense Past: Cultural Essays in Memory and Trauma*. Edited by Paul Antze and Michael Lambek. London: Routledge.

Larson, Pier M. 2000. *History and Memory in the Age of Enslavement: Becoming Merina in Highland Madagascar, 1790–1822*. Portsmouth, N.H.: Heinemann.

Law, Robin. 2004. *Ouidah: The Social History of a West African Slaving 'Port', 1727–1892*. Athens, Ohio: Ohio University Press.

Lawrence, A. W. 1964. *Trade Castles and Forts of West Africa*. Stanford, Calif.: Stanford University Press.

Lee, Robert E. 1994. "On the Meaning of the Slave Forts and Castles of Ghana." Unpublished paper presented at the Conference on Preservation of Elmina and Cape Coast Castles and Fort St. Jago, Elmina in the Central Region, May 11–12.

Lever, J. T. 1970. "Mulatto Influence on the Gold Coast in the Early Nineteenth Century: Jan Nieser of Elmina." *African Historical Studies* 3: 253–61.

Leys, Ruth. 1996. "Traumatic Cures: Shell Shock, Janet, and the Question of Memory." In *Tense Past: Cultural Essays in Trauma and Memory*. Edited by Paul Antz and Michael Lambek. New York: Routledge.

Lovejoy, Paul E. 1983. *Transformations in Slavery: A History of Slavery in Africa*. New York: Cambridge University Press.

Lovejoy, Paul E., and David Richardson. 2003. "Anglo-Efik Relations and Protection against Illegal Enslavement at Old Calabar, 1740–1807." In *Fighting the Slave Trade: West African Strategies*. Edited by Sylviane A. Diouf. Athens, Ohio: Ohio University Press.

Mamdani, Mahmood. 1996. *Citizen and Subject: Contemporary Africa and the Legacy of Late Colonialism.* Princeton, N.J.: Princeton University Press.

Massey, Doreen. 1994. *Space, Place, and Gender.* Minneapolis: University of Minnesota Press.

Matory, J. Lorand. 1999. "The English Professors of Brazil: On the Diasporic Roots of the Yorùbá Nation." *Comparative Studies in Society and History* 41: 72–103.

———. 2005. *Black Atlantic Religion: Tradition, Transnationalism, and Matriarchy in the Afro-Brazilian Candomblé.* Princeton: Princeton University Press.

Mbembe, Achille. 1992. "Provisional Notes on the Postcolony." *Africa* 62(1): 3–37.

———. 2003. "Necropolitics." *Public Culture* 15(1): 11–40.

McCarthy, Mary. 1983. *Social Change and the Growth of British Power in the Gold Coast: The Fante States, 1807–1874.* Lanham, Md.: University Press of America.

McCaskie, T. C. 1990. "Nananom Mpow of Mankessim: An Essay in Fante History." In *West African Economic and Social History: Studies in Memory of Marion Johnson.* Edited by David P. Henige and T. C. McCaskie. Madison: Board of Regents of the University of Wisconsin.

McSheffrey, Gerald M. 1983. "Slavery, Indentured Servitude, Legitimate Trade and the Impact of Abolition in the Gold Coast, 1894–1901: A Reappraisal." *Journal of African History* 24(3): 349–68.

Memmi, Albert. 1967. *The Colonizer and the Colonized.* Boston: Beacon Press.

Meriwether, James H. 2002. *Proudly We Can Be Africans: Black Americans and Africa, 1935–1961.* Chapel Hill, N.C.: University of North Carolina Press.

Meyer, Birgit. 1995. "'Delivered from the Powers of Darkness': Confession of Satanic Riches in Christian Ghana." *Africa* 65(2): 236–55.

———. 1998. "'Make a Complete Break with the Past': Memory and Postcolonial Modernity in Ghanaian Pentecostal Discourse." In *Memory and the PostColony: African Anthropology and the Critique of Power.* Edited by Richard Werbner. London: Zed Books.

Miller, Joseph C. 1988. *Way of Death: Merchant Capitalism and the Angolan Slave Trade 1730–1830.* Madison: University of Wisconsin Press.

Ministry of Education. 2001. "Teaching Syllabus for Social Studies (Junior Secondary School)." September.

Ministry of Tourism. 1996. "Tourism Development Plan for the Central Region, Draft Final Report."

Mitchell, Timothy. 1988. *Colonising Egypt.* Cambridge: Cambridge University Press.

Morrison, Toni. 1987. *Beloved.* New York: Knopf.

Mudimbe, V. Y. 1988. *The Invention of Africa: Gnosis, Philosophy and the Order of Knowledge.* Bloomington: Indiana University Press.

Nandy, Ashis. 1983. *The Intimate Enemy: Loss and Recovery of Self under Colonialism.* Delhi: Oxford University Press.

Neptune, Harvey. 2003. "Manly Rivalries and Mopsies: Gender, Nationality, and Sexuality in United States-Occupied Trinidad." *Radical History Review.* 87(Fall): 78–95.

———. 2007. *Caliban and the Yankees: Trinidad and the United States Occupation.* Chapel Hill, N.C.: University of North Carolina Press.

Nkrumah, Kwame. 1970. *Consciencism: Philosophy and Ideology for Decolonization.* London: Panaf.

———. 1971 [1957]. *Ghana: The Autobiography of Kwame Nkrumah.* New York: International Publishers.

———. 1976. *I Speak of Freedom: A Statement of African Ideology.* Westport, Conn.: Greenwood Press.

Nora, Pierre. 1994. "Between Memory and History: *Les Lieux de Memoire.*" In *History and Memory in African American Culture.* Edited by Genevieve Fabre and Robert O'Meally. New York and Oxford: Oxford University Press.

Nunoo, Seth Nii Akele. 1998. *Daily Graphic Supplement,* July 30.

Ong, Aihwa. 1999. *Flexible Citizenship: The Cultural Logics of Transnationality.* Durham, N.C.: Duke University Press.

Opoku-Agyemang, Kwadwo. 1992. "A Crisis of Balance: The (Mis)Representation of Colonial History and the Slave Experience as Themes in Modern African Literature." *Asɛmka: A Literary Journal of the University of Cape Coast* 7: 63–77.

———. 1996. *Cape Coast Castle: A Collection of Poems.* Accra: Afram Publications.

Ortner, Sherry. 1995. "Resistance and the Problem of Ethnographic Refusal." *Comparative Studies in Society and History* 37(1): 173–93.

Penningroth, Dylan C. 2003. *The Claims of Kinfolk: African American Property and Community in the Nineteenth Century South.* Chapel Hill, N.C.: University of North Carolina Press.

Perbi, Akosua Adoma. 1996. "The Legacy of Indigenous Slavery in Contemporary Ghana." *FASS Bulletin* 1(1): 83–92.

———. 1999. "How the Slave Trade is Taught in Ghana." Paper presented at the UNESCO Regional Workshop, Nantes, France, January 28–30.

———. 2004. *A History of Indigenous Slavery in Ghana from the 15th to the 19th Century.* Accra: Sub-Saharan Publishers.

Phillips, Caryl. 2000. *The Atlantic Sound.* New York: Vintage.

Phillips, J. V. L. 1995. "Preface." In *Save Elmina 2.* Accra: Save Elmina Association, November.

Pierre, Jemima. 2002. *Race across the Atlantic: Mapping Racialization in Africa and the African Diaspora.* Ph.D. diss., Department of Anthropology, University of Texas at Austin.

Piot, Charles. 1999. *Remotely Global: Village Modernity in West Africa.* Chicago: University of Chicago Press.

———. 2001. "Atlantic Aporias: Africa and Gilroy's Black Atlantic." *South Atlantic Quarterly* 100(1): 155–70.

Piper, Keith. 1996. *Go West Young Man.* Digital animation commissioned by the Arts Council and Channel 4.

Poku, K. 1969. "Traditional Roles and People of Slave Origin in Modern Ashanti—A Few Impressions." *Ghana Journal of Sociology* 5(1): 34–38.

Price, Richard. 1998. *The Convict and the Colonel.* Boston: Beacon Press.

Priestley, Margaret. 1969. *West African Trade and Coast Society: A Family Study.* London: Oxford University Press.

Quist, Hubert. 1999. *Secondary Education and Nation-Building: A Study of Ghana, 1951–1991.* Ph.D. diss., Columbia University, New York.

Ransdell, Eric. 1995. "Africa's Cleaned-Up Slave Castle." *U.S. News and World Report,* September 18: 11, 33.

Rattray, R. S. 1932. *The Tribes of the Ashanti Hinterland.* Oxford: Clarendon Press.

———. 1969 [1929]. *Ashanti Law and Constitution.* Oxford: Clarendon Press.

Reindorf, Carl Christian. 1950 [1895]. *The History of the Gold Coast and Asante.* Basel: Basel Mission Book Depot.

Report of the Committee on Functional and Adaptive Uses Related to the Preservation of Cape Coast and Elmina Castles and Fort St. Jago. 1994. Ghana Museums and Monuments Board Report.

Report of the Committee on Philosophical and Historical Considerations Related to the Preservation of Cape Coast and Elmina Castles. 1994. Ghana Museums and Monuments Board Report.

Reynolds, Edward. 1974. *Trade and Economic Change on the Gold Coast, 1807–1874.* New York: Longman.

Richards, Sandra L. 2005. "What Is to Be Remembered?: Tourism to Ghana's Slave Castle-Dungeons." *Theater Journal* 57: 617–37.

Richardson, David. 1989. "Slave Exports from West and West-Central Africa, 1700–1810: New Estimates of Volume and Distribution." *Journal of African History* 30(1): 1–22.

Riddell, J. Barry. 1992. "Things Fall Apart Again: Structural Adjustment Programmes in Sub-Saharan Africa." In *Journal of Modern African Studies* 30(1): 53–68.

Rimmer, Douglass. 1992. *Staying Poor: Ghana's Political Economy, 1950–1990.* Oxford: Pergamon Press.

Robertson, Claire C. 1983. "Post-Proclamation Slavery in Accra: A Female Affair?" In *Women and Slavery in Africa.* Edited by Claire C. Robertson and Martin A. Klein. Madison: University of Wisconsin Press.

Robertson, Claire C., and Martin Klein, eds. 1983. *Women and Slavery in Africa.* Madison: University of Wisconsin Press.

Robinson, Vienna Imahküs. 1994. "Is the Black Man's History Being Whitewashed?" *Uhuru* 9: 48–50.

Rodney, Walter. 1966. "African Slavery and Other Forms of Social Oppression on the Upper Guinea Coast in the Context of the Atlantic Slave-Trade." *Journal of African History* 7(3): 431–43.

———. 1969. "Gold and Slaves on the Gold Coast." *Transactions of the Historical Society of Ghana* 10: 13–28.

———. 1982. *How Europe Underdeveloped Africa.* Washington, D.C.: Howard University Press.

Rømer, Ludewig Ferdinand. 2000. *A Reliable Account of the Coast of Guinea (1760)* Translated and edited by Selena Axelrod Winsnes. Oxford: Oxford University Press.

Rosaldo, Renato. 1989. *Culture and Truth: The Remaking of Social Analysis.* Boston: Beacon Press.

Rosenthal, Judy. 1998. *Possession, Ecstasy, and Law in Ewe Voodoo.* Charlottesville: University Press of Virginia.

———. 2002. "Trance against the State." In *Ethnography in Unstable Places: Everyday Lives in Contexts of Dramatic Political Change.* Edited by Carol J. Greenhouse, Elizabeth Mertz, and Kay B. Warren. Durham, N.C.: Duke University Press.

Saaka, Yakubu. 2001. "North-South Relations and the Colonial Enterprise in Ghana." In *Regionalism and Public Policy in Northern Ghana.* Edited by Yakubu Saaka. New York: Peter Lang.

Sanjek, Roger. 1977. "Cognitive Maps of the Ethnic Domain in Urban Ghana: Reflections of Variability and Change." *American Ethnologist* 4(4): 603–22.

Sarbah, John Mensah. 1968a [1897]. *Fanti Customary Laws.* 3d ed. London: Frank Cass & Co. Ltd.

———. 1968b [1906]. *Fanti National Constitution.* 2d ed. London: Frank Cass & Co. Ltd.

Schein, Louisa. 1999. "Of Cargo and Satellites: Imagined Cosmopolitanism." *Postcolonial Studies* 2(3): 345–75.

Schildkrout, Enid. 1979. "The Ideology of Regionalism in Ghana." In *Strangers in African Society.* Edited by William A. Shack and Elliot P. Skinner. Berkeley: University of California Press.

Schwenkel, Christina. 2006. "Recombinant History: Transnational Practices of Memory and Knowledge Production in Contemporary Vietnam." *Cultural Anthropology* 21(1): 3–30.

Scott, David. 1991. "That Event, This Memory: Notes on the Anthropology of African Diasporas in the New World." *Diaspora* 1(3): 261–84.

———. 1999. *Refashioning Futures: Criticism after Postcoloniality.* Princeton, N.J.: Princeton University Press.

———. 2004. *Conscripts of Modernity: The Tragedy of Colonial Enlightenment.* Durham, N.C.: Duke University Press.

Sekyi, Kobina. 1970. "Extracts from 'The Anglo-Fanti.'" In *The Negro: An Anthology.* Edited by Nancy Cunard. New York: Frank Ungar Publishing Co.

———. 1974. *The Blinkards.* London: Heinemann.

Sharp, Lesley A. 2001. "Youth, Land, and Liberty in Coastal Madagascar: A Children's Independence." *Ethnohistory* 48(1–2): 205–36.

———. 2002. *The Sacrificed Generation: Youth, History, and the Colonized Mind in Madagascar.* Berkeley: University of California Press.

Shaw, Rosalind. 2002. *Memories of the Slave Trade: Ritual and the Historical Imagination in Sierra Leone.* Chicago: University of Chicago Press.

Shumway, Rebecca. 2004. *Between the Castle and the Golden Stool: Transformations in Fante Society in the Eighteenth Century.* Ph.D. diss., Emory University.

Simmonds, Doig. 1972. *West African Historical Museum Project: First Annual Report to the University of Cape Coast and the Ghana Museums and Monuments Board.* May.

———. 1973. "A Note in the Excavations in Cape Coast Castle." *Transactions of the Historical Society of Ghana* 14(2): 267–99.

Singleton, Theresa. 1999. "The Slave Trade Remembered on the Former Gold and Slave Coasts." In *From Slavery to Emancipation in the Atlantic World.* Edited by Sylvia R. Frey and Betty Wood. London: Frank Cass.

Songsore, Jacob, Aloysius Denkabe, Charles D. Jebuni, and Steven Ayidiya. 2001. "Challenges of Education in Northern Ghana: A Case for Northern Ghana Education Trust Fund (NETFUND)." In *Regionalism and Public Policy in Ghana.* Edited by Yakubu Saaka. New York: Peter Lang.

Southon, Arthur E. 1934. *Gold Coast Methodism, The First Hundred Years, 1835–1935.* Cape Coast: Methodist Book Depot.

Stoler, Ann Laura. 1989. "Making Empire Respectable: The Politics of Race and Sexual Morality in Twentieth Century Colonial Cultures." *American Ethnologist* 16(4): 634–60.

———. 1995. *Race and the Education of Desire: Foucault's History of Sexuality and the Colonial Order of Things.* Durham, N.C.: Duke University Press.

Stoller, Paul. 1995. *Embodying Colonial Memories: Spirit Possession, Power and the Hauka in West Africa.* London: Routledge.

Talton, Benjamin A. 2003. "The Past and Present in Ghana's Ethnic Conflicts: British Colonial Policy and Konkomba Agency, 1930–1951." *Journal of Asian and African Studies* 38(2–3): 192–210.

Tenkorang, S. 1973. "John Mensah Sarbah, 1864–1910." *Transactions of the Historical Society of Ghana* 14(1): 65–78.

Thomas, Deborah A. 1999. "Emancipating the Nation (Again): Notes on Nationalism, 'Modernization,' and Other Dilemmas in Post-Colonial Jamaica." *Identities: Global Studies in Culture and Power* 5(4): 501–42.

Trouillot, Michel-Rolph. 1995. *Silencing the Past: Power and the Production of History.* Boston: Beacon Press.

———. 2002. "The Otherwise Modern: Caribbean Lessons from the Savage Slot." In *Critically Modern: Alternatives, Alterities, Anthropologies.* Edited by Bruce M. Knauft. Bloomington, Ind.: Indiana University Press.

Tsing, Anna. 2005. *Friction: An Ethnography of Global Connection.* Princeton, N.J.: Princeton University Press.

Tsing, Anna Lowenhaupt. 1993. *In the Realm of the Diamond Queen: Marginality in an Out of the Way Place.* Princeton: Princeton University Press.

van Dantzig, Albert. 1980. *Forts and Castles of Ghana.* Accra: Sedco Publishing Limited.

van den Nieuwenhof, Michel. 1996. "The Government Garden." In *Save Elmina 3*. Accra: Save Elmina Association, August.

van Dijk, Rijk. 1997. "From Camp to Encompassment: Discourse of Transsubjectivity in the Ghanaian Pentecostal Discourse." *Journal of Religion in Africa* 27(2): 135–59.

Van Dyke, Charles. 1996. "Town Culture in Nineteenth Century Elmina." In *Save Elmina 3*. Accra: Save Elmina Association, August.

Vogt, John L. 1973. "The Early Sao Tome-Principe Slave Trade with Mina." *International Journal of African Historical Studies* 6(3): 453–67.

Walcott, Derek. 1990. *Omeros*. New York: Farrar, Strauss, Giroux.

Wallerstein, Immanuel. 1987. "World-Systems Analysis." *Social Theory Today*. Edited by Anthony Giddens and Jonathan H. Turner. Stanford: Stanford University Press.

Walters, Ronald W. 1993. *Pan Africanism in the African Diaspora: An Analysis of Modern Afrocentric Political Movements*. Detroit: Wayne State University Press.

Ward, W. E. F. 1934. *Africa before the White Man Came*. London: Longmans Green, and Co.

Wartemberg, J. Sylvanus. 1950. *Sao Jorge d'El Mina, Premiere West African European Settlement: Its Traditions and Customs*. Ilfracombe, U.K.: Stockwell.

Werbner, Richard. 1996. "Introduction: Multiple Identities, Plural Arenas." In *Postcolonial Identities in Africa*. Edited by Richard Werbner and Terence Ranger. London: Zed Books.

Wertsch, James V. 2002. *Voices of Collective Remembering*. Cambridge: Cambridge University Press.

White, Geoffrey M. 1995. "Remembering Guadalcanal: National Identity and Transnational Memory-Making." *Public Culture* 7(3): 529–55.

Wilks, Ivor. 1993. *Forests of Gold: Essays on the Akan and the Kingdom of Asante*. Athens, Ohio: Ohio University Press.

Williams, Eric. 1994 [1944]. *Capitalism and Slavery*. Chapel Hill, N.C.: University of North Carolina Press.

Wolf, Eric. 1982. *Europe and the People without History*. Berkeley: University of California Press.

Wright, Richard. 1954. *Black Power: A Record of Reactions in a Land of Pathos*. New York: Harper and Brothers.

Wrigley, C. C. 1971. "Historicism in Africa: Slavery and State Formation." *African Affairs* 70(279): 113–24.

Yarak, Larry W. 1986. "Elmina and Greater Asante in the Nineteenth Century." *Africa* 56(1): 33–52.

———. 1989. "West African Coastal Society in the Nineteenth Century: The Case of the Afro-European Slaveowners of Elmina." *Ethnohistory* 36(1): 44–60.

Yoneyama, Lisa. 1999. *Hiroshima Traces: Time, Space, and the Dialectics of Memory*. Berkeley: University of California Press.

Zachary, G. Pascal. 2001. "Tangled Roots: For African Americans in Ghana, the Grass Isn't Always Greener—Seeking the 'Motherland,' They Find Echoes of History and a Chilly Welcome." *Wall Street Journal*, March 14.

Zachernuk, P. S. 1998. "African History and Imperial Culture in Colonial Nigerian Schools." *Africa* 68(4): 484–505.

INDEX

Page numbers in italics refer to illustrations.